WRESTLING'S
ONE-RING CIRCUS

WRESTLING'S ONE-RING CIRCUS

The Death of the World Wrestling Federation

SCOTT KEITH

CITADEL PRESS
Kensington Publishing Corp.
www.kensingtonbooks.com

CITADEL PRESS BOOKS are published by

Kensington Publishing Corp.
850 Third Avenue
New York, NY 10022

All Kensington titles, imprints, and distributed lines are available at special quantity discounts for bulk purchases for sales promotions, premiums, fund-raising, educational, or institutional use. Special book excerpts or customized printings can also be created to fit specific needs. For details, write or phone the office of the Kensington special sales manager: Kensington Publishing Corp., 850 Third Avenue, New York, NY 10022, attn: Special Sales Department, phone 1-800-221-2647.

CITADEL PRESS and the Citadel logo are Reg. U.S. Pat. & TM Off.

First printing: October 2004

10 9 8 7 6 5 4 3 2 1

Printed in the United States of America

Library of Congress Control Number: 2004106014

ISBN 0-8065-2619-X

Contents

Contents

Acknowledgments

A list of the people without whom my life would be a lot less interesting:

Thanks to my parents for the usual parental stuff.

Thanks to Huy Tong, John Rybak, Tyler LaSalle and his weak rhymes, Zen Porohowski, Rahim and Karim Jetha, Jody Serner, Brian Hill, and everyone else who hangs out for the pay-per-views every month.

Thanks to Lindsay Grad, Taryn Long, Pam Malinowski, Donna Underhill, and Nicole Mullen for being cool chicks.

Thanks to Frank Scatoni for being my agent.

Thanks to Richard Ember for the great job in editing my ramblings down.

Thanks to Pete Fornatale for getting this all started.

Thanks to David Bixenspan, Michael Jenkinson, Josh Grutman, Stephen Beveridge, and Derek Burgan for suggestions and early feedback.

Thanks to the people within the WWE who have asked not to be named for all the cool info.

Thanks to Dave Meltzer and the *Wrestling Observer Newsletter*, who *I can* name, for all the other cool info.

Thanks to John Petrie for influencing the format of the reviews.

Thanks to Don Becker for his webmastery over the years.

Thanks to Darren Smith for all the photos.

Thanks to Matthew Heckel for the HHH stuff.

Thanks to Christian Tremiseux, Ryan Ouellette, and Chris Dibble for nothing in particular, but I figured I'd give them a thrill.

And thanks to many other people who I'll probably offend by not remembering them. But I'm trying, honest.

Introduction

In 1995, Steve Austin was fired from WCW by Eric Bischoff, over the phone, after a fairly infamous incident where he failed to report an injury and decided to miss a show as a result. He bounced through ECW briefly before landing in the World Wrestling Federation, where they came up with the brilliant moniker of Ringmaster for him. It was a play on words, see: wrestling happens in a ring, and the best wrestler would presumably be the Ringmaster. Austin went on to become the biggest star in the history of wrestling, thus living up to his initial billing.

It's doubly ironic that the name could also apply to Vince McMahon, head of the (then) World Wrestling Federation and general guru of the so-called sport of wrestling, because he's been ringmaster of a circus since 1983, where the animals are his wrestlers and the traveling show hits two cities a night with little regard for the welfare of the people doing the work. The circus also has another connection to wrestling that many newer fans aren't aware of: professional wrestling in its current form evolved from the circus and carnival performers at the turn of the nineteenth century, who would speak in code and stage wrestling matches between ringers and "marks" (or common patrons who didn't know better). The "carny" terminology sur-

vives today in many forms, from the disdainful term "mark" being applied to the common fan, to "kayfabe," the secret code of wrestlers. At heart, today's highly paid musclemen, who think of themselves as TV stars and matinee idols, are little more than updated circus performers, speaking in gibberish to keep the fans uneducated. Thankfully, the newer generation of wrestlers has embraced the fanbase a bit more and opened up lines of communication, but the business is still controlled by those who come from the "old school" way of thinking, which has long been part of the problem.

Of course, "ringmaster" sometimes refers to a person pulling the strings behind the scenes, and if you want to go into another layer of irony, you run into HHH, one of the top stars of the WWE since 1999, and husband of Vince's daughter, Stephanie. It's often been argued that he's the kind of evil genius who's been running the show all along since ascending to power. This would seem to contradict Vince's long-running company line about the inmates not controlling the asylum, but he's always had a soft spot for Stephanie. But while you can argue the morality of HHH's constant politics, you certainly can't argue the effectiveness, as he has managed to maintain a position as top guy on RAW through a series of clever maneuvers and by never losing to anyone who can hurt his position. Unfortunately, his skills as a performer haven't been able to keep up with him.

As of 2004, it's looking good that HHH will switch careers to Hollywood after the strong buzz from his role in *Blade: Trinity* and hopefully leave RAW to the wrestlers again. I plan to buy 1200 tickets to his next movie, just in case.

Ultimately, the side effect of all these strings being pulled was a jumbled mess in place of a cohesive wrestling promotion: a one-ring circus in place of a three-ring one. So this, then, is the story of World Wrestling Entertainment, why they changed their name from the World Wrestling Federation, and how things got so bad for them.

But more specifically, it's the story of two men who brought it both up and down again: "Stone Cold" Steve Austin and HHH. Although their methods were wildly dissimilar, the end result was the same. We'll examine how they got to the top, and who ended up winning their little war.

This is not strictly a history of what happened from 2001 until 2003—such a thing would be boring, and I strive not to be that. I don't always succeed, but then look at the material I have to work with a lot of the time. This is more my examination of everything that happened in that period, and a look behind the curtain at the thought process that made the people involved do what they do. And since I'm all about the wrestling, in between the psychoanalysis and bad jokes, we'll examine the defining matches of the era and why they were great enough or bad enough to warrant inclusion.

Finally, be warned up front that I am heavily biased and opinionated, and I make no apologies about it. Objective journalism is for pussies, I say.

And now, find your seat, because the curtain is rising. . . .

Cast of Characters

Hurry, hurry, step right up and witness the wonderful spectacle and powerful prestidigitation that is World Wrestling Entertainment. A reminder, no refunds once the show has started. And now, for your edification and education, presenting the performers who will titillate and tantalize this evening:

Vince McMahon

The owner and main creative force behind the WWE, and also the evil TV character known as Mr. McMahon to his enemies. Doesn't deal well with change and criticism. Catchphrase: "What do you mean shock TV is dead?"

Kevin Dunn

Vince's chief advisor and production guru, he was instrumental behind the revival of the promotion in the '90s, but has a decidedly soap-opera slant on what wrestling should be. Catchphrase: "We might not ever watch *Six Feet Under*, but we can sure as hell use it to justify our excesses."

Hulk Hogan

Aging former superhero who was on top of the promotion from 1984 until leaving for WCW in 1993. Also known as Mr. America in 2003. Catch phrase: "Add $2 million to that number and make me champion again, and you've got a deal."

Shawn Michaels

Aging former main event draw who was on top of the promotion from 1996 until his retirement in 1998; he found Jesus in 2002 and God told him to return to the ring and pad his downside guarantee. Catchphrase: "Praise the Lord and pass the Percocet."

Kevin Nash

Aging former Breck model masquerading as a professional wrestler for going on twelve years now, best known for his immaculate haircare and tendency to injure himself tying his shoes. Catchphrase: "I used to be World champion, you know. Honest."

The Undertaker

Aging former zombie, turned patriotic biker, turned redneck submission grappler. Much like the undead, just won't go away. Catchphrase: "I'm not feeling it."

Steve Austin

Aging former biggest draw in the history of wrestling, whose back injuries forced him into retirement in 2003 after authorities forced him into detox due to a spousal abuse charge. Catchphrase: "Austin 3:16 says I just beat up my wife."

HHH

Supposed biggest star in the company, eternal World champion, and son-in-law of Vince McMahon, a run of great matches in 2000 put him on top of the promotion and his marriage to Vince's daughter cemented him there despite a series of leg injuries that left him a shell of his former self. Catchphrase: "On this show, I am God!" (And that one's not a joke answer!)

Kane

Supposed younger brother of the Undertaker (depending on which version of continuity the writers are following at a given time), he may also have been a necrophiliac drunk driver in his younger days and may or may not actually have been burned beyond recognition by a fire in his youth. Catchphrase: "Who am I related to this week?"

The Rock

Hollywood badass and a star so big that no wrestling promotion can contain him, he spent much of 2002 hyping "The Scorpion King" and shooting a followup movie that went through several name changes. Despite not needing to, he still returns every few months to spruce up the shows. Catchphrase: "Call my agent."

Kurt Angle

Your Olympic hero and one of the best wrestlers in the world today, Angle hung in midcard limbo for much of 2002 before suffering another serious neck injury and then shrugging it off with a miracle operation. Catchphrase: "Here, go ahead, break this bone, I can work through the pain."

Chris Benoit

Canadian hero and another one of the best wrestlers in the world today, all he does is provide great matches, but spent much of the year mired in meaningless tag feuds, all of which were great matches. Catchphrase: "You want me to put him over, too?"

Edge

Long-haired pretty boy who seemed assured of a breakthrough push to the main event before the dreaded neck injury put him on the shelf, perhaps for good. Catchphrase: "Ouch, my neck!"

Booker T

The only true survivor of the WCW invasion in 2001, he was able to adjust to the WWE's style and forge out a solid career of being held down by HHH. Catchphrase: "Do I get to win this time?"

Chris Jericho

Eternal #2 heel behind HHH despite being more popular as a babyface and more hated as a heel, he at least got smart in 2002 and started telling everyone who would listen how happy he was to be putting guys over instead of being burdened with the money and respect of being World champion. Catchphrase: "I love my job!"

Shane McMahon

Vince's son and president of the new media division of the WWE, he disappeared from TV in 2001 after a rumored real-life falling-out with his sister and now remains in a backstage role and has no interest in the wrestling operations of the company, aside from a stint in late 2003. Catchphrase: "Can I run another division of the company, Mom?"

Stephanie McMahon

Vince's daughter and head writer, she is married to HHH and is apparently seeing the buffet table on the side. Favors slimming black suits while on TV and thinks of herself as the biggest babyface on Smackdown. Well, she's half-right. Catchphrase: "Conflict of what? Pass the gravy."

Big Show

Signed to a ten-year contract in 1999 during the heat of the wrestling wars, the result is a top push for him every other year to justify the money. Weight fluctuates between 350 and 500 pounds depending on his mood. Catchphrase:

"Who's the sucker who signed me to a guaranteed contract, anyway?"

Brock Lesnar

The freakishly large and agile ex-NCAA champion and natural rival for Kurt Angle, he debuted the day after Wrestlemania XVIII and was in the main event of Wrestlemania XIX a year later. Seems content to be a modern-day Bob Backlund. And that's not a good thing. Catchphrase: "Smile!"

Rob Van Dam

Continually misused, charismatic, and high-flying, Rob learned firsthand what the glass ceiling was in 2002, but then they were probably worried that he'd sell the World title belt for a nickel bag. Catchphrase: "Dude . . . like . . . um . . . yeah . . . dude."

And also featuring:

Rey Mysterio	Zach Gowen
Jamie Noble	Ric Flair
3 Minute Warning	Randy Orton
Christian	Dave Batista
Test	Sean O'Haire
Matt Hardy	Eric Bischoff
Jeff Hardy	The Dudley Boyz
Eddie Guerrero	Sable
Chavo Guerrero	Trish Stratus
Team Angle	Victoria
Torrie Wilson	William Regal
Dawn Marie	Lance Storm

Glossary of Terms

I don't normally like to delve into these sorts of things because I tend to assume that anyone reading this book would know all this stuff already, but in case you don't, here's the basic, "scribblings on a bathroom wall" version of terms you'll run across during the course of this book:

A. Stuff You NEED to Know to Understand What the Hell I'm Talking About

Angle The series of events that sets up a particular match or storyline.

Babyface The "good guy"—a protagonist. Usually abbreviated to "face."

Bump Falling down in a realistic manner to simulate impact. A "ref bump" is where the referee takes the fall and magically becomes unconscious for as long as the heel needs to cheat.

Feud A series of angles and matches between a heel and a face, usually with a storyline reason behind them.

Gimmick The character or mannerisms that a wrestler adopts in order to get himself over (see "over").

Heat Crowd noise and reaction, either positive or negative. If it's pre-taped and played back to give the illusion of a bigger reaction than actually exists, it's "canned heat." It can also refer to real-life problems between people (i.e., "John had heat with management over his new character").

Heel The "bad guy"—an antagonist.

Job To lose a predetermined match. The opposite of "go over."

Over Having a character who elicits a strong reaction from the crowd, either positive or negative. Can also apply to general concepts (i.e., "The Hell in a Cell match really got over with a crowd that's normally tough").

PPV Abbreviation for "Pay per view," the monthly shows run by the WWE.

Sell To act like an opponent is causing you pain, which is the basis of professional wrestling. The opposite is "no-sell," which is to ignore their moves and pretend they have no effect. Faces making their comeback will generally no-sell heel moves for a short period of time to get the crowd going.

Work As a verb, "to wrestle." Workrate is the quality of the wrestling from a quantitative standpoint—the speed and amount of moves done. Also refers to the art of fooling the audience.

B. Stuff You Need to Understand My Match Reviews

Blade Used as a verb, to cut yourself and draw blood from the forehead. Used as a noun, what you hide in your wrist tape to accomplish this. The act is referred to as a **bladejob**.

Comeback When the face has decided that he's had enough of the heel and starts to fight back during the match. Generally leads to the finish.

Finish The ending of the match, generally set up with a big series of moves by one or both wrestlers. A wrestler's biggest move is called his **finisher.** A particularly irritating variation of the finish is the **Dusty Finish**, where one or more referees are knocked out and the decision is reversed by another authority figure (be it a referee or someone higher up) as a result of what happened while the referee was knocked out.

Go Over Win a predetermined match. The opposite of "job" blowoff—the big finale to a feud, where the face gets his big revenge.

Hot Tag When one member of a face tag team gets pounded on for an extended period of time, only to make a miracle comeback and tag in his partner. This tag usually results in positive heat from the crowd, so it's a "hot tag."

Resthold A chinlock, sleeper hold, surfboard, nerve pinch, or any other move that allows both wrestlers to stay on the mat without significant movement for long periods of time.

Screwjob A finish during a match that involves something illegal and leads to an inconclusive ending such as a disqualification or countout. Generally disliked by fans.

Spot A specific move or series of moves within the match, which is usually part of a wrestler's regular repertoire. A "highspot" is a move designed to elicit a big reaction from the crowd, usually a high-flying move or a dive outside the ring.

C. Stuff That's Just Good to Know

Booker The guy who determines the outcomes to the matches—also referred to as "the writers" or collectively as "creative," because the WWE doesn't like to be associated with old wrestling terms anymore.

Buyrate The percentage of the total audience who buys a particular PPV.

Carny In one sense, the general attitude of the older wrestlers, as though wrestling was still a carnival sideshow and the people were nothing but stupid sheep to be herded into the arena. In another, the idiotic pig latin that wrestlers speak in, giving you "hizzouse" instead of "house," etc.

Jobber A wrestler who always loses.

Main Event Style A strange term that has only developed in the past couple of years, which indicates the heavily scripted and choreographed kick-and-punch matches that inhabit the main event levels of the WWE. More deliberately paced than matches further down the card and generally featuring multiple reversals of the finishers and one or more run-ins and ref bumps, this derivative and repetitive style is part of the reason why the top of the WWE has been so stagnant in recent years.

Mark A fan of wrestling. Derived from the carnival and grifter slang for someone who exists only to give their money.

Push To emphasize someone on TV and generally book them to win a lot of matches as a result.

Road Agent/Agent Ex-wrestlers backstage who coordinate the matches and generally work out finishes beforehand. Also used to "keep the peace" and set a good example for the other wrestlers.

Rub The theoretical boost that a lesser wrestler gets from working with a more established veteran—by beating him or looking competitive against him, the younger guy is said to be "getting the rub." Unfortunately, this has become a lost art these days.

Swerve To lead the fans to think that one outcome for a storyline or angle is coming, and then switch it up with something else.

Turn To switch a character from face to heel or vice versa.

Rating the Matches

At some points in this book, you'll come across star ratings for certain matches. The star ratings system is the smart mark's best friend, because it's a (supposedly) universal way for wrestling fans to compare the quality of the matches, although it rarely works out that way. The basic premise is that a match is "rated" from DUD (0 stars) to ★★★★★ (5 stars), using scary words like workrate, psychology, transitions, heat, and other intangibles to define just how good it was. It was invented by managers Jim Cornette and Norm Dooley and has since been taken by the Internet community and modified for their needs. Here's how it works:

★★★★★	Match of the Year candidate
★★★★½	Almost perfect
★★★★	Excellent
★★★½	Extremely good, but with some important flaws
★★★	Good, but lacking in many ways
★★½	Above average, but nothing special
★★	An average match—most of the wrestling matches on TV will top out here due to time constraints
★½	Below average, but watchable
★	Bad match, but enough action to make it worthwhile
½★	Terrible match
DUD	No value whatsoever
Negative numbers (e.g., −☆)	Completely offensive to the viewer in every way

WRESTLING'S ONE-RING CIRCUS

1.

The Invasion, Redux

Whatever you do, do it with all your might. Work at it, early and late, in season and out of season, not leaving a stone unturned, and never deferring for a single hour that which can be done just as well as now.
—P. T. Barnum

Some days give you hope for the future, and some days yank the rug from underneath your feet and then stomp on your head for fun. That's kind of what I was feeling like as a wrestling fan at the beginning of 2002.

The year 2002 was, for what is now the WWE, a total financial disaster created by rampant problems within creative and egos out of control in the back. That doesn't really hit home with the average viewer because we as fans aren't privy to the fallout from that sort of thing, but I think for me it was a disaster because for the first time, wrestling ceased to be fun for me. It started to become a job, something for which I used to care a great deal, but now did out of habit more than anything else. There were good moments and things that kept me interested, but the same signs were starting to appear as when dearly departed rival WCW died out in the spring of 2001, with a whimper rather than a bang.

The biggest potential money-earning angle in the history of pro wrestling, the so-called "InVasion" of WCW, had been a spectacular flop on every level possible. Think about this for a moment: ex-manager and promoter Jim Cornette once said that wrestling fans had become so jaded by years of the business being exposed that the only thing left for people to believe in was the rivalry between different promotions, specifically WCW versus WWF. You could throw the fake nature of the so-called sport in the faces of the fans as much as you wanted, but by god we all knew that deep down Vince McMahon and Eric Bischoff really hated each other, and someday the only way to settle that feud would be in the ring, with the top stars from the WWF facing off against the top stars of WCW. Not a hard concept, if you think about it. The NFL has the Super Bowl, baseball has the World Series, MTV had Celebrity Deathmatch (before they cancelled it—bastards). For years, fans had dreamed of a kind of "Super Bowl of

Wrestling" featuring the dream matches that we had longed to see since childhood. Maybe not with the same people, sure, but the star versus star idea was still there in the hearts of all the fans of both promotions.

> **The WWE's version of this theory was to split the rosters, then present the millionth version of Undertaker v. Kane as an interpromotional match.**

Take for example Hulk Hogan's departure for WCW. Now, even up until the mid-90s, the fanbase for WCW was comprised mainly of "old school" fans, who had a more hardline stance on the wrestling wars and were spawned from the fanbase of the defunct National Wrestling Alliance. The NWA, in most of its iterations over the years, stressed a more athletic product over the kind of one-ring circus presented by Vince McMahon and the WWF. Hulk Hogan was the very embodiment of everything "wrong" with the business, at least to those fans who had grown up on the more athletically mature product offered by the NWA. To then turn around and have the offspring of that promotion, namely WCW, sign the person who was the enemy in a long-standing cold war, was akin to treason for wrestling fans. Many of the more "serious" fans of the promotion, such as myself, abandoned WCW completely rather than face a world where the Orange Goblin wore the gold belt that was supposed to symbolize the excellence inherent in wrestling. You can imagine my feelings when he went on to win that thing many more times.

But an interesting thing happened, as a result of a mistake that the WWF had made

years earlier. Back in 1991, the WWF had signed away Ric Flair, the disgruntled top star and NWA champion, in the heat of a contract dispute with his employers. In the WWF, the feeling was that if you hadn't made it there, you hadn't made it anywhere. Thus, Flair was made to "earn his spot" like everyone else instead of being immediately promoted as the NWA World champion and put into the main event of the next PPV against Hulk Hogan to see who the real champion was. In fact, that shot at the WWF title went to upcoming WWF in-house product Mark Callaway, a.k.a. the Undertaker. Flair was used as little more than a tool to help Undertaker defeat Hogan and create a new main event star. Flair and Hogan *did* meet in singles matches, but they were on poorly promoted house shows with goofy finishes that left fans of both men feeling unsatisfied. Flair was eventually given the WWF title himself and turned into the focal point of the promotion for a while, but you had to feel that nagging at the back of Vince McMahon's mind was the anger toward the NWA for building someone who could be perceived as a star without the stamp of Vince McMahon on him. So Flair and Hogan never had a match on PPV, never fought to determine who the real World champion was, and when Flair quietly dropped the WWF title to Bret Hart in the middle of Saskatchewan in 1992 and left the promotion, people were still looking for that match between them to settle things once and for all.

Enter WCW.

Now, no one ever accused the people running that promotion of being brain surgeons, but they did do one thing right after signing Hogan. They realized that the audience who was begging for dream matches was still out there and still looking for the satisfaction of seeing which side really was better. So the first thing

WCW did after picking up Hogan's contract was to book a PPV main event match for their big summer show, Bash at the Beach, between Hogan and Flair, for the World title. Winner take all, who was really better after all those years? Of course, being Hogan, he also brought all his friends with him to shore up the "ex-WWF" side of things, and being WCW, they immediately let all the WWF alumnus win every match and confirmed what the fanbase suspected all along: WCW as a collective entity was suffering an inferiority complex and had become a sort of corporate self-loathing manic depressive. Rather than being too full of pride, like Vince McMahon and the WWF, they took the opposite road and didn't let their fans get behind the homegrown talent at all, instead choosing to let Hogan and his cronies run roughshod over the promotion.

But that's another story.

> **Hogan tried this very tactic again in mid-2003, complaining that Brock Lesnar and Kurt Angle were being treated as bigger stars than him. Go figure. Vince fired him soon after.**

The point is that even the most brain-dead bean-counting promotion in the world, WCW, was smart enough to know that if given your enemy on a silver platter, you can make money by matching him up against your own top stars. Apparently, that lesson was too simple for the WWF to figure out, because they managed to fuck it up in record time.

In fact, the WWF was given two of the top promotions as a result of striking when the iron was hot—they bought WCW for a song in early 2001 and then got ECW and its assets (with bankruptcy proceedings pending at the time) when they snagged Paul Heyman to be a writer. The fans still believed, but Vince didn't.

The invasion by WCW was a comedy of errors, and those errors are as follows:

1. They immediately screwed things up from the get-go by turning the final episode of WCW Nitro into a launching pad for yet another angle involving the McMahon family. In this specific case, Shane McMahon was instituted as the new "owner" of WCW, having signed it away under Vince's nose. So right away you're telling former fans of WCW that their promotion isn't important enough to exist by itself, without a McMahon figurehead running the show behind the scenes. Now, in reality, having spoken to some of the production crew for the WWF around this time, they really were planning to spin off WCW into a separate entity and promote shows under the WCW brand name. Shane McMahon would get to run the promotion by himself, in theory. Shows were booked for dates in May and June, and the idea was that some of the big WWF stars would "jump ship" to the new WCW and shore up the star power. Ah, but what star power? That leads into my next point.

2. The major names of WCW were left unsigned, for financial reasons. The thinking was this: If we ("we" being the WWF) were to carry the contract of someone like Bill Goldberg (who was making upwards of a million dollars per year under his WCW contract) while our own top stars make far less than that, locker room morale would fall apart and the universe would

collapse in on itself. Thus, Vince essentially issued an edict from on high: Only those stars from WCW making less than one million per year would be signed by the WWF as part of the sale, unless they gave up their cushy Time-Warner money and took a smaller deal with the WWF. Thus, Goldberg and most of the other "big names" left after the fire sale and decided to sit out the next couple of years, while midrange names like Booker T and Diamond Dallas Page went groveling to the WWF for work, at greatly reduced rates. Who was right here? Tough call, frankly. Even though the WWF was insanely profitable at the beginning of 2001 (they bought another PROMOTION, for pete's sake!), there's no guarantee that picking up millions of dollars in bloated contracts would have allowed them to stay that way. And was anyone from WCW really worth the money? Goldberg hadn't drawn a dime for WCW since 1998. Ditto for people like Sting and the Steiner brothers. Really, the best hope for making their investment back was to take the lesser names and build them into bigger stars as a part of the WWF machine. Ah, but then there was another problem.

3. The WWF immediately showed a reluctance to allow anyone from outside of their usual system of talent development to develop as talent. They had a huge influx of raw talent like Lance Storm, Sean O'Haire, Chuck Palumbo, Billy Kidman, and another dozen others, but what happens to them? They're given nosebleed seats at Wrestlemania and made to look like observers at the biggest show of the year. The message is: You are on the outside looking in while Undertaker and HHH lumber around near the main event and show you how to work WWF Main Event Style. Those on the fringes of stardom were brought in later, past the point

when it would do the most good, and the younger set were sent to the WWF's training facilities in the OVW promotion to "learn how to work." Admittedly, WCW's own training programs were, shall we say, less than stellar, but keeping a monster like Sean O'Haire in the minor leagues for nearly two years, after he was fresh off becoming the next big thing in WCW, strikes me as slightly counterproductive. Ah, but would those names brought in from WCW have meant anything in the long run anyway, as compared to training kids on a show like *Tough Enough* and developing them from scratch? That depends, really—a lot of the developmental talent from WCW was so far gone or far out of the bounds of what could be turned into something useful (David Flair, son of legendary wrestler Ric with all of the blond hair and none of the talent, is a prime example) that it was doubtful any of them had a chance to escape the training facilities to begin with. A guy like Mark Jindrak, who was given a fairly big push in WCW due to his size and look, was given a brief look by the WWF in the big leagues before essentially being abandoned in the developmental system once it became apparent that he had almost no retention of the minimal skills taught to him by WCW and no desire to learn how to work the WWF's own style of matches. In a note of supreme irony that demonstrates exactly what the mindset in wrestling really is, Mark Jindrak was brought back to the big leagues nearly two years after being abandoned to developmental hell, with no appreciable improvement in performance but a nice body and a good haircut, and given a minor push. But back to the problem at hand—normally I would say, "Huzzah, never mind them and their stupid WWF style, I'm glad these kids have the balls to stand up for themselves and stick with what they know," but really, you've got to be realistic and think that kids as green as those pulled from the flaming wreckage of WCW would be more of a danger to themselves and others than someone with better training working for less money.

> As a coda to the Mark Jindrak saga, he was put in a tag team with fellow greenhorn Lance "Garrison" Cade and was quickly forgotten, months after being touted as the fourth member of HHH's planned Evolution stable. So really the system *does* work sometimes.

4. A new problem developed in May, when the WWF's main programming carrier, TNN, refused to green-light a proposed WCW TV show, citing the lowered value of the WWF in general and the lack of star power for such an endeavor. The idea behind a potential WCW show was artificial competition to replace the departed WCW, an idea that would later resurface in 2002 as the Brand Extension. Without an outlet for the WCW brand name to redevelop on its own, however, the idea was as good as dead and things took a drastically different turn. This wasn't necessarily the WWF's fault, but it was a big stumbling block in getting the WCW name relaunched and one of the main reasons for the failure of it. It's interesting to look back on the potential plans for such a WCW offshoot and what things were going to look like as a result. Most of the

rough plans had HHH and the Rock moving to the "new look" WCW Nitro for star power, while Steve Austin and Undertaker held court on RAW. Boy, those were the days, back when the same four guys held all the main event positions with no room for others to break through to the top. Oh, wait, that's still true today, with a couple of exceptions.

5. Without any of the major names from WCW to lead an invasion and without a separate TV show to put the WCW name onto, this was obviously not the ideal time to launch the biggest money-making angle in history. But they tried anyway, bringing in C-level names like Lance Storm and Hugh Morrus to lead the charge, months after the initial purchase and announcement of the sale to Shane McMahon. By this point, they might as well have given up, because by June they were asking the fans to buy into Booker T as the leader of the WCW faction, and, furthermore, they were portraying the outsiders as babyfaces and asking fans to boo Vince McMahon in his fight against them. The psychology behind the invasion was strange, as well, because you had B-level midcarders banding together and giving speeches about how the WCW invaders hadn't yet earned their spot in the WWF locker room, which was both strange because no one outside of the wrestling business would understand the references to "earning your spot," and also because many of the people rallying around the WWF name were former WCW defectors themselves who had only been back in the company a few months (i.e., Raven and Haku) and thus shouldn't have had any loyalty to the WWF name to begin with. Meanwhile, the people who DID have loyalty to those initials, namely the fanbase, were being asked to treat the loser brand WCW as their

new heroes in order to facilitate support for a new TV show featuring that brand, along with two or three of the top stars on the WWF shows, who would then be perceived as traitors to their own cause (at least, that's my own speculation) and probably sink the whole idea from the beginning. This was not what you could call a well thought out plan, to be sure. Luckily, this phase of the invasion plans only ran from June until early July, at which point they scrapped the entire thing and started fresh from the drawing board.

6. Okay, so July sees the drafting of Plan B. Unfortunately, right off the bat they showed a fundamental misunderstanding of what people wanted from WCW, because the first guy they brought in was Buff Bagwell. The problem here was that no one in the WWF had actually watched WCW's programming and thus didn't know about the limitations Bagwell had as a wrestler (i.e., he sucked like a hooker at a Viagra convention). Bagwell's hiring was based on a live crowd months earlier squealing with delight at the mention of his name, not on anything tangible like talent or merit. They attempted to put a "WCW match" as the main event of a RAW in July, featuring attempts to mimic the look and feel of WCW's dead Nitro program by dimming the upper lights and adding Scott Hudson as the commentator for the match. (In another ironic note, months later, attendance would drop so sharply that they would be dimming the upper lights to disguise the empty seats, rather than as a stylistic choice.) Unfortunately (or fortunately, depending on how you look at it), the crowd shit all over the match, booing both Bagwell and opponent Booker T out of the building without giving them so much as a shot to get over on the value of the match.

Rather than doing something constructive like examining the cause of the problem and finding talent for the WCW brand that people might want to see, however, they took the opposite tack and panicked. If in doubt, go with what you know, I always say.

7. Now, those of you who have read my previous book probably understand better than most what the WWF's usual panic mode involves: more people named McMahon. Or Undertaker. But in this case, McMahon. Specifically, the ECW name that they assumed was theirs when they brought bankrupt owner Paul Heyman on board a couple of months previous, and a plan to revive it as a part of a three-way feud between fake promotions. However, they made a slight error in judgment with regards to who should be running the show. See, ECW (being extreme and all) was based around certain concepts with regard to its audience, namely blood, guts, and the manly arts. Women were used in ECW as evil manipulative bitches all the time (possibly due to mother issues with Paul Heyman, but that's another discussion) who would lie and connive their way into the upper hand and then get piledriven by Tommy Dreamer as their comeuppance. It was, indeed, an unapologetically misogynistic group of people, which is why resurrecting the brand name and then immediately appointing STEPHANIE MCMAHON as the figurehead owner of it was so perplexing to so many people. Because if there's one thing that ECW fans would never in a million years have stood for, it was a woman telling the tough guys who inhabited ECW what to do. The decision was even stranger since Paul Heyman, himself forever associated with ECW as the owner and figurehead all wrapped into one, was then put in a submissive role to Steph and made to

play spokesman and lapdog for the group, basically castrated by the almighty Steph. The whole thing with Stephanie was also part of a deeper problem with the fanbase, which is that a major portion of the audience that ECW appealed to were sexually frustrated fourteen-year-old boys who, unable to release their aggression in normal ways, lived vicariously through their "hardcore" heroes, with spurts of blood and dives off ladders replacing sexual release on their part. In other words, to bring back the name and then appoint a woman as leader is to chop off the figurative dick of every male who watched ECW. That strategy never made sense to me, especially since Vince is a sleazemonger who makes millions capitalizing on the base instincts of his knuckle-dragging audience, and certainly taking out pent-up hostilities against women is one of the neuroses that he's had no problem exploiting over the years (cf. *Chyna v. Jeff Jarrett*, 1999).

> **In 1999, Jeff Jarrett was forced to do a humiliating job to Chyna on his way out of the promotion, which essentially destroyed any chance of his ever drawing money in wrestling again. Vince Russo booking him in WCW didn't help, either.**

8. So, having established ECW as the plaything of Stephanie McMahon, they immediately merged it with Shane's loser brand, WCW, to ensure that it would never get over. This hap-

pened in the same show as the ECW comeback, which was pretty weird to begin with because that could have been a storyline that took months to play out. I mean, hotshotting to pop a rating is one thing, but introducing an entire PROMOTION within the bigger WWF and then immediately merging it with WCW, in the same show, is insanely wasteful. The storyline possibilities from that twist alone could have lasted until November. But it was somewhat understandable—due to bankruptcy proceedings against the former ECW—that the WWF couldn't just use the name and likeness whenever they wanted, and thus they needed a combined name for the teams. (In fact, it wasn't until June 2003 that the ECW name and library went to the former WWF once and for all!) And here's where all the money they were paying the former sitcom writers really paid off, because the name that was hammered out for the new team was . . . The Alliance. Oo, scary. But first, a word on Team ECW, if I may. Another problem with the group was not just the naming convention, but the fact that the group itself wasn't truly representing anything new. They did have two new acquisitions from the former ECW—Rob Van Dam and Tommy Dreamer—but for the most part, Team ECW consisted of current lower-midcard to midcard WWF stars who put on a new t-shirt with the ECW logo and were supposed to be totally new characters. This is what I like to refer to as the nWo mindset. Back in 1998, when the New World Order storyline was running rampant through WCW, it had become so overexposed and driven into the ground that their big idea for keeping it alive was to split the group into two subgroups: one would wear white and black colors, and the other would wear red and black colors. So instead of interesting character development, what you ended up seeing week after week was wrestlers donning a new t-shirt and thus changing allegiances via their clothing rather than their actions. Same basic deal here—the Dudley Boyz, for example, retained the same mannerisms and catchphrases, and thus were the same stale team, but they happened to have an ECW shirt on. The fans had no reason to care about their sudden change of heart.

9. Speaking of no reason to care, the grand mal bonehead move of 2001 was turning Steve Austin heel at Wrestlemania X-7, in more ways than one. After a lackluster period midway through 2001 that saw Austin cowtowing to HHH's bull dyke act, the world breathed a sigh of relief as Hunter tore his quad and thus got put on the shelf for months. But this left Austin with nothing to do, so the solution was to align him with the WCW-ECW Alliance as their new leader. Now, this presented another conflict of character, because in "real life" everyone knew that Austin hated everything WCW stood for (since they fired him in 1995 and all) and would never align himself with such a group. But that aside, they made an even worse mistake by having Austin become the alpha male of the group, forcing everyone in it to bend to his will and hogging all the segments for himself. The Alliance, supposedly this fearsome group of outsiders out to destroy the WWF, were portrayed as Austin's sniveling henchmen, while Austin himself went through a weekly nervous breakdown and demanded attention from his peers. Austin's character focus was on singing "Kumbaya" with Vince McMahon backstage and trading silly gifts with Kurt Angle as part of comedy sketches, while the invading Alliance were treated like second-class citizens. And, in fact, seemingly on a weekly basis they would be

humiliated by Austin for losing their latest match or letting him down. By September, the group was so ineffective that people like Rob Van Dam, previously the focus of the group only weeks earlier, were effectively split away from it so as not to damage future drawing power by saddling him with the image of being part of that gang of losers. Of course, RVD was then buried by politics, but that's a different issue.

> To be fair, Rob got so sick of the political bullshit in 2003 that he would go on radio shows and complain about the situation. Most thought this would seal his fate, until he proved to be a huge hypocrite by signing a new contract soon after.

10. Titles, and way too many of them. A secondary effect created by the Invasion storyline was the importation of the WCW World title, World tag team title, Cruiserweight title and United States title. Add that to the WWF World title, World tag team title, Light heavyweight title, Intercontinental title, Hardcore title, European title, and Women's title, and that's a shitload of titles! How was the common schmoe watching at home supposed to keep track of ELEVEN different titles, let alone who all the champions were? For example, in August, the WCW and WWF tag team titles were traded around a few times, leaving the oddball team of Booker T and Test as one of

the few duos ever to hold both sets of titles. This pairing was so innocuous that after losing them, they broke up, never feuded, and were never even acknowledged as former partners again by the writers and announcers! And just to use a personal example, there were points when I would be having a conversation with a friend about wrestling, and he'd ask a simple question like "I haven't watched in a couple of weeks . . . who are the such-and-such champions?" and I'd draw a complete blank because I'd already seen five title changes in that time period and could no longer keep track. And I'm a guy who used to be able to recite all the Intercontinental champions by memory, complete with cities where they won the title. The title situation was becoming so meaningless that unification matches between the WCW and WWF tag champions and singles champions headlined house shows across the country and drew *worse* in a lot of cases than previous shows in a given city!

11. The worst offense of all, I think, is that by October, the Invasion was no longer a threat, or even something special, it was just another part of a scripted television show featuring guys who had become associated with the WWF brand name by osmosis, occasionally spewing rhetoric about how the WWF sucks or whatever. The "specialness" was long dead, replaced by the kind of general ennui and boredom that the fanbase had become used to by that time. Was it really that big of a deal when WWF tag champions The Dudley Boyz were fighting WCW tag champions the Hardy Boyz (or maybe it was the other way around—see point #10) in the same match people had been watching since 1999? The appeal of an outsider angle is making the fanbase believe that what they're watching is "real"—that the people involved really hate each other and that the survival of your favorite promotion is in real jeopardy if the people representing it lose their match. What did we get here? Green rookies Sean O'Haire and Mark Jindrak doing an ignominious job to the APA, Diamond Dallas Page getting squashed by Undertaker's wife, and the future of the WCW name being fought over by a guy who hates it (Austin) and a guy who was barely out of his rookie year when the promotion folded (Angle). How does any of that make me, as a fan, think that anyone's job is actually in jeopardy?

To date, and this is the really scary one, they've probably made more money taking a few of the WCW archive matches and putting them on DVDs as extras than they did from the entirety of the Invasion angle.

Credit where it's due here: Since they've gotten their head out of their ass regarding using their huge library of footage, they've put out some *awesome* DVDs—and sales figures back that opinion up.

Which brings us to 2002.

2.

Ch-Ch-Ch-Changes

If I shoot at the sun, I may hit a star.
—P. T. Barnum

As the year drew to a close in 2001, the dreadful invasion angle was put out to pasture completely at Survivor Series 2001, as a WWF-led team captained by the Rock defeated an Alliance-led team captained by Steve Austin. In typical fashion, it featured almost no one from the original WCW side on the WCW team. Rob Van Dam in fact was better associated with ECW than WCW, and it was fairly surprising that he was even allowed into the main event scene again, as his rapid rise to popularity rivaling the top stars' was ruffling more than a few feathers on top and causing the usual suspects to freak out. The process of burying him began in earnest, with losses to Edge, and HHH (and Kurt Angle's wife of all people) began a smear campaign against him decrying the evils of his kicks, as did Steve Austin (who defended the WWF title against both Angle and RVD at the No Mercy PPV in October 2001). The end result was a guy stuck in the doldrums of his career, quickly realizing that the glass

ceiling was very real. Let's take another look at the match, shall we?

The Background: The match actually went through quite a few forms during the planning stages, as the initially announced team for the WWF had Vince McMahon in place of Big Show, while the Alliance team was lacking Kurt Angle because he hadn't turned from the WWF side of things at that point. In fact, originally Chris Jericho was supposed to turn from Team WWF to Team Alliance, but the writing team thought that would be too obvious and so chose Kurt Angle instead, thus ruining a months-long run as top babyface and sending him crashing into the midcard again. Paul Heyman actually cut the promo of a lifetime on Smackdown to build up this match, airing every bit of dirty laundry he had against Vince and venting all his frustrations, and it probably helped the buyrate by about 10 percent, too, which would have covered merely a portion of the money that Vince lent him over the years to keep ECW afloat.

The Stipulations: The losing side is dissolved

and is never seen on Vince McMahon's programming again. Clearly a joke that would never be bought into by the cynical fanbase, but it was just designed to get rid of the Alliance once and for all anyway. Shane and Stephanie were banished from TV. Stephanie's banishment didn't last quite as long as you'd hope, but Shane didn't want to be a TV personality any longer and so hasn't really been around since then, excepting a brief stint in 2003.

The Overall Importance: As a match, not much. It marked the first time in years that a Survivor Series elimination match was actually headlining the show that made those matches famous, but the stipulations proved to be forgotten weeks later, as everyone who was "fired" from the WWF as a result of losing the match was rehired via a goofy loophole or literally just appearing for no reason later on. It did mark the first time that Rock pinned Steve Austin in their respective WWF careers. Also, three people turned in the same match, as Jericho turned on Rock, Kurt Angle turned babyface on Austin (and then heel the next night) and Austin was turned de facto face with the loss.

Survivor Series 2001, November 18, 2001, Greensboro, NC

Winner Take All: Team WWF (Big Show, Undertaker, Kane, Chris Jericho, and The Rock) versus The Alliance (Shane McMahon, Kurt Angle, Rob Van Dam, Booker T, and Steve Austin). Show was looking positively svelte compared to his weight just two years later, although he was consistently announced as 500 pounds his whole WWF career. Just to show you the kind of logic behind this entire angle, Rock (leader of Team WWF) was the WCW champion, while Steve Austin (leader of Team WCW) was WWF cham-

pion. And speaking of which, Austin and Rock slug it out in the corner to start, and Austin gets a quick Thesz Press and F-U elbow for two. Rock returns fire with his own Thesz Press and F-U elbow for two, but Shane saves. Booker comes in and pounds Rock, who comes back with a flying clothesline for two. Shane saves again. Jericho comes in and chops Booker, setting up a flapjack and a dropkick to the back that brings RVD in for the Alliance. Jericho grabs a headlock and overpowers him, but they crisscross until Jericho gets a leg lariat and a vertical suplex. They slug it out, won by Jericho, but he misses a dropkick and Rob gets a handspring splash for two. Rob dodges a charge in the corner and tries a rana, but Jericho blocks with the Walls. Shane again saves, becoming more of a pest by the minute, and Kurt Angle comes in to give it a go with Kane. Angle can't win with punches, and in fact gets his clock cleaned as a result. Corner clothesline, but Angle goes underneath and fires off a german suplex. Kane comes back with a sideslam and goes up with the flying clothesline, which gets two. Shane, of course, saves again. He's so gonna die.

Now it's Undertaker's turn, and he pounds on Angle in the corner, but runs into a boot. Booker comes in and gets nowhere, walking into a big boot. Legdrop gets two, and guess who saves again. Taker works the arm with the ROPEWALK OF DOOM and a hanging knucklelock. Taker bars the arm, foreshadowing his later "submission skills," and gets two, as Shane saves again. Austin comes in and fires away on Undertaker, but misses a charge to the ropes and falls victim to the ropewalk. That gets two and Shane saves for the millionth time. Austin brings UT into the heel corner, however, and it's a four-on-one situation as the heels beat on him. Angle slugs away on Taker, who fights back, but falls victim to a neckbreaker that gets two. Taker keeps slugging, and a DDT follows.

Big Show tags in, full of piss and vinegar, and clotheslines Angle in the corner, then tosses him around. Rob comes in and gets more of the same, but Angle goes low and hits the Angle Slam on Show. Booker comes in with the axe kick and pre-babyface spinarooni, and then it's RVD's turn, as he frog splashes Big Show. Finally, Shane's turn with a flying elbow to finish Show at 12:39. I assume this was during one of Show's frequent punishments. Shane gets cocky, however, and Rock comes in to take him to the proverbial woodshed. In counterpoint to the finishers on Show, all the faces come in and tee off on Shane with their finishes: Kane's chokeslam, Undertaker's tombstone, and Jericho's lionsault for the pin at 14:28.

Angle comes in next and they fight over a suplex, but Jericho forearms him down to set up a backbreaker for two. Angle takes him down in turn and slugs away, allowing Booker to come in with some slams and a kneedrop. RVD comes in and kicks away in the corner and pounds Jericho with shoulderblocks, but gets rolled up for two and clotheslined. Kane comes in and hammers on his future tag team partner, but gets kicked in the head. Kane clotheslines him coming out of the corner and powerslams him, then stops to deal with a wayward Booker. This allows Rob to pop up with a frog splash, which Kane no-sells. Chokeslam is stopped by Booker and everyone brawls, leaving RVD to dropkick Kane for the pin at 18:17.

Undertaker goes for RVD immediately, pounding him in the corner as well as Booker. Then Austin in another corner. Then Angle in a fourth corner, and he runs back and forth clotheslining

all of them. Pride goeth before the fall. Snake eyes for Angle and a big boot set up the powerbomb, but Austin sneaks in with a KICK WHAM STUNNER and Angle gets the pin at 20:00 to put the Alliance up four on two. So it's Jericho and Rock alone. Booker stomps on Rock, who fights back and slugs away, but gets caught with a spin kick. Rock suddenly no-sells and DDTs Booker for two. They slug it out, won by Booker, but he walks into a samoan drop for two. Austin saves. That's a pretty devastating samoan drop if it needed a save. Rock rolls up Booker for the pin at 22:30.

RVD comes in for his team and hammers away in the corner. He goes up, but gets powerbombed off by Rock for two in a slick spot. Hot tag Jericho, who cuts off RVD's tag with a dropkick and a forearm. Neckbreaker gets two. He unloads the CANADIAN VIOLENCE and bulldogs RVD to set up the Lionsault, but it misses and Rob spinkicks him. Split-legged moonsault, but it hits the knee and Jericho hits the Stroke for the pin at 24:49, and it's down to a regular tag match. Everyone brawls, as Angle hammers on Jericho in the corner and Austin catapults Rock into the post with MUSTARD, leaving Angle to chinlock Jericho. He powers out, but Angle stomps him down for two. Austin comes in with chops and brings him up for a superplex, which gets two. They mess up a crisscross spot and Austin powers him into a suplex and drops an elbow for two. Angle keeps pounding him and chokes away. Back elbow gets two. Jericho counters a rollup to an anklelock, but Angle counters out of it and clotheslines him. Austin comes back in and suplexes Jericho, but miscalculates a potential elbowdrop off the top and has to abort it. Weird.

They bring Jericho into the heel corner and continue the beatdown, with Austin getting some pretty aggressive stomps in. He goes back to the chinlock on Jericho, who powers out and slugs away, but they collide and both are out. Finally, it's the hot tag to the Rock, who goes nuts on Angle and suplexes him out of his boots. Dragon-screw legwhip into the Scorpion King Deathlock, and Angle taps at 31:54. That was suspiciously quick. So it's Austin alone against Jericho and Rock. Austin rolls through a bodypress by Jericho and gets two. Jericho tries the Walls, but Austin pokes him in the eye to break. He gets his own Austin crab, but Jericho powers out of that to block. Austin goes up for an axehandle, but Jericho nails him coming down. Austin lifts the knees to block the Lionsault, however, and gets two. They go up top, but Jericho fights him off and gets a missile dropkick for two. He chops away and gets a rollup for two, but Austin counters for the pin at 34:29, leaving us one-on-one.

Rock and Austin slug it out while Jericho protests, and then shows his true colors by turning on Rock with the Stroke and going heel for the long haul. Austin only gets two off it, however. Both guys are out, and Austin starts pounding on the mat and stomping away, but Rock fires back. Rock gets tossed in dramatic fashion and they brawl outside, where they inevitably end up on the Spanish announce table. Back in, Rock stomps him and chops away, but walks into a spinebuster and Austin gets his own version of the sharpshooter. Rock makes the ropes, but Austin holds on until forced by the ref. That's smart tactics in general. Austin grabs the title belt, but misses and gets locked in Rock's sharpshooter. Austin makes the ropes, but Rock pulls him off. Back to the ropes, where Austin goes low behind the ref's back and tries a stunner, which Rock reverses to his own. That gets two. Evil Referee

Nick Patrick punks out the original ref, allowing Austin to hit Rock Bottom for two. Austin takes out his frustrations on Patrick and decides he likes Hebner better after all, but he gets bumped again. A KICK WHAM STUNNER for Rock, but the ref is, of course, dead. Should've stuck with Nick Patrick. Kurt Angle then runs back in, turns on Austin, and Rock Bottom blessedly kills the Alliance at 44:45. Most of the match actually ended up being filler, but once it got to the final four men, it was good stuff the rest of the way. ★★★½

My original rating was ★★★★, so I liked the match a little less on second viewing. I think this was due to the slower portions that opened the match and the fact that I was three years removed from the original drama of the stipulations.

The RAW that took place the day after that fateful show was actually quite interesting in itself. With the end of the invasion storyline, Paul Heyman no longer had a viable reason to be an onscreen character, so he was removed from the color commentator position and replaced again by Jerry Lawler (who had come to an agreement with the WWF after leaving months earlier and from all accounts being miserable the whole time he was gone). Heyman remained on board as a part of the creative team.

A word on Jerry Lawler, if I may.

I personally am not a fan of Lawler's style of "commentating" (it generally has less to do with calling the match and advancing storylines and more to do with leering at the women twenty years his junior), but the crowds generally like him, so it was a positive move for them to make. It's strange, though, that someone so accomplished in the ring and able to train younger wrestlers in the fine art of working a match would be wasted as a TV announcer, while Big Bossman was used as a trainer. Since no one in the promotion outside of Lawler knows how to throw a really good-looking worked punch, you'd think someone would take advantage of his knowledge of the business and teach the newer workers. Lawler's story is quite sad and interesting at the same time, however, as his split with the WWF came in April 2001, when an argument with management over not using wife, Stacy Carter (a.k.a. the Kat), enough turned into a very ugly walkout on Lawler's part. Lawler cried over his beer in very public fashion, via his personal Web site, and the story got even sadder when Carter (nearly twenty years his junior) dumped him for independent wrestler Mike Hard (and with a name like that, you just knew there was gonna be a picture leaked onto the Internet of the new couple having sex, which there was) and left him spiraling into depression, a senior citizen with a taste for young women, who was no longer able to get them. His Web site updates became more routinely pathetic and whiny, as he was basically begging Carter to come back to him and getting nothing back from her. Finally, after working a couple of shows for upstart promotion XWF, he returned to the one place where he could feel at home, the WWF, but his glory years as a color commentator were obviously far behind him.

But I digress.

The really big thing on that post–PPV RAW proved to be the long-awaited debut of Ric Flair, nine years after his departure from the company in 1993. It was interesting to bring him in AFTER killing the WCW angle, because Flair (in the minds of many) was just the guy to bring the credibility and spark to the WCW brand, since he had been associated with it for close to twenty years. They had a different plan in mind, however. Vince's pet project had long been the establishment of two different "brands" of WWF programming, in an attempt to create his own competition. Even Vince was smart enough to know that without his nemesis in the form of WCW, his own promotion wasn't going to be as effective. Of course, you're opening up a can of worms about whether competition itself or simply Vince's mind-set was causing his own demise, but he sure *thought* the lack of competition was the cause, and I guess that's the important thing. And on a rather ironic note, it was around this time that preliminary negotiations with the original members of the nWo (Scott Hall, Kevin Nash, and Hulk Hogan) began, and they symbolized the exact opposite of all the traits of WCW that Flair symbolized. It just goes to show that they really had no idea where any of this was going.

So Flair was brought in to play his new

> **Apparently we just didn't realize what a great use of the greatest wrestler of all time HHH had in mind—as his simpering lackey. Who *wouldn't* be honored with that kind of role?**

nemesis, and here's where things get a bit complicated. You see, back when Shane and Stephanie "bought" WCW and ECW, respectively, the explanation for why they had such sums of cash lying around was that they sold their shares in the WWF to someone, but it was never mentioned who the buyer was. So when Flair debuted, he announced that he was the representative of a "consortium of investors" (never seen on TV and never mentioned again), and therefore he was now the 50 percent owner of the promotion.

Now, you may be thinking to yourself, "Hey, that would have been a cool way to bring in a big name from WCW back when it would have meant something!" and of course you'd be right, but that kind of logical thinking never stopped the WWF from doing something dumb and/or six months too late before, and it sure as hell didn't stop them at that point, either. Now apparently the whole "feuding figureheads" thing hadn't been beaten into the ground quite enough by the previous five years of Vince Russo storylines yet and they felt there was still fertile ground for exploitation of a tired storyline. The funny thing is that the night that Flair was introduced as the new babyface figurehead, commissioner–owner–Grand Poobah, Mick Foley (the previous holder of the lame-duck commissioner title) quit the promotion entirely after months of dissatisfaction with the storylines and the generally stale nature of his character. Well, it's more funny-sad than funny-haha, but then I have a weird sense of humor anyway. Money apparently speaks louder than integrity, because Mick returned in 2004.

Flair's arrival also heralded another major change in the direction of the company, as Steve Austin's months-long (and hugely failed) heel turn was abandoned without warning, after

he cost his Alliance teammates the win at Survivor Series. First order of business: recycle another storyline, as he began feuding with Vince McMahon again, just as he had done for years previously. He was still the WWF champion and was pinned the previous night by the Rock, holder of the World championship (nee WCW championship) in the final segment of a ten-man elimination tag match that was the main event of the evening. Of course, not only was putting the WCW World title on the Rock, who had never even worked for WCW in his career, a retarded thing to do, but then to have the WWF and WCW champions meeting for the first time ever on PPV without so much as promoting it as a singles match puts the whole creative team beyond "nuts" and into "the entire Planters factory."

And speaking of "nuts," that leads into a discussion about another charming period in the WWF's history, as Vince McMahon, ever one to push the envelope in directions that no one in their right mind would want to go, decided that there was something vital to the equation still missing from the programming. Something to draw in audiences composed of women and children as well as the usual male demographic. Something that families could get together and watch during dinner. Yes, I can only be speaking of one thing: hot man-on-man ass-licking action, otherwise known as the Kiss My Ass Club. Okay, check out this high-concept stuff: WCW's side lost the big match at Survivor Series, and therefore everyone on that side is fired and can no longer compete in the WWF. However, this being wrestling and stipulations in general being a joke, you need a way to get everyone back on TV again, preferably within two weeks and with a minimum of thought required. So you get Vince offering ex-WCW guys their jobs back, on the condition that they pucker up and kiss his bare ass on live TV. Now, I'm a heterosexual male and as secure in my manhood as the next guy, but, FUCK, could this have been any more gay? Sample segment: Vince demands that Steve Austin bend over and kiss his ass, but he refuses. Announcer Jim Ross thinks this is hilarious, so Vince has him hauled into the ring (in Oklahoma, which is well known as Jim's home state, since he talks about it during *every show*) and has new ally Undertaker force Jim's face into his bare ass. Then (and this is the best part), he gallops around the ring while wearing Jim's famous cowboy hat. Now, we all know the deal with Vince—he's a power freak who gets off on humiliating talent just because he can. Thankfully, this particular fetish was wrapped up after a couple of weeks (despite great ratings due to the Jerry Springer "I'll watch anything once just to see how bad it can get" mentality of the wrestling audience) when Rock took the initiative and forced Vince to kiss Rikishi's ass.

As a sidenote to the whole thing, Undertaker turned heel and joined with Vince, forcing Jim's humiliation in his hometown. There were an awful lot of turns done in this brief period, including Jericho turning on Rock to go full heel, Kurt Angle going from the WWF to the Alliance and back again, Austin changing back to superhero babyface after the Survivor Series, Rob Van Dam going full-fledged babyface with the death of the Alliance, and a bunch of other minor turns in the midcard. Big Show turned as well, but then he did it so much from his debut in 1999 until 2002 that it was something of a running joke by that point anyway.

Speaking of Chris Jericho, an odd push for him began in early December, sort of. For years, Jericho had been fighting to break through the

> **Miraculously, Show's heel turn in 2002 proved to be the one that not only stuck but proved to be the most effective.**

glass ceiling and escape the midcard, and the closest he had ever gotten was a win over HHH on RAW in April 2000 that was immediately overturned. The plan for Wrestlemania X-8 was for Jericho to get the big belt and defend it against the conquering hero, HHH, so that the universe could be right again and so forth, because god forbid anyone go more than a month without HHH having a title again.

So anyway, here was the thinking from Vince McMahon's end of things, and see if you can follow along here: they want to get rid of the WCW title, which is understandable. The worthless U.S. title was already unified with the slightly less useless Intercontinental title at Survivor Series, as Edge (the U.S. champion at the time, for those keeping track) defeated Test (the Intercontinental champion) to win both belts. Ditto for the tag titles, as the Dudley Boyz unified the belts by defeating the Hardy Boyz. But the big one, the WCW World title, somehow survived the scorched-earth unification match policy because they wanted to keep it around and book a unification match between the WCW and WWF titles once and for all and hopefully draw a big buyrate for it. However, the first thing they did was rename the WCW World title into a more generic-sounding the "World title," so as to erase any memory of WCW from it. Of course, without the memory of WCW on the title, there really wasn't any *point* in doing a unification match for the belt.

And then it gets really good—instead of promoting a singles match between the two biggest stars of the modern era in a straight one-on-one match (Rock and Steve Austin, the respective champions at that point), they set up a minitournament for the Vengeance show in December, with Rock facing Jericho for the World title and Austin facing Angle for the WWF title, and the winners then facing for the supposed Undisputed World title at the end of the night. But they essentially promoted the show as a guaranteed Rock-Austin final, which first of all negated any heat that either Angle or Jericho might have gotten by being promoted as a part of this thing. Ah, but if you're an astute fan you're probably thinking to yourself, "If they were going to do a Rock-Austin match, you'd think they'd just promote it straight up instead of messing with a tournament, so obviously something was up." And indeed, what was up was that they wanted to make the money off the Rock-Austin match without actually delivering it by putting Jericho over the Rock and setting up Jericho-Austin for both belts as the eventual main event. Tricky fellow, that Vince.

The Background: This was the finals of a one-night, four-man tournament to determine an Undisputed champion. Steve Austin defeated Kurt Angle in 15:01 of a ★★★¼ match, while Jericho upset the Rock in 19:05 of a ★★★★½ classic that was forgotten a few weeks later. The really strange buildup to this match was Jericho's antipush leading up to it, as he lost match after match in order to make fans think he had zero chance at winning the title. Well, that sure succeeded with flying colors. In fact, Steve Austin essentially squashed him on RAW the week before this match in order to really throw us fans off the scent. Mission accomplished. Austin was engaged in a minifeud with Booker T that featured much politicking on Austin's part, as he vetoed the use of Booker's brother Stevie Ray for an angle, and essentially felt that Booker wasn't at his level. He also refused to do a clean loss to Jericho, which explains the nature of the finish.

The Stipulations: This was World (WCW) champion versus WWF champion, winner takes both belts.

The Overall Importance: This was the first sign that someone outside of the Big Four (Austin, Rock, HHH, and Undertaker) could be given a shot to the main event with the main title of the promotion, although really Jericho was just being set up as a lame duck for HHH later on. It also marked the end of Steve Austin's final reign as champion, something that no one thought would come at the end of 2001.

Vengeance 2001, December 9, 2001, San Diego, CA

Undisputed World title: Steve Austin versus Chris Jericho. Jericho rolls over for two, then stomps away. Forearm, and he pounds away. Corner clothesline, but Austin spears him and gives him some turnbuckle sandwich. Stunner is blocked, so Austin tosses him and they brawl. Austin dumps him on the railing and gives him the post ala Angle in the previous match. He pulls up the mat, but Jericho preps the Spanish table and tries the Walls of Jericho there. Austin powers out, though, and suplexes Jericho on the floor. They head back in, where Austin charges and hits the post. Jericho goes to the arm, but misses a dropkick and gets catapulted for two. Jericho floats over out of the cover, into a Herb Kunze armbar, using the ropes for leverage. As a note, this move is more properly called a Fujiwara armbar, but it gained the name of an online wrestling columnist in the early days of the Internet, due to his overriding irritation at moves exactly like this, which are submission moves, being used without any attention to details such as inflicting previous pain on the arm beforehand. Suplex and he goes up, but Austin nails him coming down. Austin comes back, but Jericho rolls into the Walls of Jericho, getting a good pop. Austin makes the ropes. Ref is bumped, so Jericho goes low and stunners Austin. Vince brings out Nick Patrick: Evil Ref to count (at this point, Nick Patrick was a freelance biased ref, whereas before he had favored exclusively WCW guys), but Ric Flair in turn pulls him out, and Vince in turn punks out Flair. In the ring, Austin chases Vince and punks him out, then heads back in for a Thesz Press and the Walls of Austin. Jericho is tapping, but Booker T runs in, nails Austin with the belt, and Jericho unifies the titles at 12:37. ALL HAIL CANADA! Too much tomfoolery, what with the ref bumping and the run-ins and the screwjobs and all. ★★★

> **My thoughts on this match remain the same—a decent, well-worked match that was ridiculously overbooked in the name of placating Steve Austin.**

Largely undermined by the booking that was supposed to make him a big star, Jericho was now a lame-duck champion with a title that no one believed in. Not a good position for someone who was supposed to be breaking through the glass ceiling, is it? You'll be happy to know that people within the WWF cleaned up on the match, however, as a betting agency in Britain was dumb enough to take wagers on who would be the champion at the end of the year. Many people within the promotion put money on Jericho, knowing the future plans, and cleaned out the agency as a result.

The same sort of character burial thing that was happening to Jericho was also happening to Rob Van Dam (without the subsidiary betting action), as he lost the Hardcore title to the Undertaker on the same show, in what was presumed by some (who were in turn laughed at by others such as myself) to be an opportunity for Undertaker to return the favor to RVD and put him over bigger than before. That, of course, didn't happen. At least the match was decent. But then that seemed to be becoming the rallying cry for despairing fans everywhere: "Well, this guy's career is dead, but at least the match was decent." I'm sure I'll go to my grave mumbling that. Jericho and RVD were then programmed together in a feud that was supposed to pay off at Royal Rumble and become the first show since December 1997 not to feature one of Rock, HHH, Steve Austin, or Undertaker in the main event, but we still had a while to wait for that.

The Vengeance show also featured an interesting advertising campaign, as all the TV promos were heavily centered around HHH, who was still a couple of weeks away from returning from his quadriceps tear in July 2001. However, HHH wanted to return in Madison Square Garden later than planned, so the plans to have him return on this PPV (or indeed even make a token appearance to satiate fans who bought the show based on the incessant hyping of his appearance on TV) were scrapped and people were left scratching their heads at how a previously organized company like the WWF could let a boner like that one slip by them.

The year ended on a tragic note, as developmental talent, Russ Haas, fresh off receiving a clean bill of health from the WWF's medical team a few weeks earlier after suffering a heart attack, suffered another one and died. His brother, Charlie, briefly changed his in-ring name to RC Haas, but switched back when he was called up to the majors later on. No serious questions about why he was allowed to continue competing and why his heart was in such bad condition were ever asked.

3.

A Whole Lotta H's

Every man's occupation should be beneficial to his fellow-man as well as profitable to himself. All else is vanity and folly.
—P. T. Barnum, *The Humbugs of the World*, 1866

As 2002 began, it seemed to signal a change from the old to the new, although that would swing wildly in the other direction within a few weeks and the company would begin to not only show cracks in the façade, but fall apart completely.

Gone since July 2001 with a torn quad, HHH was set to make his triumphant return to the WWF on January 7 at the mecca of wrestling, Madison Square Garden. The assumption was generally made that he would be a babyface, since he had been given literally months of buildup with a video package set to U2's "Beautiful Day" (all of which were very well done thanks to the crack production crew) and endless vignettes about his courage in the face of suffering the injury and how he trained like a madman to come back again. However, there were two mitigating circumstances that made people wonder if the HHH returning from six months on the sidelines would be the same as the one who won Wrestler of the Year in 2000:

1. Wrestling as an artform is extremely dependent on leg strength and the ability to be mobile enough to take the bumps necessary to tell a story in the ring. The injury suffered by HHH, which was akin to his leg muscle rolling up like a window shade due to stress on the tendons, was considered so serious that doctors essentially doubted he would be able to return at 100 percent if at all. To suffer that sort of injury and expect to come back at the same level as before the injury would be optimistic thinking in the extreme, but HHH not only expected that, he expected to be immediately pushed back into a main event position again with an iffy leg. So in order to compensate for the bum leg, he concentrated his "training" in another direction.

2. When he returned in January, he had mysteriously gained a good thirty to forty pounds of bulk. Not fat, and not muscle, but sheer bulk. Long an admitted mark for bodybuilders, HHH reshaped his body into what was almost a

parody of what wrestlers are considered to look like by the general public, with the intention (in my humble opinion) of keeping his spot by being physically bigger than everyone else on the roster (and in some cases bigger than a couple of people on the roster put together) and disguising the lack of mobility from the injury with a new power-based offense that would make everyone in the audience go, "Gosh, what a monster that HHH is, let's buy ten tickets for the next show and tell all our friends." Or something like that.

The results of the "new" HHH, as you might be able to tell, were not encouraging. While I was willing to give him the benefit of the doubt to a certain point because of his prior performances in 2000 and 2001, it was immediately apparent his movement and move-set had become so reduced by the injury and added weight that carrying matches in the main event would require a miracle from his opponent. And since HHH is the smartest man in wrestling, he programmed himself against Kurt Angle, who was just such a miracle worker most of the time. Good first step, but another problem became apparent: After the initial fan response to his water-spitting act and the big rating for his return, the numbers and reactions plummeted back to earth within a week. This was the first real sign that it was no longer wine and roses as far as Vince's promotion went—fans had become so burned out on big returns and the mishandling of the people involved (Rock's return from shooting *The Mummy Returns* in mid-2001 is a prime example) that when the promotion really needed fans to believe in a top babyface (and said babyface had so much stroke that it was highly unlikely he'd ever get mishandled), the strategy backfired and the fans chose to wait and see. In fact, whereas

Rock's big return had pulled RAW's ratings to respectable levels for a period of a month or so in August 2001 (to a peak rating of 5.7, up from levels of 5.0 or thereabouts), HHH's big return only popped the rating for a week, and even then the ratings had gotten so low (falling below 4.0 during the Christmas holidays) that the big boost was only to a 4.9, and it fell back to 4.4 the next week and didn't show any upward trends until later in the year.

That was the kind of stuff that the common fan didn't really care about, but even within the mark community, their initial reaction wore off rather quickly, as HHH's overexposure during the build to his return burned a lot of people out on him before he even came back. Another tidbit on him also came out at this point, as he was doing the publicity tour and went on Howard Stern to discuss his relationship with ex-girlfriend Chyna among other things, and it came out publicly for the first time that he was dating head WWE writer Stephanie McMahon. That had kinda been the worst kept secret in wrestling for a long time, before they were "outed" on an Internet radio show. Many people started questioning the inherent conflict of interest in being pushed to the top of the promotion while being romantically linked with the boss's daughter (*and* head writer to boot), but HHH simply shrugged it off by claiming to be the most talented and hardest working guy in the promotion, and thus most deserving of the attention given him by the TV product. Most fans were just wondering whether HHH's tits were bigger than Stephanie's after all the steroids. However, a little more than a month after being removed from WWF TV "forever" (with the Alliance loss at Survivor Series), Stephanie was back on TV again with the return of HHH, reminding everyone that they were still married (in storyline terms—in real life, the wedding wasn't until October 2003) and thus she somehow deserved to be back on TV again. This was clearly gearing toward a breakup angle, which under the Kevin Sullivan rule of wrestling, was a very bad idea for HHH. The rule states that any relationship that breaks up on screen will also break up off screen because wrestlers are freaks who get so far into their character that they can't tell reality from their twisted storyline world. Or words to that effect. In an amazing stretch of acting ability, Stephanie got to act like a whiny, screeching nag and general pain in the ass every week on TV.

HHH also had a rather brilliant way to appear to be a company guy while still manipulating things behind the scenes entirely around himself—he would sell and/or do jobs for guys lower down the card, but would ensure that they were low enough down that they would never be a threat to his position. So, for instance, he would be fine with going out and losing to someone like D-Von Dudley (a lifelong tag wrestler who had zero chance of ever advancing as a singles wrestler) but would always make sure to pin Chris Jericho in every possible scenario where they faced each other. In this way, if questioned about sitting in on booking meetings and criticizing others, he could claim to be helping to make new stars while still being on top of the promotion with no challengers in sight.

We'll get back to HHH in a little bit.

Moving onto an *entirely* different line, a team that would become important later on was formed in January, as multiple-time washout Billy Gunn was paired with Alliance survivor Chuck Palumbo in a new tag team that fulfilled the three rigorous demands of being top-level WWF superstars: both were tall, muscular, and had full heads of hair. However, in a twist that might have been edgy in 1962, it was hinted that they might be a little bit more than just tag team partners, wink wink nudge nudge. Now, while I'm all for character development and a more three-dimensional approach to the people who inhabit the WWF world, wrestling fans don't particularly like to be reminded of the homo-erotic undertones of the sport they love so much, and this sort of thing was just rubbing salt into the wound. I mean, it's bad enough that you've normally got two guys with short tights and oily bodies rolling around on the mat and trying to grab onto each other, but to then have that same portrayal exaggerated to the point where you're dealing with obviously gay characters is pretty insulting. To the credit of the creative team, however, it was just innuendo for most of the year. Again, we'll get back to Billy and Chuck (like all "WWF Divas," they lost their last names) later on.

Speaking of flaming homos (or people who play them on TV, not that there's anything wrong with that), the buildup for the Royal Rumble match included a couple of rather odd names, as Goldust (last seen in the WWF appealing to Vince for breast implants to help the character and getting fired over it) and Mr. Perfect (last seen in WCW being drunk on live TV and in the short-lived XWF as their champion) were both announced for the match as surprise entrants. The Goldust one was particularly shocking since he left on such bad terms and was one of the people fired on the live Nitro/RAW simulcast in early 2001. But as they say, forever is a short time in wrestling.

HHH's return was geared toward his entrance in the match, where the winner would get a shot at the WWF title. While the buildup was obviously toward making HHH seem like the second coming of Jesus, there was still a push, even if it was a half-hearted one, to make Chris Jericho (you know, the guy with the Undisputed title, who beat both Rock and Steve Austin in the same night?) into something that might possibly resemble a champion before HHH inevitably squashed him. The Rock, long a good friend and supporter of Jericho in real life, was game to help him out any way he could, and the result was another great match between them, this one at the Rumble PPV.

The Background: Jericho, having turned heel after winning the titles at Vengeance, was slowly developing his own stable of lackeys, all of whom were Canadian. While this idea never panned out, the involvement of the so-called Canadian Horsemen (okay, it was mainly me who called them that) seemed to indicate a tainted victory for Jericho was coming. Rock himself earned the title shot by defeating Booker T in a #1 contender match, which isn't exactly a daunting feat. The buildup was the standard for such a match, as Rock generally got the advantage over Jericho in tag matches, while Jericho squeaked out wins over lesser contenders to make the fans think he was ripe for the picking. Oddly enough, the entire feud between them that lasted for much of the fall of 2001 was ignored in setting the stage for it.

The Stipulations: None, just a standard match for the Undisputed World title.

The Overall Importance: It was the year's first serious contender for Match of the Year, and it probably would have established Jericho as a top guy in the promotion with no further help. But other things interjected themselves, and all did not go according to plan. It did, however, foreshadow the stable that would be known as the Un-Americans later in the year.

Royal Rumble 2002, January 20, 2002, Atlanta, GA

Undisputed WWF title match: Chris Jericho versus The Rock. Jericho does some trashtalking, so Rock kicks his ass to start. Samoan drop gets two. Jericho beats a hasty retreat and runs right into a Rock spear and ground'n'pound routine. "Ground 'n' pound" is shorthand from the mixed martial arts world for taking an opponent down to the mat and hammering on him with punches. Jericho hits the forearm and a clothesline, but charges and hits the post. Rock walks into a hotshot and Jericho kicks away and adds some CANADIAN VIOLENCE, but gets elbowed. Jericho leg lariat gets two. Suplex and the arrogant cover get two. You know, he really needs to do the full spiel because he could get it over huge. Those who watched him in WCW will know what I mean. Jericho removes the turnbuckle (just in case a spare one is needed later) but Rock attacks. Jericho takes him down and tries the Walls, but gets reversed out of it. Jericho clotheslines him and pounds away, however. Jericho goes up, missile dropkick gets two. He hits the chinlock, but Rock fights free. Jericho back up top, but the Rock crotches him and chops him on top. Superplex puts both guys down. Rock comes back with the belly-to-belly for two, but Jericho bulldogs him and hits a pair of Lionsaults. ROCK IS DEAD! Oh, wait, it only gets two. Well, he's lucky that Jericho wasn't really trying that time. Jericho argues the blatantly anti-Canadian bias issue with Earl Hebner, but gets caught in a Scorpion King Deathlock as a result. Lance Storm and Christian run in to protest Rock's obvious use of the tights (and possibly a foreign object) while Jericho bangs on the mat to alert Hebner to the illegal submission move being used. Some may insist he was tapping out, but some are biased against Jericho and Canadians in general, so I ignore them. Is there no impartial refereeing to be found?

Rock, caught in his web of deceit, tries to cover up by tossing Storm and Christian out of the ring, but walks into the Jericho Bottom (a move invented by Jericho and stolen by Rock, mind you) for two. Senton sets up the Canadian People's Elbow, but Rock kips up and tosses Jericho in dramatic fashion. Rock preps the tables, and Rock Bottoms him from one table to the other. Back in, Jericho is in trouble, but Rock only gets two. Rock Bottom is blocked and Jericho gets the Walls of Jericho, but Rock makes the ropes. I'm pretty sure he was yelling "I quit!" but that bastard Hebner ignored it. What terrible refereeing. Back to the Walls, but Rock reverses for two. Ref is bumped (good riddance), so Jericho proudly shows off his belt, and Rock's head accidentally runs into it and knocks him out. What a klutz. Finally, some good refereeing, as Nick Patrick comes in to count two. Rock DDTs Jericho, but Patrick's Numeric Referitis is acting up again and he can't remember what comes after "1." Instead of dealing with the very real and very serious condition with an open mind, Rock resorts to violence and takes out Patrick. I'm shocked and appalled. People's Elbow, but since Rock chose violence over compassion, there's no ref. Jericho hits Rock low, rams him into the exposed turnbuckle, and then rolls him up with his feet on the ropes for the pin at 18:41. See, a good clean, scientific win by Jericho. ★★★★¼

The rub given to Jericho would prove to be short lived, unfortunately.

> My feelings on this match remain the same, as the match aged very well, and Rock and Jericho had tremendous chemistry together and could have done great things given a better push as a major program.

The opposite of short lived would of course be Hulk Hogan, who is quite long lived. And as January was ending, the deal to bring in the nWo was sealed, triggering my hypocrite alarm.

The WWF had been toying with the idea of bringing in former stars Scott Hall, Kevin Nash, and Hulk Hogan off and on since November 2001, but negotiations only got serious in January. It came down to the WWF's desperation for some big names to boost business, thus overwhelming the bad idea of hiring someone with a track record as bad as Hall, and locker room heat as bad as Hogan and Nash. The feeling was that if they could pop one big buyrate for either No Way Out in February or Wrestlemania in April, then they would have paid off their contracts and justified the trouble. But it did raise some pretty disturbing moral questions, specifically in regards to Scott Hall. For instance, only three months before, Eddie Guerrero was fired for a DUI charge, despite an honest effort on his part to clean up his act. Jerry Lawler's son, Brian (a.k.a. Grandmaster Sexay), was caught coming across the Canadian border with unspecified amounts of drugs and was arrested and terminated by the WWF soon after. And yet Scott Hall, who had numerous public battles with drugs and alcohol and even lost custody of his children at one point due to his demons, was being welcomed back into the fold with open arms and a big paycheck. Now, I'm all for second chances and all that crap, but this is a guy with multiple DUI charges and even an infamous incident where he fondled a fifty-year-old woman while drunk. I'd say his employment card should have been punched for the last time long ago.

And then you have Kevin Nash, a guy who was being called a locker room cancer as part of the official WWF company line while he was in WCW, a guy who nearly set the record by tanking two major promotions within a three-year period by winning their respective World titles and drawing record low houses and buyrates for his matches, a guy who spends more time on his hair than his training regimen, and a guy who thinks that by making a little framing gesture before an elbow that it makes him look cool. The worst thing about Nash is his very sad sense of denial, as he grew his hair to rock-star lengths while having to dye it away from the natural grey it was becoming by 2002. There's nothing more uncool than a forty-something wannabe hipster who has to use Grecian Formula to keep from looking like someone's grandpa. By this point, Big Daddy Cool was more like Granddaddy Cool. It also stunk of hypocrisy for the WWF to push crap about "not knowing how to work" and then signing a guy whose big highspot is lifting his leg in the air. Admittedly, we can't all be eighteen years old and ready to jump off ladders and land on moistened rags, but it's starting to stretch the bounds of credibility when people are running in fear from a guy who takes five minutes to limp to the ring and spends another five lifting his fist in the air. I'm reminded of *This Is Spinal*

Tap, and specifically the DVD commentary, where Derek Smalls justifies the cliché fist-in-the-air act by noting that he's "projecting strength" by doing it. Nash is the strongest of men, then, fearing nothing but split ends.

In a tragic note that nearly ruined the whole year for me, Nash lost a haircut match to Chris Jericho in August 2003, resulting in his graying locks being sheared off on live TV. I was so moved by it that I wrote a haiku to express my pain:

Nash's flowing locks
Never to be dyed again.
Grecian gone bankrupt?

On the opposite side of the hair-care rainbow you have Hulk Hogan, who much like herpes, always returns when you want him around the least. Er, um, so I've heard. But with money to be made and people to be held down, you'll always find Hogan nearby. This signing was one of the most bizarre, because Vince spent the better part of ten years following Hogan's departure spinning the history of the WWF so that Hulkamania and the boom of the '80s was all his doing rather than Hogan's. They buried him on screen and off, most famously with the Huckster versus Nacho Man parody match in 1996, and constant jabs at his age via Jim Ross the night after WCW PPVs. Hogan testified against Vince in the steroid trials of 1994 (although his testimony came close to single-handedly saving Vince from jail, thus backfiring on the government), which is something that NO ONE thought Vince would ever forgive. Hell, just look at Kevin "Nailz" Wacholz, who both testified against him and sued him, a lethal combination toward ending your career if there ever was one. It seemed as though Hogan's legend was exposed for good in 2000 when he departed WCW on bad terms, which made the signing (for a good chunk of money, although later questions arose as to whether there was even a contract signed) all the more perplexing.

But regardless, there they were, whether I liked it or not. And believe me, I didn't like it. Sadly, Vince didn't call me for advice on the situation and spent millions instead. Can you believe the nerve? Ah, but you've got this potentially killer angle, for which you're paying big money, with three people who are in theory the biggest stars available on the free-agent market at that point—so how to set things up for them? By getting a McMahon involved, of course! And that happened at Royal Rumble, as the dueling owners faced off in a street fight.

The Background: Flair and McMahon had been doing the clichéd "feuding authority figures" storyline since November 2001, when Flair made a surprise appearance as the new coowner of the WWF. There wasn't really any one specific incident that caused this match to be signed, although Vince did a weird impression of Flair using a blond wig and one of his robes to really get him good and cheesed off.

The Stipulations: Just good old pride and bragging rights.

The Overall Importance: As a match, not much, but the result caused major ramifications for the WWF the next night on RAW, as Vince

went insane and vowed to destroy his own company, and Flair got involved in a feud with the Undertaker that led indirectly to the eventual split of the promotion in March.

Royal Rumble 2002, January 20, 2002, Atlanta, GA

Ric Flair versus Vince McMahon. The Flair family is at ringside, and Reid is a badass. When did this kid grow two feet? Screw Scott Steiner, they should have signed him. We already saw him taking Bischoff down on Nitro, so we know he's got the goods on the mat. Vince overpowers Flair to start and does some posing. Nice to see George Zahorian is keeping himself busy. I've gotta think that going to prison was the best thing to happen to old Dr. George—I mean, talk about your seller's market! I wonder how many prison bitches you can buy for a month's worth of HGH? Vince applies the dreaded SIDE-HEADLOCK OF DOOM to show off his arms. And he wonders why the legitimate media treats him like a joke. Besides threatening to beat up reporters. He overpowers Flair again, this time adding a strut. Flair takes him down and starts pounding him in the corner, but Vince goes low. Diesel elbow and Vince adds some chops, but Flair gives it back with extra mayo on top. Vince goes to the eyes and hits one of those weird stiff-arm clotheslines that Scott Steiner does since he can't move his arm anymore. Flair Flop and Flair Flip put Flair on the apron, where Vince knocks him down. The aluminium sign of grotesque dismemberment triggers a manly Flair bladejob, and Vince adds a garbage can for good measure. Just to clarify, a bladejob is defined as manly if done by someone with blond hair, and the resulting blood stains it red. Vince posts him and introduces him to the stairs, then steals a camera from Flair's wife Beth and takes a picture of the bloodied Flair. I'm curious if Vinnie Mac actually shows up on film, but I guess if he really WAS the agent of Satan we wouldn't get the honor of seeing him on video-tape every show. Or maybe I'm thinking of vampires. Same thing. Back in, Vince works the leg in a manner even he should be ashamed of, as he can't even get his legs extended into the air for the kneedrops to Flair's knee.

He grabs a toehold, then goes back to the knee. He goes to the figure-four (and sets a good example by actually putting it on the correct leg—straight leg is the injured one), but Flair reverses. Vince bails and grabs his phallic lead pipe, but Flair gives him a solid shot to the Hogan to stop that. He dishes the chops like a waiter at Dusty Rhodes's dinner party, and they brawl outside, where Flair smacks Vince in the face with a monitor to bust him open. Back in, Flair drags him out again and bites the cut in front of Beth. What a romantic. Back in for real, and Vince is all hold the mayo! Flair keeps on

the cut before switching up the psychology and canning him again. I think I should make it an official policy to add one star for every time Vince gets hit in the nuts. Flair puts him down with the lead pipe, and before Vince can live up to my expectations by jumping up and doing a hulking-up act, Flair puts him in the figure-four and puts him out of his misery at 14:54. For those who don't think Flair is still God, STFU. Keep your Outsiders, I like real wrestling. He not only provides entertaining matches, but tons of material for me. ★★★

The next night on RAW, everything changed, as Vince promised a "lethal dose of poison" would be injected into his promotion (no truth to the rumor that Bret Michaels was watching and thought Vince wanted to tour with him), because he would prevent Flair from killing his creation by being the one to do it himself. And with an impending lawsuit, there was more than a little real-life foreshadowing in that statement.

In February 2002, it was time for the nWo.

4.

WWF Presents New World Order™®©, All Rights Reserved, Patent Pending

Nobody ever went broke underestimating the intelligence of the American people.
—Attributed to P. T. Barnum

You knew there was gonna be problems with the nWo angle right away, as Vince revealed their presence on Smackdown, by spinning around in an office chair that had the nWo logo painted on it in white, with what appeared to be liquid paper, and done backward so that it could be read in a mirror that was placed behind Vince.

Vince at this point was playing a character going increasingly senile (which some thought might have been pretty close to the truth considering the way his promotion was being run), and using the Hogan-Hall-Nash tandem was one of the biggest indicators of both his on- and off-screen insanity. He was smart in one thing, holding off the group's debut until the No Way Out PPV in February 2002, but there was no in-

dication that they would actually be *doing* anything there, just appearing. The really odd thing about the way the buildup of the group was handled was that it wasn't really the nWo bad boys from WCW, but it was more of a sanitized WWF version of the group, with cleaned-up graphics for their anarchic video packages and official WWF-licensed t-shirts with copyrighted logos. And what they really needed to do with the nWo was sit down and actually explain the concept to people who weren't watching at the time, rather than just recycling WCW clips and hoping the vague "intrigue" factor would sell the show. Because it didn't—there was no storyline there, it was just "These guys will show up at this show, guaranteed." Well, that's great for the people who are actually silly enough to pay $30 for the honor of seeing the Three Liverspots (Nash's new catchphrase: "That's not a liver spot, that's my spot . . . oh, wait, I guess that *is* a liver spot."), but for everyone else you need at least some kind of more specific warning. I mean, sure, most of us jaded online geeks knew that the nWo was going to run in and beat up Steve Austin to allow Jericho to retain the title, but you've gotta nudge the marks in that direction so they can figure it out for themselves. I mean, the surprise factor had already been shot once you've ANNOUNCED that they're showing up. Ooo, they're such badboys that they're going to appear in a contractually mandated World Wrestling Federation Entertainment Event after being introduced by highly polished and well-produced videos. This wasn't Led Zep reuniting the band, it's Coverdale-Page with Robert Plant doing a walk-on cameo to shill his new line of Robert Plant Brand Hernia Trusses. It may bang a good buyrate in the short term (which it did, although not as good as hoped), but it's still not a new idea, it's just a sanitized WWF version of a previous WCW gimmick. They were on the right track by using the nWo name, but missing the point of the gimmick: It's about new blood starting a revolution by force and using fascist tactics and propaganda because the clean-cut Turner suits wouldn't let them express themselves otherwise. What did the WWF have to say there? "We're so desperate to find a direction that doesn't suck that we're willing to bring in the WWA's castoffs"? It's just applying the cosmetic outer shell of the angle without cracking it open to see the angst-filled center, so to speak.

See, the whole appeal of the nWo was originally the anarchic nature of the beast, and then eventually the fascist aspect that lured the cynical fourteen year olds in. Do you have any idea how many doofy-looking kids you'd see walking down the street on a given day wearing an nWo shirt of some sort? *Tons.* Why? Because it was a cool thing to do. It's black and white, it looks menacing, it's just the kind of thing to piss off parents and other authority figures. It's the kind of thing they could wear and have their parents be vaguely worried about the origins, without actually having grounds to stop them wearing it. That's a successful t-shirt, my friends, because if you can find a way to facilitate young boys annoying their teachers, you can start lighting your cigars with $100 bills.

Now, I've made this comparison before in one of my columns, but for those of you joining us a few years too late, I'll recap. Basically, the nWo played on the most important principles of the facist regimes in order to hook the kids and keep them there. In no particular order:

- Bleak, contrasting colors. Black and white. Grey. The occasional red. Ever seen Star Wars? Of course you have. You know why the Death Star is so cool and the Imperial forces look evil? Because everything is jet black (like Darth Vader's suit) or gleaming white (the Stormtroopers' armor) and they're always throwing that contrast on the screen to say, "HEY, WE'RE EVIL!." It all looks cold and mechanical, and that's what disillusioned teens *eat up.* Sure, Luke Skywalker walks out of the movie as the big hero, but who wants to be Luke Skywalker? Everyone wants to be Darth Vader, baby. Well, maybe not after seeing *Attack of the Clones*, but you know what I mean.

- Propaganda. Here's where Eric Bischoff's creative team was not only years ahead of his time, but years ahead of Vince McMahon as well. While the WWF was doing goofy vignettes featuring the Stalker and TL Hopper, the nWo was out there doing these bizarre, black-and-white, scratchy, out-of-sequence videos that said nothing more than how great they were, and looked like something out of *Triumph of the Will*. Whereas you could tune out the latest Todd Pettingill interview segment, this stuff hit you right in the sack and said, "Hey! This is something new and different and you need to pay attention!" It was a visual and auditory assault on the senses, with the picture jumping around and the audio repeating out of nowhere, and it was just generally completely different from anything else at the time. The WWF even lifted a few of those techniques for D-Generation X, and even in diluted form it *still* made them millions. And at the same time, it didn't matter if Hall, Nash, or Giant had anything more constructive to say than "Buy the shirt!" because it LOOKED important, and so people believed it was important. The mistake in 2002 came when the WWF tried to produce those same videos themselves, but since the people doing them were so slick and technically proficient, it just came across as being something out of The Establishment.

- Hand gestures and catchphrases. Notice how fans were buying into Steve Austin's "What?" bit in 2001 and still did long after he retired? Heel catchphrases sell, and the simpler the better because people are basically stupid and they get lost easily. Notice the two original nWo catchphrases: "Too sweet!" and "4 Life." Two syllables, nothing over five letters to remember, instant money. Both can be reasonably spelled by even the dumbest teenager and put onto a sign. The Nazis also used this important principal, as even today

everyone knows that the Nazi verbal salute is "Seig Heil." See? Quick, easy, effective. Handsigns are also important: The nWo lifted the "clique sign" so that Nash and Hall could have their sort of secret handshake, and the fans picked it up quickly. Look at the Nazis again, and their famous salute. Look at any fraternity, with the secret handshakes and beer-chugging anthems. Give the kids something to chant, something to do with their hands, and you've hooked them again.

This is all basic psychological stuff that any good advertising executive could probably tell you in a heartbeat. Obviously, however, none of the WWF's creative team have psych degrees, and maybe they *should*.

And it was all right there, too. The names don't even matter—the message is the important thing. When they were running the Invasion, they could just as well have had DDP, Lance Storm, and Mike Awesome interrupt the usual boring twenty-minute interview and rage against Billionaire Vince for bankrupting their home promotion and stealing their jobs from them. Now there's some angst, there's some motivation to start fucking with the WWF and cost *them* their jobs. That's the spirit of revolution from within that kickstarted the nWo, not just because they had the big names and the fancy production. And since they don't understand that one simple, but important, distinction, this was doomed to fail just like every other Direction of the Week failed.

But enough about the nWo for the moment, let's spread around the hatred and talk about the insipid HHH storyline that began around the same time.

Now, as you probably know, in storyline terms HHH was married to Stephanie McMahon in late

1999, with a wedding straight out of a story-book—you know, groom drugs daughter of company owner in Vegas, marries her in shotgun wedding via a drive-through service by impersonating her, rapes her on the honeymoon, and then beats up her father to gain prestige within the company until she decides to turn to his side and admit they planned it all along. Along the way in real life, they became romantically linked and Joanie "Chyna" Laurer got dumped by HHH and ended up so distraught and mentally deranged by the experience that she actually opted to date Sean Waltman years later, obviously still not in her right mind. Poor woman.

> **The bizarre romance of Sean Waltman and Joanie "Chyna" Laurer eclipses in sheer weirdness anything that wrestling's writers could ever think up . . . Keep in mind we're talking about the people who thought Kane shooting fire out of ringposts was a good idea.**

At any rate, the on-screen relationship between HHH and Stephanie had always been rocky, ranging from blissfully evil together in early 2000 to being on the verge of a breakup midway through 2000 when Kurt Angle got caught in the middle. But when HHH was injured in July and Stephanie was booted off WWF "forever" in November, it seemed as though the happy couple was indeed going to be off our screens for a good long while. Unfortunately, that proved to be a pipe dream. With HHH back in January, Stephanie returned as well, albeit in a storyline where she was unable to get on TV because of her suspension. Now, how's this for the surreal nature of professional wrestling writing—an angle where someone is on TV every week complaining that she's never on TV. The intention was to finally split them on TV for good, so Stephanie began taking on the persona of a hen-pecking wife who nagged HHH constantly and felt she should be a part of his comeback. This unfortunately required Stephanie to flex her acting muscles again. Now, for those of you who haven't really felt the awesome power of Stephanie's acting, it's much like the WWF's version of Meryl Streep. You see, picture Streep getting into wrestling, and taking one chair to the head too many until she had so many concussions that she was unable to see two feet in front of her face and delivered her lines in a shrieking voice that caused Rosie Perez to go "Damn, that's annoying." Then picture her thirty pounds heavier. Now you've got the idea.

The payoff for her acting forays was to ramp up the sympathy factor for HHH and make him into a bigger babyface, but you have to understand that Hunter was walking a pretty narrow political tightrope there—even though he was the only one in the promotion who was actually allowed to stand up to Stephanie and not look like a total pussy in her presence, you knew that Stephanie was still going to get the last word at some point. I mean, I'm totally opposed to violence against women and glorifying domestic violence in general, but if ever someone needed a good smack upside the head, it's

Stephanie. But sadly, that didn't happen. What *did* happen is Stephanie's badgering increased week after week, until HHH finally grew a set of balls (he likely needed a new one after years of steroid use anyway) and dumped her.

And then, in a storyline turn so stupid that it would only be eclipsed by the crap pumped out months later, she demanded that they renew their wedding vows because she was pregnant. Now, despite everyone in the audience (and keep in mind how dumb wrestling fans are—no offense to those reading this book, who are obviously intelligent and discerning readers who are mature beyond their years) being about three weeks ahead of the writers in terms of where the storyline was going, HHH still had to play along with believing that she was telling the truth and acting like he was thrilled that she was going to give birth to his child. My own feeling was that the storyline stretched plausibility, since Stephanie is the daughter of Satan and HHH is a Neanderthal and thus they wouldn't be compatible. Had HHH (the character) been smart, he would have seen through her obvious lie and been an even bigger babyface. But because Stephanie had to be reinforced as a master manipulator, HHH (the actor) was forced to play along with a storyline where everyone thought he was a putz for believing that she was actually pregnant. That was a small, but important, factor in his gradual fall from the heights of top babyface. Stephanie's split from her "husband" was completed when they actually went through with staging a wedding renewal ceremony on RAW (with the entire crowd not buying a word of it) and during the show HHH discovered that the "doctor" who had diagnosed Stephanie's pregnancy was in fact a travel agent. This led to an enraged HHH dumping Stephanie on the altar (after an excruciat-ingly boring fifteen minutes of singing and vow-trading that killed the live crowd) and delivering a Pedigree to Vince McMahon. You know you're watching wrestling when a wedding ends up with the father of the bride getting Pedigreed. The whole thing did nothing to build up the PPV rematch between HHH and Kurt Angle, which by that point was completely secondary to the storyline between HHH and Stephanie, and got even worse with the announcement that Stephanie would be refereeing the match!

Never more than in wrestling is there such an obvious gap between what the fans want to see and what the performers want to do. The main problem in building a feud between HHH and Stephanie is the lack of a payoff: when HHH's opponents are seen as secondary to a twenty-four-year-old girl, it reduces their importance to the point where it's actually hurting them to be feuding with the supposed biggest star in the promotion. That's actually what happened to Kurt Angle, although since he's practically Superman he survived it without hardly even denting his charisma.

The Background: HHH eliminated Kurt Angle to win the 2002 Royal Rumble, so being a good heel Angle whined and cried about the elimination until he had talked himself into a singles match at No Way Out. Most of the buildup focused on Stephanie as referee, however.

The Stipulations: The winner would get the title shot at Wrestlemania. HHH was technically supposed to get it no matter what due to winning the Rumble, but this is wrestling, where even first-born children can be won or lost in rigged matches.

Overall Importance: This was HHH's first big PPV match back after the injury and would probably set the stage for how his in-ring performances would go for the rest of the year.

No Way Out 2002, February 17, 2002, Milwaukee, WI

HHH versus Kurt Angle. Angle gets a pair of fast counts from Stephanie, but HHH punches him down. Angle slugs away, but HHH uses that stupid choke takedown and stomps a mudhole. Short-arm clothesline, but Angle suplexes him. Steph gets bumped already as HHH backdrops Angle and tosses him. Back in, neckbreaker gets two from Tim White. Angle hits the rolling germans for two. HHH bails, and back in Angle gets an elbow for two. Overhead belly to belly gets two. Another one gets two. A third one gets two. He goes to the sleeper, which is a sure sign that the match is going nowhere if done this early. Angle keeps slugging away, but gets powerbombed out of the corner. They slug it out and HHH gets the high knee and a spinebuster for two. This was also the start of a disturbingly silly trend in the main events, as seemingly everyone above a certain point in the card had to use a spinebuster and/or a sleeper during the course of their matches. Facebuster gets two, and Angle bails. Ref is bumped (#2 on the match), allowing Angle to get a lowblow and Angle Slam. Steph bounces out for the near-fall, but HHH blocks the Anglelock and she's bumped again (#3). HHH DDTs Angle, no ref. Tim White gets revived and bumped again (#4) so Angle grabs a chair. KICK WHAM PEDIGREE, so Tim White comes to, counts two, and he's out again (#5!!!!). HHH goes after Stephanie like a moron, KICK WHAM CHAIRSHOT from Angle (okay, I made up the KICK and the WHAM but the last bit was accurate) and the Angle slam finishes at 14:40. Silly me, I thought the point of doing a biased ref gimmick was to build up some suspense for a foregone conclusion and then have the babyface overcome the amazing odds to win in the end and thus not look like a huge fucking pussy. But hey, if HHH wants to be portrayed as a loser, more power to him. Someone's gotta be the jobbers of the future. Match had nothing special between the five ref bumps and screwjob finish. ★★½

The shock of seeing Angle win the title shot (which wasn't really that suspenseful since they did the exact same gimmick in 2000, when Big Show won the title shot from Rock prior to Wrestlemania 2000, only to see Rock back in the match later on) was erased the next night on RAW as HHH got his win back against Angle. In fact, that became a major symptom of a lot of the WWF's problems in 2002: people doing things on PPV one night and having them negated the next night by "fifty-fifty booking," where no one is allowed to look dominant and get over. Except HHH, of course. With the Angle problem out of the way, everyone figured that they'd put Stephanie with Chris Jericho in a managerial role and begin pushing that feud heavily, but HOO BOY were we wrong about that one. The rest of the PPV was relatively uneventful—the nWo's much-hyped debut saw them deliver an interview that didn't exactly electrify the crowd, and then interfere (as predicted) in the Austin-Jericho title match to give Jericho the cheap win. There was more going on there as well, which I'll get into a bit later.

However, with the build to Wrestlemania needing to begin, something really strange and unique happened the next night on RAW. Gone from the promotion for nearly ten years by that point, most people thought that Hogan's big return would be as an occasional legend who got a minor nostalgia reaction and then disappeared back to Florida again. But when he came out for a solo interview in Chicago to challenge the Rock for a match at Wrestlemania, people immediately bought into Hogan's former star power and treated him like a returning hero. Even though Hogan was doing the same spiel he had done for years in WCW, the Hogan-starved WWF fans ate it up with a spoon and soon the one-on-one interview between Hogan and Rock had money written all over it. It was truly one of the few remaining "dream matches" that the WWF had left to bank on, and Hogan later took credit for the sold out Skydome (which was sold out months before he was even signed) and potential buyrate boosts (the show actually did worse than the previous year).

Unfortunately, all the good will was killed by the second part of the segment, which featured Hall and Nash jumping Rock and then having him loaded into an ambulance, which Hogan then ran down with a semitrailer. The only thing stupider than Hogan's facial expressions was the obvious switch between prop ambulance and real one. This whole segment really showed the chasm between old-style wrestling angles that can draw money and the "Russo style" angles that focus on trying to trick the fans into thinking someone is injured and using over-the-top theatrics and exploding vehicles. My feeling is that once HHH survived a forty-foot drop from a crane in a car without a scratch, every other vehicular injury angle from then on was dead in the water.

Speaking of being dead in the water, back to Chris Jericho. By this point, a mere two months into his reign as champion, the front office had literally lost all confidence in him as champion and the obvious conclusion—that HHH needed to go over at Wrestlemania and save the company—was reached. Well, it was obvious if you're HHH or Stephanie, I guess. But they didn't

just give up on Jericho, they buried him. While normally pairing the World champion with a woman would be so that she could augment his act and help to get him over, the situation was reversed leading to Wrestlemania. In this case, Jericho was seemingly there to get Stephanie over, being treated like a subordinate to her on screen and being ignored in building up the match for the title, as the focus was seemingly on whether HHH could give his ex-wife a Pedigree or not. The low point for the entire storyline was reached a week before Wrestlemania, as Jericho and Stephanie kidnapped HHH's beloved dog, Lucy (introduced only in that show, and boy there's nothing that makes fans cheer for a guy more than him kissing a dog), and Jericho was turned into a dog walker by the person who was supposed to be getting him over leading up to the biggest show of the year. And in the big heel act to send him into the stratosphere, he accidentally ran over the dog while it was tied to a limo and ran away like a bitch so that he wouldn't have to face the wrath of HHH.

There's a phrase in movies called "dog heel" that I think applies here. In westerns, you generally have a villain, and then three or four secondary henchmen who do the dirty work for him and act as cannon fodder for the hero to go through on the way to rescuing the girl. But there's a hierarchy of those villains: the main guy gets to kill the sheriff, the second guy kills the deputy, the third guy kidnaps the girl. But after that, there's a big gap in truly evil things to do, so the screenwriters were generally forced to have any lower villains commit some sort of generic act, like killing a dog. Thus, a "dog heel" is someone so low on the evil totem pole that he's not even worth mentioning as a main foe of the hero. That principle also applies to wrestling, but I just never thought that a promotion would actually apply that standard word-for-word like that.

And just when you thought it couldn't get any worse, as March began, the World Wrestling Federation lost an appeal in court to the World Wildlife Fund, and things got REALLY bad.

I got that bit of lingo from the DVD commentary for *Die Hard*, for all you aspiring film critics out there.

5.

Brand-Extend *This* !

More persons, on the whole, are humbugged by believing
nothing, than by believing too much.
　—P. T. Barnum

As March, and in turn Wrestlemania, approached, things were going on behind the scenes that would have long-term ramifications for the promotion, most of them not good.

People within the company were already second-guessing the wisdom of signing the nWo, as ratings weren't skyrocketing upward as predicted, and the buyrate for their first appearance at No Way Out wasn't looking to set the world on fire, either. So with Wrestlemania approaching, it was pretty much make-or-break as far as Hulk Hogan's continued career with the promotion was concerned.

The Background: Both guys were considered larger-than-life, mainstream stars, and a challenge was issued for a match to settle things once and for all. Hogan tried to kill him by locking him in an ambulance and running it over with a semi, but Rock returned with the ubiquitous taped ribs a week later and looking none the worse otherwise. Hogan pinned Rock clean with the big boot and legdrop in a six-man match

to set the stage, and the match was rehearsed extensively with the help of Pat Patterson a few weeks beforehand.

The Stipulations: None.

The Overall Importance: Huge, as the gigantic Toronto crowd turned Hogan babyface before he even made it to the ring and thus altered the course of WWF history for that year. Canada has long been the stronghold of the WWF, completely ignoring WCW even during their huge run and even forgiving Vince for the Montreal screwjob (sort of), and people in Toronto associated Hogan with the WWF and Wrestlemania. This was totally unexpected, to be sure, and it resulted in a hasty postmatch angle whereby the nWo turned on Hogan and fired him from the group, replacing him with X-Pac a few nights later. Feel free to make your own jokes about *that* tradeoff. While the intention was for Hogan to pass the torch to Rock, Hogan came out of it the bigger star, leading people to wonder who really *was* the smartest man in wrestling by that point.

Wrestlemania X-8, March 17, 2002, Toronto, Ontario, Canada

The Rock versus Hulk Hogan. Hogan of course gets the monster pop from the Toronto crowd, who are eternally stuck in the '80s due to Canada's longtime relationship with the WWF. WCW didn't exist as far as this country was concerned, so it was like Hogan was returning from retirement rather than exile. Even Hogan seems shocked when the entire crowd starts chanting his name right away. Hindsight being twenty-twenty, this should have gone on last. They do Hogan's now-cliché "fight over a lockup" spot, which Hogan of course wins. The crowd goes INSANE just for that, and never turns back to Rock's side again. Hogan grabs a headlock and overpowers Rock, and the crowd eats up his posing. Hogan pounds him down with forearms and a clothesline, as Rock sells his goofy offense before coming back with a flying clothesline, which the crowd boos. JR and King are trying their darnedest to ignore it at that point. Rock slugs away and Hogan goes out and regroups. Back in, Hogan starts selling an ankle injury that may or may not have been real. Rock slugs him down and goes for Rock Bottom, but Hogan fights out and elbows him down. He drops the elbows and hits a corner clothesline, but they mess up what looks to be a boot in the corner. Rock tackles him down and pounds away in another spot that Hogan was off-kilter on. Hogan comes back with a backdrop suplex for two. Abdominal stretch into a rollup gets two. That looked sloppy, too. He starts using backrakes, which again Rock is nice enough to sell. Hogan does the punches in the corner for the crowd to count along with, but Rock returns fire with chops. Hogan charges and hits elbow, but comes back with something vaguely resembling a chokeslam and some choking. Rock fights back but gets dumped, as he continues to do all the physical work in the match.

Rock rams him into the table a few times, but the ref won't let him use a chair. That allows Hogan to clothesline him, and they head back in for a collision with the ref. Rock gets the spinebuster (which Hogan can't even get up into the air for properly) and that sets up a Scorpion King Deathlock, which the crowd hates. Hogan makes the ropes, but there's no ref, so Rock pulls him back out while Hogan taps. Rock starts working his heel mannerisms back in, realizing the crowd has turned on him, and Hogan goes low and hits him with a Rock Bottom of his own, for two. Hogan starts beating him with the weightlifting belt, but Rock takes the high road and DDTs him. But then he decides that the low road looks pretty good, too, and uses the belt on Hogan. Hey, it's Toronto, they deserve it. This sets up Rock Bottom, which gets two. Hogan hulks up, and the crowd goes NUTS. I mean, stone cold crazy. Hogan does his usual big boot and BIG FAT STINKY WART INFESTED GIANT KILLING LEGDROP OF DEATH, but it only gets two. Crowd doesn't like that one. Another boot, but the legdrop misses this time and Rock hits him with another pair of Rock Bottoms to set up the People's Elbow for the pin at 16:23, at which point the crowd turns back to Rock again. On first viewing the structure was impressive, but time has not been kind to this match, as the work falls apart under scrutiny and it's painfully obvious who is carrying the match. Hogan's broken-down body made for some ugly spots, too. ★¾

While the Rock was getting the main event slot at Wrestlemania against Hulk Hogan in a "battle of the icons" type deal, #1 draw in the history of the universe Steve Austin was stuck in a dead-end feud with the useless two-thirds of the nWo, Hall, and Nash. And since Nash wasn't physically able to compete at that point, that left Hall. Austin squashed him like a bug at Wrestlemania to end that particular rivalry, but not before we got to sit through some of the most horrendously acted skits between the two ever seen, including Austin getting a cinder block broken over one leg on RAW, and selling the injury on the other one on Smackdown! It was pretty apparent during the feud that Austin was running on fumes, creatively speaking, and didn't really care enough to put his full effort into selling the threat of a drunk and a cripple. Hall, meanwhile, was seemingly too busy showing up late and/or in no condition to work to put forth an effort to get any better in the ring, and the result was a train wreck at Wrestlemania where Austin had the finish changed from a screwjob win for Hall to a convincing blowoff victory for himself. And even then things weren't good with Austin, as he disappeared the night after Wrestlemania and didn't show up for RAW. That of course didn't stop them from advertising Austin for the next few shows and all the house shows in between. More on that later. Hall, by the way, was already on thin ice with the company and this wasn't helping matters.

The night after Wrestlemania began yet another change in direction for the company, as the long-rumored brand extension was announced. And what an announcement it was! After months of on-and-off feuding by Ric Flair and Vince McMahon, and a particularly dull and loathsome show-long angle two weeks previous where Vince had Flair temporarily stripped of power because of his "embarrassing" behavior in terms of warring with the Undertaker, no explanation was given for the move, other than Flair and Vince being unable to get along. Smell the money!

The idea behind the "brand extension" was, at the very least, something they needed to try. With WCW dead and Vince thriving on competition, the business wasn't going to survive with Vince existing as a monopoly. The idea of splitting the WWF into separate RAW and Smackdown brands was an idea that had been toyed with since November, and the idea of splitting into WCW and WWF brands had been toyed with since buying WCW in early 2001. So after all those months of planning and delays, what was the explanation we got? Nothing. It also left more questions about the painfully complicated power hierarchy of the storyline WWF boardroom, but by that point everyone had given up trying to figure out who was *really* in charge anyway. I won't even go into Vince's speech to the board where he got Flair removed from power, where his argument was that Flair was engaged in conduct unbecoming the owner of the company. This coming from a guy who had his wife (and CEO of the company!) drugged and kidnapped, rode around the ring with his pants down while wearing a cowboy hat, nearly snapped and attacked Bob Costas on HBO, actively encouraged other men to literally kiss his ass on his TV programming, and brought in the nWo to destroy the company in February. That was, by the way, the only time that Vince was linked with the group he supposedly brought in to kill the company. After that, they were on their own and that plot point was never mentioned again. It was also announced that a draft would be held the following week to split up the rosters evenly, with Vince controlling Smackdown and Flair controlling RAW. Just for completeness sake, I should note that the rumors were RAW going to Vince and Smackdown going to Flair all the way until the moment that Linda announced the opposite, and I have no idea why plans were changed.

Speaking of plans changing, the original idea was for Austin to be on RAW as the top star, and Rock to be on Smackdown, and thus they would anchor each side. Unfortunately, that plan got somewhat waylaid when Austin walked out for a week due to unhappiness with a variety of things, and had to be talked into coming back to the RAW side of things later.

The initial draft went on March 25 and saw the following picks made for the top ten (the rest were done off screen in what was basically a random draw, with many people only finding out which show they'd be on by checking the WWF.com Web site!):

RAW:

1. Undertaker.
2. The nWo (Hall, Nash, and X-Pac)
3. Kane
4. Rob Van Dam
5. Booker T
6. Bubba Dudley
7. Big Show
8. Brock Lesnar
9. William Regal
10. Lita

Smackdown:

1. The Rock
2. Kurt Angle
3. Chris Benoit
4. Hulk Hogan
5. Billy and Chuck
6. Edge
7. Rikishi
8. D-Von Dudley
9. Mark Henry
10. Maven

The most common comment was that RAW seemed to be immediately the weaker show, with too many lumbering giants like Big Show, Kane, and the nWo, although it was initially the higher-rated show until the ratings balanced out again later in the year.

HHH, Jericho, and Austin were all exempt for various reasons, although HHH ended up on Smackdown after losing the title, Jericho was put on Smackdown, and Austin eventually signed with RAW. The initial setup was that the Undisputed champion would "float" between brands, defending against challengers on either side, as would the Women's champion. That would change later in the year, but it began well enough that way. There was also a bizarrely complicated formula for RAW and Smackdown challengers for the title getting shots at alternating PPV shows, but that idea fell apart after the first show in April.

The interesting thing about this draft is that only a year later, nearly the entire thing was meaningless. On the RAW side, Undertaker was switched to Smackdown at the end of the year, the nWo broke up soon after this, Big Show was traded to Smackdown, Brock Lesnar jumped there later, and Lita broke her neck and missed an entire year. The guy most closely associated with RAW as of 2003, HHH, wasn't even drafted by that show. On the Smackdown side, Rock goes where he wants now, Benoit was sent to RAW with no explanation and sent back with no explanation later, D-Von jumped back to RAW as part of the Big Show trade, as did Maven. In other words, literally half of the people drafted weren't even on the show a year later. Even sillier, Flair drafted hated enemies like the Undertaker and the nWo with no explanation given as to why. With Vince's silliness you at least know it's because he has the attention span of a fruit fly, but Flair is generally more discerning with his friends.

The whole goal behind the split was financially oriented, so they would have to find a way to differentiate, since the ultimate idea was to run nightly house shows with both brands, and eventually eighteen PPVs a year, with two WWF shows per month for the "B" months and co-branded shows for the "big four" (Wrestlemania, Summerslam, Survivor Series, and Royal Rumble) and extra shows from the United Kingdom. With prices going from $29.95 to $34.95 at the same time, many people thought this was nothing more than a pipe dream on their part. While a necessary evil toward rebuilding the company, no one really bought the whole deal, least of all the writers, who broke the "rules" of the split on a consistent basis. They eventually made an effort to distinguish the visual styles of the shows, as RAW was skewed toward red and got a new set, while Smackdown was made blue and silver, but really it was all Vince McMahon behind the scenes and the two shows didn't become that different until Paul Heyman got creative control of Smackdown.

Speaking of Heyman, the RAW after Wrestlemania is traditionally a show that introduces new characters into the mix, and 2002 was no

---

The first brand-exclusive PPV, *Bad Blood,* finally happened in June 2003, and despite the awesome drawing power of Kevin Nash on top, only did OK money-wise. It's been pretty much downhill from there for the concept.

---

exception, as phenom Brock Lesnar burst onto the scene with Heyman managing him and started obliterating those smaller than him (which was pretty much everyone). Brock was an interesting case, as he came up through the amateur wrestling system and was a former NCAA champion, which led many to think a natural rivalry with Kurt Angle was forthcoming. The odd thing is that despite his freakish size and scary tattoos, he wasn't one of the showcase stars of the OVW training facilities. While big and impressive, most felt that Rico Constantino and John "Prototype" Cena were the true breakout stars who would be created by Jim Cornette. Rico debuted on the same week as Lesnar, playing Billy and Chuck's gay hairstylist. Guess which gimmick got over better. But never discount Vince's love of big guys, and soon enough Lesnar was powerbombing little guys with the best of 'em, doing a unique finish where the ref would stop the match rather than have him inflict more damage on his opponents. HHH had that one stopped soon after because he felt threatened.

Speaking of HHH, he (in a shock to no one) won the Undisputed title from Jericho at Wrestlemania in a lackluster match with a dead crowd (they were burned out from the Hogan-Rock match) and quickly found himself in a delicate political situation. Well, not immediately—first he made sure to humiliate Jericho again by having him team up with Stephanie, in a match where Steph had to leave "forever" (there's that word again) if she was pinned. Which she was. Jericho's involvement was pretty much secondary. And Stephanie was back a few weeks later. How about that. But as mentioned, HHH had a delicate situation to deal with: Hogan was now back on top of the babyface mountain, having turned himself against Rock, and it seemed that

Vince was going to strike while the iron was hot and wanted Hogan to headline the next PPV. Against HHH. You could almost hear people running to the bookies to place bets on who would win that particular war of wits. Oddly enough, the original planned (and announced on TV!) main event for the Backlash show in April was HHH versus Undertaker, but three days later they did a 180 and switched it to Hogan on Smackdown. Either one would have been a terrible match, and neither would have drawn, so it was pretty much a push as far as I'm concerned.

Things were getting bad for the company in general, financially speaking, and everyone not already in the main event was scaled back to downside guarantees in the neighborhood of $125,000 a year. I figure this is as good a time as any to explain how contracts and revenues work in wrestling.

Take, for instance, Chris Jericho. The exact terms of his contract in 1999 were never really released, but I'm pretty sure the downside was $300,000 a year or thereabouts. Even if it wasn't, pretend it is for the sake of argument. Okay, now that money is guaranteed him—if he broke his neck in his first match and didn't wrestle the entire year, but remained under contract, he would make $300,000. That sounds like a lot, but given the costs of travel and eating out every day, it's not that much. However, in order to give the wrestlers incentive to improve their standing, there's generally several extras built into the contract. If he wrestles on a PPV, he gets x dollars, usually a percentage of the gate. If he wrestles in the main event of that PPV, he gets x+y dollars, a bigger chunk of the pie. If he works a certain number of house show dates, he gets a chunk of that pie, too. If he sells a certain number of t-shirts, he

gets a piece of that. A really *big* piece in fact—merchandise is pretty much the #1 moneymaker for wrestlers, which is why they take such an active role in designing their own stuff. That's how "salaries" are paid out in wrestling—rather than a set weekly salary like in baseball or other sports, you get a chunk of the revenues from shows that you work. So at the end of the year, all the PPVs and house show and merchandise revenues are added up. If he made less than his downside guarantee, then the WWE cuts him a check for the remainder, because he's guaranteed to have made at least $300,000 from the PPVs and house shows by the end of the year. If he made more than his downside, then great, everyone's happy.

Main eventers usually have downside guarantees ranging from $500,000 to $1 million a year, depending on length of time with the company and money drawn. Chris Benoit has a downside of about $500,000, and Undertaker makes close to $1 million. Midcarders start at $100,000 and go up to about $600,000 (e.g., DDP was making $600,000 in his WWF run). Jobbers generally have a set rate of $500 a night, although they're not used much anymore outside of Velocity and the like.

The effect of this cut in downside was simple: guys who depended on house show and merchandise revenue to feed their families began rushing back from what would normally be a serious injury. Under the WCW system, for instance, you were given a guaranteed contract, pay or play, and so there were actually a lot less serious injuries because guys would slow down and not do crazy stuff to justify the money. Also, once they were injured, they'd generally milk the time off for all it was worth. In the WWF, however, it was wrestle or starve, so things got to the point where seeing Dr. James Andrews (a famous sports-medicine doctor) became kind of a running joke, because you could almost walk in with your leg hanging on by a tendon and he'd tell you to tape it up and continue working through the pain if you were able. While this didn't immediately make its effects known, later in the year the injuries were starting to pile up and wouldn't stop.

So switching back to the brand extension for a while, RAW was actually an interesting show in the first couple of months, as a legitimate attempt was made to make something out of the talent given by the draft. Bradshaw, split off from the APA and turned into a singles wrestler again, was made into Steve Austin's Texas buddy (complete with cowboy boots and hat) and turned into his de facto partner in the continuing war with the new and not-so-improved nWo. Booker T and Goldust, with nothing better to do, were turned into the most unlikely of teams, initially with a "Men on Film" gimmick and then just as two friends who respected each other. What a concept. And Eddie Guerrero, after being fired for a DUI in 2001, was brought back again as a foil for Rob Van Dam, because you can never have too many Guerreros in the midcard. As well, Bubba Dudley was made into a single and did quite well for himself with a twenty-first-century Dusty Rhodes gimmick, making a name in the midcard before getting squashed in a TV match by HHH and sent spiraling back into the tag team ranks again. The initial energy displayed by the guys reflected in the ratings for a bit, but soon enough the overwhelming suck of the nWo and the debacle with Steve Austin would drag it back down again.

The energy of the split carried over in some ways to the first postsplit PPV, Backlash. While in some ways (like the main event, or a terrible Bradshaw versus Scott Hall match that stunk up the joint) it was a disaster, in others, guys like Brock Lesnar really tried to step up to the plate and deliver as a future main event talent for the first time. Unfortunately, in Brock's case, he was hampered with office darling, Jeff Hardy, in a feud where the crowds in the Northeast were dying to see the badass beast Lesnar crush the pretty boy Hardyz once and for all, but Jeff was very protected. One guy who wasn't energetic or happy was Steve Austin, as he faced Undertaker in a #1 contender's match that was so boring it inspired my first-ever stream of consciousness review.

The Background: In a desperate attempt to recreate the magic of Steve Austin versus Vince McMahon, Austin gets involved in a program with Ric Flair, who would soon turn into an Evil Owner and feud with the Rattlesnake. This match featured Flair as a referee, ostensibly to make sure hated enemy Undertaker lost, but in reality to make sure he won.

The Stipulations: The winner would receive the RAW side's shot at the Undisputed title in May, against either HHH or Hulk Hogan, depending on who won in the main event that night.

The Overall Importance: This was Austin's last major PPV match of 2002, and what I believe was his final match ever against the Undertaker, leaving the series tied at a billion wins apiece. Ric Flair's red boots were such a fashion faux pas that people still laugh about them to this day. Well, I do at least.

Backlash 2002, April 21, 2002, Kansas City, MO

Undertaker versus Steve Austin. Speaking of fashion faux pas, Ric Flair appears to have stolen Ernest Miller's red slippers, sticking out like a sore thumb in a ring with two guys dressed all in black. Isn't there some rule about wearing red boots after Wrestlemania? I'll have to ask Martha Stewart once we both end up burning in hell. They do the big staredown to start and dance around in lieu of actually doing anything. Undertaker grabs a headlock. FEEL THE ELECTRICITY! Austin gets overpowered and Undertaker dances again. ★★★★ classic! Oh, sorry, thought I was watching Rock-Hogan again for a second. Okay, Austin recuperates from that devastating shoulderblock and he's ready for action again, so they're back to it, and now he grabs his own headlock. Irony! Oh man, we're getting closer to ★★★★★ by the minute. Undertaker dances again. I can't stand the excitement much longer. Okay, back to the lock-up, and Undertaker gets another headlock. Austin clotheslines him, however. Now we're getting somewhere. More stalling follows. Well, they're old.

Now Austin wants a test of strength, but then he DOESN'T. Oh, TAG. He's so the master of psychology. UT overpowers him again, but Austin gets a hiptoss and armdrag, and I'm pumped for a mat-wrestling exhibition until Ric Flair's red boots ruin the mood. Austin works the arm while JR explains the psychology as though anyone watching gives a damn. Austin goes to the pounding, but UT clotheslines him for two. Then goes to the arm. ROPEWALK OF DOOM looks to pep up the match, and it gets two. Man, I just can't stop focusing on those boots. It's like mangled bodies in a car wreck. Oh, wait, it's the thesz press and FU elbow, with extra FU. That gets two. Plus it knocks the bandana off, which is like the universal symbol of "time to whoop ass" among the over-forty set these days.

They brawl out and head back in as UT exchanges bon mots with a fan, but Austin dumps him again. Well, that was a pointless exchange.

They head over to the announcer table and Austin rams him into the devastating plastic addition, but he spends too much time adjusting his knee brace and walks into a big boot. Undertaker decides to give him back some of the devastating plastic, and they struggle for control of the stairs like two aging, crippled generals on the battlefield of life. Or whatever. Into the crowd for lack of anything sensible to do to fill time, and Undertaker actually stops to clear the timekeeper's table before getting rammed into it. He's not only a badass, he's well organized.

The exciting brawl continues as Austin tries a piledriver, but UT reverses it. Well, geez, when do you ever see that? That was a totally unexpected development from where I sit. Undertaker calls a spot into the camera while the drunk and his luchadore "friend" wander out (known in some circles as Scott Hall and X-Pac) to do nothing in particular. The crowd is so into the thrilling Austin-UT brawl that they chant "X-Pac Sucks." Austin meets the stairs and you know he's devastated because he keeps clutching at his forehead, as if to say, "Ouch, knave, thou hast injured my forehead!" X-Pac continues looking intimidating, in a "gay street toughs" type of way, while Undertaker legdrops Austin on the apron. JR has no logical reason for them to be there. And yet there they are, on camera. Go figure.

Undertaker now goes to work on the leg of Austin after spending the last ten minutes hitting him in the head and neck, which makes me think he should have planned his attack a bit better beforehand. I mean, the guy's wearing KNEE BRACES for god's sake, this ain't rocket science. Austin makes the ropes, but UT hangs on. You know he's still hanging on because he nods his head as though that adds extra pressure to the hold. A DDT gets two and he hits the chinlock, as the focus shifts again back up to the neck. Dude, pick a body part and stick to it already. Be decisive—I mean, look at Flair, he's out there with boots so fruity that Jeff Hardy would probably go "Dude, you look gay" if he saw them, and he didn't think twice about wearing them. Austin tries a sleeper, but gets suplexed. Is the sleeper the new spinebuster for the main eventers or something? Is Entertainment Weekly *gonna* do one of those lists where it's like "red is the new yellow" and "the sleeper is the new spinebuster" next week? Austin tries the stunner, but gets clotheslined for two. UT is so upset at this that he rubs his forearm into Austin's face. The nWo is so upset that they stand around and do nothing. I leave it to you to judge which attack is more devastating.

Austin fires back with an attack not so much designed to punish as it is to get the crowd chanting "What?" in time with the punches, but UT clotheslines him to stop it. He goes for the turnbuckle, which Flair ignores completely, but Austin whips him into it. Wow, never seen that before, either. Double clothesline, but Undertaker seems more annoyed than knocked out. Flair isn't counting anyway. Austin slugs back, again giving the fans a chance to chant "What?" rather than doing something useful like going after the leg or pointing a locker room disturbance and then stunning the distracted Undertaker, but alas Ric Flair, sixteen-time champion, gets bumped by a simple shoulder block and Austin gets his KICK WHAM STUNNER with no referee present. In a world where Flair gets bumped by a shoulderblock, Austin shouldn't be getting clean wins anyway. UT goes low and signals for the chokeslam (which might be seen as telegraphing the move by someone more cynical than myself), but it only gets two. I don't know if Austin is guttier to kick out, or to participate in this boring match for twenty minutes without falling asleep.

UT grabs a chair to no avail, but changes gears and gets a big boot for two. I'd stick with the chair next time. Austin gets a spinebuster for two. That's like, so last week. I read that in Entertainment Weekly. Austin tells Undertaker to get up, but Flair is bumped again. Well, politeness might have helped his case somewhat and avoided that whole situation. Chairshot gets two for Undertaker. See, that's what rudeness gets you. Austin reverses the dragon sleeper into a clothesline for two. He goes for his own, but UT escapes and goes for the chair again. Austin slugs him down again. I sense a limited offense from Austin tonight. Austin grabs the chair, but gets booted and pinned at 26:58. Austin's foot was on the ropes, but dwelling further on the subject might prolong the match, so we'll move on. That Austin—he can't work WWF style. ★ He gets his heat back after the match, however, as he spins his fists like Dusty Rhodes before punching UT and delivering a KICK WHAM STUNNER. Oh, TAG.

"Oh TAG" is a joke I started using in early 2002 in honor of Lita, who made that particular stupid remark as a way of indicating that Matt Hardy had gotten in an especially witty dig on William Regal. The thing that put me over the top on it was that she actually smacked him while saying it, as though actually playing Tag with him. You can't make stuff like that up.

The writers were bending over backward to keep Austin happy, but it was apparent that he had no interest in doing anything other than reviving old feuds again, as in the case of the "Austin versus authority figure" feuds that had seemingly been running forever.

And speaking of feuds that had been running forever, as May began, the WWF lost their last appeal in the war with the World Wildlife Fund, and the World Wrestling Federation officially died as a result on May 5, 2002.

6.

World Wrestling What?

Long ago I learned that to those who mean right and try to do right, there are no such things as real misfortunes. On the other hand, to such persons, all apparent evils are blessings in disguise.
—P. T. Barnum

On May 5, after months of legal wrangling and fruitless appeals in the highest courts of the United Kingdom, the World Wrestling Federation finally surrendered to the inevitable and changed their name. Very quietly, World Wrestling Entertainment (or WWE for short) was born, putting an end to the legacy of Titan Sports, Inc. nearly twenty years after Hulk Hogan made the WWF name a household word.

The interesting thing about the lawsuit and changeover is that the entire thing was their own fault and could have been avoided from the start.

The saga began in 1994, as the World Wildlife Fund and the World Wrestling Federation reached an out-of-court agreement to prevent potential confusion in the marketplace. The deal, which was actually proposed by the wrestling side, was that the federation would be allowed to use the WWF initials and logo within the United States, but not anywhere else in the

world. It should be noted that there was no objection on the fund's part to the WWF name being used even during the massive explosion of the sport during the boom in the '80s. Why did they suddenly object in 1994? Who knows why animal lovers do what they do. Don't even get me started on PETA.

The idea behind the agreement was that, presumably, they could be called the WWF within the United States, and everywhere else they would be promoted as the World Wrestling Federation, no abbreviation. However, and this seems to be the sticking point from the fund's side of things, in 1998 they underwent a logo change, from the classic "block" WWF logo to the "scratch" logo symbolizing the attitude era, and began a worldwide campaign to rebrand the WWF logo to that new one. And in the process, they arrogantly ignored their own agreement and started promoting themselves as the WWF everywhere in the world. The fund sued in 2000, and rightly so, on grounds that the WWF was breaking a valid contract between the two parties, with no justification for doing so other than their own assumption that they were above the legal system.

Things got worse when the federation's legal team began making ridiculously hypocritical arguments about how there couldn't possibly be confusion in the marketplace, which was strange to hear them arguing because they based a multimillion dollar lawsuit against WCW in 1997 on the exact opposite argument: That in fact using Scott Hall and Kevin Nash as characters roughly reminiscent of Razor Ramon and Diesel was infringing on the WWF's trademarks.

As expected, the judges in the United Kingdom had little sympathy for the billion-dollar wrestling promotion as it waged war against the nonprofit animal organization and ruled that the federation had to surrender the WWF name and WWF.com Web site to the World Wildlife Fund. A series of appeals went nowhere, and they ended up having to pay nearly $300,000 in legal costs to the fund as a result of the appeals and finally threw up their hands in surrender after crying about a potential name change costing $50 million. The actual amount ended up being perhaps in the $50,000 range, as a few hiccups of "WWF" were quickly squashed by the endless repetition on TV of the new name, until everyone knew that they were the WWE after a few weeks and forgot all about the WWF name.

The real silliness came later, as the draconian terms of the lawsuit forced the promotion to edit out all references to the WWF in their tape library, ring equipment, and international broadcasts by May 15. So even to this day, you'll see old footage with the WWF logo blurred out on turnbuckles. Also, they had until November 2002 to get rid of all merchandise in the United Kingdom with the WWF name on it, which made

> **The World Wildlife Fund left the WWF.com domain name unclaimed as of 2004, and another wrestling Web site swooped in and bought it—which I just think is really funny for whatever reason.**

for some *great* deals on old tapes if you happened to have a VCR capable of playing PAL-encoded video.

And speaking of disasters for the company, another one befell them as they decided to go with new Undisputed champion Hulk Hogan (who won the belt from HHH at Backlash in a match so hideously boring that I won't even talk about it further for fear of putting you, gentle reader, to sleep by merely describing it) versus Undertaker at Judgment Day. Not only did you have two *very* noticeably aging veterans squaring off for the title in a match that no one was hankering to see, but the buildup provided some of the most ludicrous moments of the year. We're talking Undertaker dragging Hogan on the back of his bike, with Hogan clearly riding a cart of some kind to protect him, in a skit that more closely resembled an advertisement for a new amusement park ride. We're talking Hogan threatening to run over Undertaker's bike with a semi, but waiting for a commercial break to go ahead with it. The feeling in putting the title on Hogan in the first place was that they had to strike while the iron was hot (which is fine as far as justifications go) but I don't think anyone anticipated just how *fast* the iron would go cold again once the title was on him. People clearly did not want to see Hogan as a champion, as ratings fell steadily when he had the belt and Backlash did a very disappointing buyrate for what both HHH and Hogan would probably feel was a "dream match." Hogan and HHH playing "out-manipulate Vince McMahon" backstage probably would have been a compelling match, but actually seeing them wrestle was not.

And then, just when it seemed like the company couldn't get any worse news, they took a swing through Europe for a house show tour, and the world was given the "Plane Ride from Hell."

The formula for such a disaster is simple: take bored wrestlers, add alcohol, put them in a cramped area for eight hours, agitate, and then watch them explode. There were four specific incidents that gained the whole excursion the infamy that it has even to this day, and they are as follows:

1. Scott Hall, recovering alcoholic and general scumfuck, began drinking beer on the bus from the arena and continued onto the plane. Hall was messed up the minute they got to England for the Insurrection PPV and wasn't even used on the show in a wrestling capacity. On the way back on the plane, he passed out, worrying people that it was going to be a bigger tragedy than just his job. He was supposedly taking an antialcohol drug to help his drinking problems, but he showed up drunk on more than one occasion in his relatively short stint in the WWE. He was officially fired on May 6 for the incident in Europe and several other reasons.

2. Goldust, also drunk, was singing love songs to ex-wife Terri, creeping her out, until Jim Ross convinced him to sit down again. Ric Flair was also prompted into party mode (which doesn't take much) and again Jim Ross had to step in and calm him down.

3. Road agent Michael Hayes, with the hair untied (there's a saying among the writers pertaining to Hayes—"Hair in a pony-tail, no need to bail. Hair undone, time to run.") and completely pissed, began picking on Bradshaw in the most juvenile ways possible, including tapping on his forehead in a spot where he had been bladed the night before. When he wouldn't give it up, and indeed proceeded to cutting wrestling promos on the other guys in the plane, a brawl erupted between Bradshaw and himself, which Hayes lost convincingly. Finally, he passed out, and in a moment of revenge, X-Pac cut off his mullet, and it was found on the bulletin board backstage at RAW the next day. This was a particularly irritating incident as far as Vince was concerned, because road agents like Michael Hayes are generally responsible for setting a good example for the other guys, not starting fights with the talent. No one was disciplined over this one, as it was felt that Hayes had it coming.

4. The big one, and most famous, saw Curt Hennig (also a noted drinker) pulling pranks on Brock Lesnar, spraying him with shaving cream and picking a fight with him. Finally Lesnar snapped and brawled with Hennig off and on throughout the plane, culminating with Brock plowing Hennig into one of the doors of the plane, which had everyone more than a little concerned for their safety. They reportedly were laughing about the situation later on once Hennig had calmed down, but it wasn't funny enough to save Hennig's job, as he was fired

over the incident the next day. There was no punishment for Lesnar that anyone has been able to discover as of yet.

This was, in summary, exactly the kind of "inmates running the asylum" nonsense that WCW turned into over the years and was eerily reminiscent of a brawl between Sid Vicious and Arn Anderson in England in 1993. It was not only a bad sign for the morale backstage, but it became *very* public knowledge almost immediately afterward, putting the company in the embarrassing situation of having to publicly discipline employees for the kind of thing that normally would be kept under wraps. Frankly, Hennig was of no further use to the promotion anyway and would have been let go for something else if not for this. However, in a tragic coda to the situation, Hennig's firing triggered a spiral of personal problems for him that led to him being found dead in his hotel room from abuse of cocaine in February 2003.

The problems for the promotion continue with the Judgment Day PPV, as Hogan and Undertaker absolutely stunk up the joint with a terrible main event that saw Undertaker pinning Hogan after tons of interference from Vince McMahon to win the Undisputed title. The show had a terrible buyrate, but there was one positive from the wreckage, as Kurt Angle and Edge had a spectacular match to round out their feud, with a stipulation not seen often in North American wrestling.

The Background: This was an attempt to elevate Edge to the level of the "big boys," by programming him with former running buddy Kurt Angle in a rather silly feud involving Edge sabotaging Angle's t-shirt business by making "You Suck" shirts instead of Kurt's desired shirt listing his lifetime achievements (it was so long that it was only available in XXXL). The "You Suck" shirts actually became a big seller. Anyway, they had a ★★★★¼ match at the Backlash PPV, which Angle won, and a rematch seemed inevitable.

The Stipulations: Since Angle was experiencing the pain of male-pattern baldness and wanted to start shaving his head, the match was made into a hair versus hair match, with the loser getting shaved bald by the winner.

The Overall Importance: It was not only a great match and a contender for Match of the Year, but the first serious attempt to make Edge into a player in the main event scene, which unfortunately would be halted by first a shoulder injury and then an "Austin injury" to the neck from years of taking bumps on his back.

Judgment Day 2002, May 19, 2002, Nashville, TN

Hair versus Hair: Kurt Angle versus Edge. Angle works a lockup to start and grabs a facelock, overpowering Edge, but falling victim to a rollup that gets two. Angle is opting for the bright orange tights tonight to go with the tacky "Angle" boots that bug me so much for some reason. Edge dumps him to set up a baseball slide and stomps him outside. Back in, Angle catches him on the way in and hammers him, but Edge comes back with a backdrop. He ties Angle in the ropes and spears him there, but goes to the proverbial well once too often and gets suplexed to the floor in a nasty bump that probably did his eventual neck injury no favors. Back in, Angle stomps him down and slugs away in the corner, and then opts for the chops instead. Edge returns those like a good Canadian, but walks into a MAIN EVENT SPINE-BUSTER that gets two for Angle. Choking follows and Kurt stays on the offense but walks into an elbow. He recovers with a DDT for two, however.

We hit the chinlock and Edge's escape is quickly cut off by a hairpull. A vertical suplex gets two for Angle, and he goes to a front face-lock. Edge fights back with an overhead suplex to set up a double KO spot. Edge comes back with a pair of clotheslines and a leg lariat, and the Edge-O-Matic gets two. Angle fires off his own overhead suplex, but Edge dropkicks the knee to send him to the floor, and follows with a suicide dive that puts both guys down. Back in, Edge goes up, and blocks the Pop-Up Super-plex to set up a missile dropkick that gets two. German suplex, but Angle fights back with his own, which Edge reverses to a rollup for two. DDT into a faceplant by Edge allows him to go up, but now Angle gets the elusive Pop-Up Superplex for two. Edge superkicks him into the corner and gets a nasty DDT out of there for two. Angle ducks a spear and the ref goes down, allowing Angle to catch him from behind with a german suplex. He grabs a chair, but Edge gets another spear (this one actually hit-ting Angle), no ref. Edge tries again, but Angle kicks him in the chest to block it, so Edge gets yet another one, for two. Super-hot near-falls for the stipulation. Edge tries the Implant DDT, but Angle hits him with his own spear and the Angle Slam, for two. Crowd was on the verge of having a heart attack (at least the female portion) thinking that Edge might have been shaved. Anklelock is countered by an enzuigiri by Edge, but Angle gets another one. Edge can't make the ropes, but he cradles for the pin at 15:30. Angle would be shaved bald later in the night, and would wear a goofy wig under a headpiece for the next several weeks. ★★★★½

May also marked a weird transition on RAW for the nWo group. Now, you may have noticed that things were getting a bit watered down for them by that point, as Hogan left right away and

My original rating for the match was ★★★½. I had problems with the reversed finishers and thought the finish was anticlimactic, but another viewing seems to have cleared up that problem, and I was just really digging it the second time through.

Hall was fired at the beginning of May, leaving Kevin Nash and X-Pac, not exactly a fearsome combination. The group was basically dead from that point on, but they kept the corpse kicking for a little while longer just to bug me. Big Show turned on Steve Austin and joined the group in a move that no one cared about, and then to really emasculate them, Evil Owner Ric Flair named Booker T as the newest member, de-spite the objections of Nash and X-Pac behind the scenes. The joining of Booker T was simply a last-minute decision to throw a "swerve" at the audience, and in fact he lost to Steve Austin immediately after joining and his membership turned into a running gag with partner Goldust trying to join at the same time. This all led to a temper tantrum before RAW at the end of May, as Nash and X-Pac threatened to walk out if X-Pac had to job twice in the same night. Unfor-tunately, they didn't follow up on that threat, and instead a gimmick was started for the nWo where if someone in the group lost, they were out. So the guys whined and complained, and were given a winning streak gimmick as a result. It was WCW all over again.

Speaking of WCW-type politics, Rob Van Dam got a shot at Undertaker's newly won title the night after Judgment Day, and if ever there was a time to shoot him to the top and create a new main event star, this was it. So, of course, they didn't. In fact, they did the famous Dusty Finish, where the fans thought RVD had won the title, only to have the referee restart the match and Undertaker destroy him for the real pinfall to retain. Rob holding the title during the fake switch was essentially the pinnacle of his career and he would never get that close again. Sort of.

Amid all the chaos, the writing team finally did the rumored split, into RAW and Smackdown teams. On the RAW side, head writer Brian Gewirtz, along with Bruce Prichard and Ed Koskey. On the Smackdown side, head writer Paul Heyman, along with Michael Hayes, Seth Mates, and Heyman progeny David Lagana. Stephanie McMahon was kind of a supervisor for everyone, and, of course, the buck stopped with Vince no matter what. There was, however, the beginning of a shift in philosophy on the shows, as RAW (under the eye of Kevin Dunn) started to shift toward a more soap-opera attitude, whereas Smackdown was going to become the "wrestling show." This was, of course, a fairly gradual change, complete with a rocky start on both sides as they worked out the best place for everyone on the roster.

Speaking of revamps, they made yet another attempt to revive the Saturday shows on TNN, as all the weekend and recap shows underwent cosmetic changes. The former fluff interview show, *Excess*, was split into two different shows, with the first hour becoming a Smackdown-branded B-show called *Velocity*, and the second hour becoming a "behind the scenes" fluff show called *Confidential*, with Gene Okerlund hosting. Generally speaking, both shows were complete flops, with the exception of shows after someone in wrestling had died,

when the WWE would pimp *Confidential* to get one final rating out of his death. As a rule, *Confidential* ranged from "mildly interesting" when there was good background material to work with, to "brutally unwatchable" when the segments were stuff like Bradshaw playing basketball with Big Show. My feelings (which have been reflected by the WWE home video department as of late) are that the show would have been better served dropping the spin-doctoring fluff and just showing classic matches from their cavernous video library, since the rating probably would have been the same or better anyway.

The month ended with some real promise on the RAW side, as they swung through Edmonton and seemingly started a program with Chris Benoit and Eddie Guerrero against Steve Austin in an effort to find Austin something to do to keep him happy, and RVD proceeded to blow the roof off the joint with a classic ladder match against Guerrero for the Intercontinental title.

The Background: Eddie Guerrero returned to the WWE after his run-in with the law and troubles with alcohol just in time for the brand extension, debuting on RAW to duel RVD for the rights to the frog splash. They had an awkward but good first match at Backlash in April, as Eddie won the title by dismantling Rob's offense in a machine-like fashion. Rob adjusted in time for a rematch at Judgment Day in May, but this time Eddie used the power of *cheating* to retain the title, frustrating him. This set up the rubber match on RAW (although really Eddie already won the series 2-0, but play along), with Chris Benoit lurking at ringside, as Guerrero was aligning himself with the evil Ric Flair and Benoit was the homecoming hero after a year on the shelf with an injury.

The Stipulations: This was a ladder match,

so the winner is the first one to climb up a ladder and snag the title belt, which was hanging from the ceiling on a hook. No rules otherwise, winner gets the belt.

The Overall Importance: One of the best matches in the history of RAW and the one that proved that Guerrero could still bring the goods, despite all his personal demons.

RAW, May 27, 2002, Edmonton, Alberta, Canada

Intercontinental title, Ladder match: Eddie Guerrero versus Rob Van Dam. Slugfest to start, and Rob gets a heel kick and Eddie bails. Rob misses a pescado on the way out, but sends Eddie to the post. Suplex on the railing sets up the guillotine, but Eddie sends him facefirst into the ladder and pounds away. Suplex and Eddie drops the ladder on him, thus breaking the supports already. Back in they go and slug it out again, and Eddie gets a vicious elbow. Eddie feeds off the crowd's booing and pounds Rob down, and posts him, which is, of course, smart psychology for a ladder match, because that way he can't climb. Even Lawler picks up on that. Eddie pounds the knee with a chair, and back in he stomps away on it. Backdrop suplex counters an RVD headlock attempt, and he works RVD in the corner. Rob comes back with a monkey flip, but Eddie gives him a powerbomb and finds the emergency backup ladder under the ring. Rob baseball slides it and follows with a quebrada onto the ladder, which pretty much takes both guys out. Benoit joins us via the crowd, with a ticket of course to circumvent getting thrown out of the building earlier, and we take a commercial break.

We return with Eddie ramming the ladder into RVD's face on the floor, and back in Eddie

makes a climb attempt. Rob missile dropkicks the ladder to stop that. That bump looked so nasty live, and on TV for that matter. Rob comes back as we try to start an "Eddie G" chant, but everyone else was into an "RVD" one. Rob gets Rolling Thunder on the ladder, which again looked brutal. My friend Roy and I are valiantly cheering Eddie on, though. Rob climbs, but Eddie knocks him off by smashing his face into the ladder and then hitting a sunset powerbomb off the ladder to kill Rob dead. Eddie heads up the ladder, and that's where a dumbass fan runs in and knocks him off. We actually thought it was Steve Austin for a moment, then we realized it was just a drunken idiot. My friend worked security for that show and they caught hell afterwards because of it.

The match continues regardless, as Eddie goes back up the ladder and hits RVD with a swanton bomb from the ladder. Good god Eddie is a maniac. Eddie grabs a chair and gives Rob what for, but Rob gives him some right back and stomps a mudhole, then walks it dry by dropkicking the chair into his face. That's one dry mudhole. Legdrop and moonsault on the ladder. SICK SHIT. Rob climbs, but Eddie yanks him down and suplexes him into the ladder, which nearly destroys another one. Ladder goes into the corner, but the fickle hand of irony sends Eddie crashing into it, and then Rob monkey-flips him into it for good measure. Looked like Eddie was about two inches away from breaking his ankle on that bump. Another Rolling Thunder on the ladder and superkick puts Eddie in the corner, and Rob climbs again. Eddie prevents that with a dropkick to the knee, but when he grabs the chair, it's Van Damination. Rob climbs in the corner, but the ladder slips and he can't frog splash him off the ladder. Earl Hebner should have helped steady the ladder there. Eddie goes up and gets dumped to cover for the blown finish previous, and Rob climbs to regain the Intercontinental title at 18:13. Messed-up finish hurt it a bit, but otherwise this was Match of the Year quality all the way, complete with sick spots and hard work on both sides of the equation. Eddie looked like a million bucks here, and hopefully he can maintain this level. ★★★★½ Steve Austin hits the ring to get him some Latino Heat, but has to fight off Flair and Arn as well. Benoit comes in to even the odds, and turns on Austin in retribution for being put out of action by him almost one year to the day. As a hometown fan, this knocked the wind out of my sails a bit, but as a wrestling fan, bring on Austin-Benoit! Sadly, it would never happen.

The heel turn of Benoit in his hometown was exactly the kind of bass-ackward booking the WWE was into doing, because no one would expect it, see?

But what no one expected was exactly what Steve Austin did later that week.

7.

Attitude Problem

Money is in some respects life's fire: it is a very
excellent servant, but a terrible master.
—P. T. Barnum

(*Note:* The following chapter is based on various conversations with people inside the WWF, who were around step-by-step for the self-destruction of Steve Austin.)

The thing with Austin had actually been brewing for months, ever since around October 2001. Steve was in the midst of a heel run that many people considered a complete flop because business dropped off during that time.

However, Steve's heel character added so many more dimensions to him instead of just being the glass-shattering, beer-drinking, heel-stunnering bad ass. He'd been doing that schtick for four years and it was time for a change.

Steve's biggest problem was that Vince didn't create new babyfaces to program with him after 'Mania and after Rock left, choosing instead to go with Kane and Taker. So Steve's heel run was hampered by not having fresh babyfaces to work with, save for Kurt Angle (who became a

babyface strictly on the greatness of his backstage bits with Steve and Vince) after the Invasion. So they programmed Steve with Kurt, and purposely held off the big Rock-Austin rematch, which was originally scheduled for Summerslam, until after Survivor Series.

But that plan was severely hurt by Kurt and Steve's match at Summerslam.

The match was supposed to be Kurt bumping Steve around, bloodying Steve, until Steve out of desperation stuns the ref to get out of the match.

That's not what happened. And this is the kind of thing that the creative team get shit for that they had no input on: they wanted Kurt to take 80 percent of the match and have Austin be a chicken shit and escape with a DQ, but when Steve, Kurt, and the agent, Jack Lanza, put the match together, that's not what happened. Steve took 75 percent of the match and bloodied Kurt, couldn't pin Kurt, so he just stunned the ref and the whole thing fell flat. The way Steve worked that match was reminiscent of kick-ass babyface Austin and didn't leave a lot of room to go with Kurt as a babyface.

And this started to open eyes about Steve's character. They found it wasn't a very giving character. His style in the ring is one of "chew them up and spit them out." His character backstage is one of DTA, and it was impossible to have anyone rub up against him and be elevated. He talked down to everyone in the Alliance and made them all seem like jobbers. He chewed up Kurt when he wasn't supposed to. He was and is to this day, the toughest character to effectively script, because as huge and as wild as his character is, it was also the one with the most limitations.

Steve didn't like working in tag matches, so when they did have a tag match involving him, it was like pulling teeth to get it approved by Vince (who was Steve's biggest ally and supporter). He refused to show the chicken-shit tendencies that all great heels possess, because the nature of the character is that if you hurt him, he comes back the next week and kills your family and burns down your house because that's the bottom line, yadda, yadda, yadda. That worked great as a babyface in 1998, but as a heel in 2001, it was counterproductive.

So after that match with Kurt at Summerslam, whatever steam he had as a heel fizzled because he wasn't wrestling like a heel, but instead as the kick-ass Stone Cold babyface. And that's when sentiments started growing that turning Steve heel was a mistake. The way Steve worked it, and the way Vince allowed him to work it, may have been the mistake. Steve's heel character was ten times more compelling than a fifth straight year of his babyface one. But regardless, it wasn't so much a creative issue that caused Steve to think about being turned back babyface, it was a financial one.

Ah, the wondrous power of merchandise.

Heel Stone Cold didn't sell as much merchandise as good ol' babyface Stone Cold. So when Steve started receiving some of those merchandise checks that were considerably lower than his old ones, Steve went to his good buddy JR and began planting the seeds. "My merchandise isn't selling as well. I don't think the fans want to boo me. I think it'd be better if we turned me back babyface."

JR then began talking to Vince, who probably talked to Steve, and before you knew it, the charge was to think of ways that Steve "could go back to being the character he was before."

Now, to the creative team this was a kick in the balls. The Kurt-Steve program was winding up, and they were prepared to start the Rock-Steve one, which would have segued into HHH-Steve, most likely culminating at the main event of Wrestlemania for the WWE title. He could turn back babyface after that. Instead, now they were looking at turning Steve back babyface after Survivor Series to feud with . . . who? Who hadn't he worked with? The Alliance? He just spent the last several months making sure his character was clearly above those guys. A freshly turned heel Kurt? They had just done the last 100 PPVs with them on top. But it didn't matter how many credible objections they had, the cries went unheard, and they were charged with turning Steve back babyface.

Anybody "new" (RVD, Jericho, Booker, etc.) wasn't seen as "on his level" and needed so much interference in the matches with Austin to still "make sure Steve looked strong" that it helped no one. The heels rarely ever looked credible, and it hurt Steve because the formula of Steve fighting from underneath against ten guys had been done for the last four years.

Meanwhile, the decision was made to unify the titles and go with something new. Jericho was put over Steve at Vengeance. But instead of Steve having a hellacious match with Kurt and being in a weakened state that the heel Jericho takes advantage of, and finally beats Steve clean after Steve almost battles the odds and pulls one out, they had to run in the Eighty-second Airborne to beat him.

That was going to lead to the main event of Wrestlemania of HHH versus Jericho with Steph involved. However, we all know how unfortunately that turned out, and believe it or not, that had a lot to do with Steve. But we'll get to that.

So now that Steve doesn't have the title, it's time for him to find someone else to work with. That's where the whole Booker T deal came in. All the bullshit of grocery stores and churches was Vince and Steve trying to recapture lightning in a bottle from 1998 and give everyone good ol' hell-raising Stone Cold. Been there, done that. That storyline also brought about the return of the Bossman, and fuck walking out, that may have been Steve's greatest sin. Bossman's spot was originally going to be Stevie Ray for a two-shot deal. He was going to attack Stone Cold in New Orleans the week before Christmas, and then Steve was going to destroy him on the RAW in Miami on Christmas Eve. However, Vince and Steph, going completely on the hearsay of others (HHH) felt Stevie Ray would actually physically hurt Steve and the decision was made to go with Bossman. Others wanted Bossman to strictly do those two shots. But Vince felt he wouldn't mean anything, so therefore it was needed to "build some heat on him" before Steve took him out. This was fucking *Bossman* we're talking about. He hadn't had heat since 1988. But to listen to Vince, Bossman was one of the greatest workers of all time and would know how to get heat on Steve so Steve could sell and the people could get behind him. Well, that didn't work.

So now after Steve had failed to help elevate

> This was during a period when they were trying to use Austin to give Booker T the superstar rub, but Austin's ideas amounted to fighting him in a grocery store and doing an extended food fight. This somehow segued into the return of Big Bossman, a period most fans have blotted out of their minds. Thankfully.

Booker, they once again were left without a way to go with him. HHH was back, so was Rock. These guys would be tearing up everywhere they went with a heel Stone Cold, but dammit, people might not buy the new Stone Cold "What?" beer coolie, so scrap that. So they needed some new heels, fast. And since it was established that Stone Cold wasn't the greatest at helping build heels, they needed some premade ones. Enter the nWo.

After the live Smackdown in Washington, D.C., on January 3, Vince wanted to get everyone's feedback on whether or not to bring in the nWo. There apparently wasn't one voice in that room in favor of bringing them in. None of the ex-WCW agents (John Laurinaitis, Fit Finlay, and Arn Anderson) were in favor of it, and neither were the older WWF agents (Pat Patterson, Jack Lanza, and Gerald Brisco) because not only did they remember all of the bullshit, but also these guys were all in their forties. Kevin Dunn reportedly put it best when he said he was trying to picture Edge versus Nash, for example. How was Nash going to keep up? But despite all that, Vince brought them in anyway because the company needed "star power," especially for the split rosters. The thought process being that they'd stir shit up and Hogan would work with Rock at 'Mania, and Steve would work with Hall (who it was felt would be a better match than Nash).

In the meantime, Steve lost the Royal Rumble to Hunter, but got the title shot at No Way Out against Jericho. This is truly where the fate of the company started to go off kilter, because going into this match, Jericho had been working with Rock and tearing the house down. Great matches, great promos, great heat, and Jericho was looking good. However, when matched against the Austin machine, all of the sudden, Jericho didn't look that great. All of the sudden, any heat Jericho built up was blown off in the same week. And all of the momentum Jericho had built up working with Rock slowly started to fade. And then came the match at No Way Out.

They knew the nWo needed to make an impact, and they knew they were going to have to need an out of the Austin-Jericho match. However, it wasn't so much the finish of that match as it was the body of the match that ruined everything. Because Steve is a guy that when he's out there listening to the audience, if he doesn't hear the "Austin! Austin!" chants, he begins to worry and chooses to start guzzling his opponents, taking all the offense for himself, instead of slowing things down and allowing the heel to build some heat and allow the fans to come to him. The end result was a shit match with a shit finish. And it was in that postproduction meeting of No Way Out, where the cracks began to form in Vince's trust of Steve.

Vince has always been Steve's biggest defender. He trusted Austin's guts more than the creative team's suggestions most of the time and changed a lot of plans to fit Steve's feelings (i.e., the babyface turn). Vince had a lot of loyalty toward Steve because of what he had done for this company. But what was more important: Steve's happiness or the success of the company? Because those two things were conflicting more and more. And so after No Way Out, it had now been three months he turned back babyface, and everyone was still waiting for him to break out and be that star again. And it wasn't happening. And all the three-on-one beatdowns on RAW, followed by Steve driving a tank with six ground-to-air missiles to the ring to raise hell on Smackdown to get revenge wasn't working. And no one wanted to say it was because Steve had raised hell for four years before this, and his hell-raising was no longer ground breaking, it was passé.

Vince lost all confidence in Jericho as champion because of this match. And Jericho went from being a hot heel champion blowing people away with Rock to being, as Vince said two weeks before Wrestlemania, "The biggest flop as WWF Champion ever." And so that match sent into action a chain of events to have Steph go with Jericho and pretty much emasculate him. But not with Jericho and Steph getting romantic, no, it was decided to go with the much stronger "business relationship." Because Vince felt no one was going to care about HHH and Jericho, but if Steph is pussy-whipping Jericho, then it'd be more HHH versus Steph and people would rather see that.

Austin was now headed straight for working with the nWo, and in particular Scott Hall. They banked on the nWo and came up craps. They couldn't keep Hogan heel for more than a month, and Scott Hall couldn't stay sober for more than a day. And Steve wasn't thrilled about having to get in there with a drunk pill popper. And can you blame him? But they were the best they could come up with.

It was once again tried to establish heat on

the nWo by having them get to Steve, but once again the nature of Steve's character was to get revenge that next night, and the fifty-fifty booking is boring. Steve's story was lukewarm heading into Wrestlemania and everyone knew it and was frustrated, but that's the hand they were given.

Originally, it was planned on Hall going over Steve (via a screwjob), to at least give the nWo something at 'Mania to help give them credibility. But when they got to Toronto the Thursday before the show, Vince decided that they were turning Hogan face after his match with Rock and putting Steve over clean, because it was the right thing to do for business by rewarding the guy who's going to be here and can be counted on (ironically enough, Steve walked out the first time the day after Wrestlemania).

Then Steve went away for two weeks. Apparently burned out, no one knows for sure.

The only people who talked to him were Vince and JR. This was around the time of the draft, and originally the plan was for Steve to be the only free agent not drafted and have him appear on both shows raising hell with Flair and Vince until he worked himself the best deal possible. This despite the fact that Steve gave confirmation that he would be back the week *after* the draft, the night *before* the draft show. Why couldn't he just come to the draft show and give it credibility?

Perhaps Steve wanted to be that free agent raising hell instead of being drafted with the rest of the herd. However, the image of Steve "holding out for the best deal" sounded more like the actions of Alex Rodriguez than crafty ol' Stone Cold. So Steve signed with RAW on the very first episode of the split shows.

It was also on that very first show where Flair made HHH versus Taker at Backlash, only to have Vince change it on Smackdown That was

because it was going to be HHH versus Taker, and Austin versus Nash. However, Nash tore his bicep and changed all that. Vince had also decided that Flair would turn heel to be the foil to Austin. Despite one of the points that was going to make the two shows different was having a babyface owner on one show, and a heel owner on the other. Immediately, the split was sputtering right out of the gate. But a lot of that can be blamed on Vince grasping at any straw possible to recapture the Stone Cold magic. The cold hard fact was that the magic was gone. People had seen it. But nobody wanted to admit that.

So the whole deal with Flair turning was predictable because you could see Flair trying to be what Vince was, and he couldn't. Fans didn't want to see it, much like every other time that a Flair heel turn was forced down the throats of people who had paid their hard-earned money to watch Flair entertain them for so many years, and just wanted to give something back to Flair in his later years. And the whole angle was fucked. People could sense it was the same old shit. They knew, but out of loyalty to Steve, kept throwing good money after bad. But the truth is that any type of alteration or enhancement to the character was met with severe resistance because "that's not Stone Cold."

So as the program with Flair plodded along to Judgment Day, Steve expressed an interest in working with Eddie Guerrero. Everyone was excited about this because everyone knew what kind of matches they could have if Steve just had the confidence to let Eddie get heat on him. So the seeds of that program were planted the day after Judgment Day with the horrible skits of Steve and Eddie at the karaoke bar. The funny thing is, Vince was the one who left the building to go shoot that. And he defended it in the postproduction meeting afterward. But it was horrible, and you could see the life draining out of Stone Cold's character. Austin went on the WWE's Internet show, *Byte This*, and said as much (albeit in much stronger terms), because he was probably the only one who could do something like that without fear of reprisal.

After the atrocious RAW, there were lots of meetings held about what to do with creative. And basically, everyone agreed on stuff that had been said for months: We need new fresh faces. Stone Cold versus Evil Owner was done. Let it go. No matter who's doing what, that formula is done. And so that led to Vince and Steph splitting the writing teams with the hope that being able to just concentrate on one show would help develop characters and long-term storylines because that person would only be concerned with writing one episode of TV a week. Brian Gewirtz became the point man on RAW with Bruce Prichard and Ed Koskey working under him. And Paul Heyman became the point man on Smackdown with Michael Hayes and David Lagana working under him. Vince and Steph oversaw the whole thing.

Now the first RAW of the split team era was the RAW in Edmonton with RVD and Eddie tearing the house down with their ladder match. Steve came in on the end of that and set up further Steve versus Flair, Eddie, and Benoit. This program had some promise because of the ability of everyone involved. However, Steve didn't like the stuff one bit and felt it was kicking the shit out of him too much on TV. Another point of contention Steve may have had was who was working on what show. Steve felt comfortable working with Paul because Paul was old school. Steve was never tight with Brian (who is responsible for Rock's stuff, Kurt Angle's stuff, Jericho's stuff, etc.) and might not have felt that great about that. But Steve's confidence in just about everything was damn near shattered by

now. It was after this show, in the car ride to the airport, that Vince asked Pat Patterson, "What would you say to us giving Steve some time off?" Giving him a break was the thing to do.

But the next week Vince talked with him and said that he could give Steve some time off, but that was the call of creative, and they didn't need to do it immediately. Because whether Steve felt it or not, the heat Eddie and Chris got him on Edmonton was very good. And the biggest concern was getting Steve hot in this program and then having him go away. RAW was in Dallas that week and had the scenario of Steve getting "off the bench" and wrestling Flair, with the loser having to be the winner's assistant. Originally, the idea of having Debra be forced to spend the night with Flair or Eddie if Steve lost was suggested, because of just trying to find some semblance of kryptonite for him. They were always asked to try and find ways to get Debra in the show (because she generally yapped to Steve about getting her "TV tapin' time"), but no one could ever use her to get heat, or have her screw Steve, or whatever. And plus, she is such a terrible actress that anything else you used her in is putrid. So with her range, and the parameters put on creative by Steve, they literally used her to her full potential when she'd answer the door before a commercial break to tell Coach she'd go get Steve. And so the idea of her spending the night with Eddie, or becoming Flair's assistant, or her screwing Steve and siding with Flair was out.

The result was a crazy idea called a "wrestling match," where punches were illegal.

The Background: Flair "benched" Austin the week before, as they ran the tired "Austin versus authority figure" angle to little success, and this was Austin's loophole to return to the roster. Earlier in the show, Austin pissed on Arn Anderson to really get Flair angry.

The Stipulations: If Austin wins, Flair becomes his servant, and vice versa. No punching is allowed, or else an immediate disqualification is called.

The Overall Importance: This was Austin's final match as a regular part of the roster before leaving.

RAW, June 3, 2002, Dallas, TX

Ric Flair versus Steve Austin. Flair and Austin trade mat-stuff and Austin works the arm. Austin resists the temptation to punch. He goes to a half-crab, but Flair makes the ropes. Chops are thrown, and Austin gets two. Flair goes to the eyes, but it's a thesz press and choking as his reward. Flair counters that and gets two. More chops, and a clothesline gets two. Benoit joins us as Austin looks to finish with a KICK WHAM STUNNER, but referee Charles "Little Naitch" Robinson is taking extra precautions to make sure that Benoit doesn't interfere. See, now that's dedication. Eddy sneaks in with a frog splash on Austin, so both guys are down. We have a break in the meantime.

Back to action, and they brawl outside. Flair gets backdropped on the floor. Back in, Austin suplexes him and chops the skin off his chest. Flair sucker-punches him, however, and clips the knee. And now we go to school. Insane chop-fest, and Flair keeps on the knee. Figure-four (using the ropes, of course) but Austin reverses. More chops lead to a double-KO spot. Flair goes up, but gets slammed (duh). Austin stomps a mudhole and walks it dry, triggering the Flair Flop. Flair goes to the eyes and cradles for two, however. Austin backslides him for two. More chops, but it's a KICK WHAM STUNNER at 14:32. Man, every time you think Flair is done, he pulls out another great match. ★★★½ *See,*

now if Flair and Austin can go fifteen minutes without a single punch, why can't everyone else?

Steve got a good win, in a good match on TV, got to drink his beers at the end of the show to send the crowd home happy, and the next week Flair was going to be his assistant. Steve was in a good mood after the match, and everything seemed cool.

So when the TV was written for the infamous Atlanta show, it was decided to *not* do the expected, namely a bunch of backstage stuff of Steve making Flair clean toilets. But in order to get the vibe of Austin having a man in power at his mercy, they looked at the RAW from October 1998 when Steve took McMahon hostage. That show ended the exact same way as the show in Dallas did. A KICK WHAM STUNNER, a beer. Rinse. Repeat. That just strengthened convictions *not* to do the same old thing. So they came up with the story of Flair getting out of the deal by giving Austin a shot at the WWE title at Summerslam by putting him in the King of the Ring tournament. Austin agrees as long as Flair doesn't allow any outside interference. Flair agrees. A KICK WHAM STUNNER. Austin walks up the ramp, and Flair drops the bombshell that Austin's opponent is going to be Brock Lesnar. Right before the match, Flair announces that a match of this magnitude needs a special referee who won't be intimidated and will make sure no outside interference will occur. Enter Eddie Guerrero. Eddie would then screw Steve, Brock goes over. Eddie escapes to the back, Austin chases, runs into an ambush of Flair, Benoit, and Arn, fights through that, and barely misses Eddie as he speeds away. Builds toward King of the Ring and gives you a dynamite main event for RAW.

Well, apparently when JR pitched the match to Steve that weekend he didn't like it. Didn't feel Brock Lesnar was ready to have a match with Stone Cold Steve Austin. Vince finally got word of this Sunday night and talked to Steve late Sunday night. Vince pitched him the creative and explained why, and Steve acquiesced and said he'd see him tomorrow in Atlanta. So they got to Atlanta thinking all is right with the world and it's a huge main event that night. However, Steve called the travel hotline that morning and booked himself a flight home. Immediately, Vince and JR try to get a hold of him. Nothing. JR finally gets in touch with Austin while he is sitting on the plane waiting to take off. JR tells him to come back and talk things out. Steve tells JR he didn't want to come back and have Vince talk him into doing something he didn't want to do. That was the last thing Steve said to anybody in the company for a long time.

Immediately, they had to rewrite the show, going with Vince becoming 100 percent owner again (which was a story they were going to do anyway because no one bought Flair as an owner, mostly because in working with Austin, he was compared to Vince and that wasn't fair). Flair turned back babyface because the only reason they turned him in the first place was to placate Austin.

The Background: Total desperation booking, as Austin walks out of the company and leaves them without their main event for RAW. Vince hadn't even been on the show since the draft, but suddenly reappears and challenges Flair to a match for total ownership of the company.

The Stipulation: The winner gets the entire company.

The Overall Importance: This one summed up what a day-by-day operation the booking really was at that point, since they had no backup plan other than this and were willing to give up a storyline that they had been building since

November in one match, thus nullifying the entire point of the split. But at this point we're picking pebbles out of our shoe while a sixteen-ton boulder is hurtling down from the sky like in a Roadrunner cartoon, so who's counting? It also ended up being both a springboard to favored status for Brock Lesnar (who was mostly fighting the Hardy Boyz and midcard comedy act Bubba Dudley by that point) and the catalyst for the introduction of the new "general managers" of the two shows, who we'll get to in a bit.

RAW, June 10, 2002, Atlanta, GA

Ownership match: Mr. McMahon versus Ric Flair. Had this stip been hyped and built up, you could have saved it for the PPV, easily. Flair attacks on the outside and chops away. They brawl and Vince ends up in the crowd. Slam on the floor, and back in we go. Vince goes to the eyes and slams him, then grabs the bell. Flair takes that and blades outside the ring. Very subtle there. Flair eats post, but chops back. Back in, Vince hammers away, giving us a Flair Flop. That gets two. Flair chops back, but Vince hits what looked like they were intended to be something not entirely unlike two clotheslines for two. Vince goes low for two. He grabs a chair, but Flair blocks it and chairs him on Vince's manly, nonchemically enhanced back. To the knee, and more chops. Arn joins us for a pointless role as Flair gets the figure-four after two low blows. I still think that Vince getting hit in the nuts, hard, several times, is the solution to ratings woes. I'd watch. But alas, it's no holds barred, so Brock comes in, hits the F5 on Flair, and Vince regains control at 9:02. Just what we needed, more Vince. This was like watching two seniors fight over the last pudding cup at the old folks' home. ★

And just when people were about to get adjusted to life without Austin in the spotlight, the unthinkable happened. Police were called to the home of Steve and Debra Williams (Austin), where Debra complained of being battered during an argument (she had a welt on the right side of her face) and also alleged that Austin hit her on the back. Austin declined to return home when called by police, but he was never under arrest due to a legal loophole. The wrestling world was stunned, to say the least, at how quickly its top star was falling from grace. The WWE, never one to miss a chance to exploit someone's pain for ratings, quickly threw together interviews with top people like Jim Ross and Vince McMahon for *Confidential*, where they gave their side of the story and discussed Steve's possible mental state. Austin was thrust into the public spotlight again, but in a way that no one wanted to see: a fading star arrested for beating his wife like common trailer trash. He eventually pleaded no-contest and was given a year's probation and was forbidden from drinking alcohol, which is ironic considering his objections to working with Scott Hall in February.

Austin has since divorced Debra and was last seen dating several beautiful younger blondes at various points in 2003–2004. But I'm sure deep down he misses married life.

Do I think Austin was right to walk out the way he did? Yes. He was obviously unhappy and bringing down everyone around him, and sticking around wasn't helping anything. Some may say that it sets a double standard for Austin to leave like that and be welcomed back months later when he gets bored and wants back in, but that just shows how smart Austin is: he knew that Vince would eventually take him back no matter what, so he essentially bought himself an extended vacation and came back hot again. Do I still respect him as a person and a wrestler? Unfortunately, no. But I understand his point of view at least.

8.

In with the New, but Not Out with the Old

While Steve Austin's departure had those within the promotion reeling, the months of June and July were somewhat notable for quite a few other people making their entrance into the newly dubbed WWE.

First and foremost, the nWo's descent into mediocrity continued, as the winning streak gimmick ended after only two weeks, and X-Pac failed to qualify for the King of the Ring tournament (which would end up being the final one). Desperate to revive the dying gimmick and equally desperate to bring in a big name to shore up the RAW side of things, Shawn Michaels was brought out of mothballs to join the nWo faction, leaving a rather goofy team of Kevin Nash, Shawn Michaels, X-Pac, Big Show, and Booker T. Now, by the this point people (i.e., us know-it-all fans) were becoming seriously concerned over the constant misuse of Booker T, who consistently got the biggest re-

actions from the crowd without ever getting pushed to the next level. After a silly feud with Edge at Wrestlemania X-8 (where the catalyst for the match was a competition over a Japanese shampoo endorsement), Booker was turned babyface as a part of the RAW side of the split, and with the limited star power on that end of things it seemed like only a matter of time before he was made into the #1 face on that show. He had a popular catchphrase ("Can you dig it, sucka?"), a popular move (the spinarooni), and a marketable look, especially to the black demographic. The only thing you could really argue against him convincingly was a lack of ratings power, but then you could make that same argument with pretty much anyone on the roster by that point. But the point (and I do have one) is that Shawn's first act after joining the group was superkicking Booker out of it, and thus kicking off what should have been a theoretical push to the top as #1 face for Booker. Didn't happen. What *did* happen was that Booker and partner

Goldust were programmed in a series of tag matches against Big Show and X-Pac, and lost pretty much all of them because X-Pac kept going over the creative team's head and whining to Vince McMahon about doing jobs.

But back to Shawn. Supposedly a born-again Christian (and given his tendencies as a compulsive liar I won't even believe that one until I see the reservation in Heaven for him) after years of stepping on the little people, Shawn apparently decided that Jesus wanted him to get Kevin Nash over again. Truly he's a noble guy. Fan reaction to him was decidedly lukewarm to begin with, since the audience at that point was basically divided into two camps:

1. Those who were watching in 1996–1998 and knew who Shawn Michaels was, and thus also knew him to be a broken-down shell of his former self who was forced into retirement by a back injury. Most of this group stopped watching wrestling entirely around 2001, and thus wouldn't be around for Michaels's return.

2. Those who started watching after 1998, and thus didn't know who Shawn was, and only saw a forty-year-old guy in a fruity beret and bad haircut dancing around in tight jeans and being suspiciously close to his big friend Kevin Nash. This group was watching wrestling, but had no interest in seeing Shawn.

So the WWE was pretty much pushing HBK on an audience that didn't really want to see him. It was no longer 1998, where audiences would yell out Shawn's name every time a potential mystery partner was announced. The assumption (confirmed by Shawn himself) was

that he had one last match in him. The only question was, which up-and-coming midcarder would he use his influence to make a superstar out of? Booker T? Rob Van Dam? Eddie Guerrero? No, even better, the nWo put out a call to HHH to join the group and defect from Smackdown. He didn't answer that challenge at that point, but the seeds were planted.

Another debut, this one a bit more innocuous, saw the long-dormant Cruiserweight division get a new contender. Funny story about the Cruiserweight title: in November 2001, when they were killing all the titles, there was the problem of what to do about the lighter weight classes. WCW had a Cruiserweight title (held by Tajiri) and the WWF had a Light Heavyweight title (held by X-Pac). However, X-Pac was, at the time, out with his millionth neck injury, leaving Tajiri to face employer William Regal in a singles match rather than a unification match with X-Pac. Now, after WCW was killed off, you'd think that the Cruiserweight title would disappear with it, but Tajiri continued defending that belt because X-Pac hadn't shown his face on TV in a while and the Cruiserweight title was right there anyway. So the WCW Cruiserweight title just suddenly became the WWF Cruiserweight title, giving them (in effect) two titles in the same weight class and (off the top of the head) maybe three people in contention for two belts. Eventually, the WWF Light Heavyweight title was simply dropped with no formal announcement, leaving an odd footnote in history, as the WCW Cruiserweight title, the lowest of the low, was given the honor of being the only surviving bit of lineage from WCW's doomed existence. But I digress.

Anyway, the Cruiserweight division wasn't exactly tearing up the wrestling world midway through 2002, as the belt was on faux superhero the Hurricane and seemingly going nowhere (although rumors were swirling that Rey Mysterio, legend of Mexico and whirlwind in WCW, was close to signing on), but an unlikely pairing would revive things somewhat. Hurricane began getting mysterious, comic-book villain type warnings from an unknown foe, who warned of being his nemesis and coming to expose him and the usual rhetoric. Most assumed it was another wrestler, but soon the clues pointed toward Tough Enough 1 winner Nidia (who had been essentially just collecting a paycheck in OVW for months) being the payoff surprise, playing Hurricane's ex-girlfriend. As revenge she brought WCW castoff Jamie Noble with her, and the duo became one of the oddest low-midcard acts seen in a while, playing an exaggerated Jerry Springer trailer trash couple who were eternally searching for the perfect double-wide and may or may not have been related at some point in their bloodline. Nidia, to the shock of many, was perfect for the role and fell into the bad accent and Daisy Duke cutoff jeans like a duck to water. Noble won the title in short order and held onto it for six months (an eternity in the WWE) before the tandem was buried for good because of heat with Stephanie McMahon backstage. Noble's redneck act was, however, an entertaining breath of fresh air in an otherwise colorless division.

Speaking of Tough Enough, another graduate of that pretty impressive class made his mark on the RAW side, as runner-up Chris Nowinski came in using his "I'm the only Harvard graduate in the WWE" gimmick and did fairly well with it for the role he was given. A feud with Maven seemed like a natural progression, but by the time they pulled the trigger on it, it was too late. Still, for someone as green as Nowinski, he held his own and didn't look like he was completely out of place on the roster, which is about all you can ask.

Another Tough Enough graduate didn't fare so well, however. Jackie Gayda (cowinner of the second season) debuted on RAW in a wrestling role rather than a safer valet role like Nidia. The result was a legendarily bad tag match on July 8, stemming from a terrible interview segment. And since I love you all so much, I'm gonna include it, just for you.

The Background: Jackie (almost visibly reading cue cards) suspects Trish of jealousy. And she wants to know what's up with Trish's cowboy hat? Ho, what a bon mot that was! And just when you think the dialogue couldn't get any more stilted and wooden, Chris Harvard adds his voice to things, also riffing on the cowboy hat with references so dated that he might as well be on *Evening at the Improv*. I mean, Yosemite Sam? Besides, it's a friggin' *cowboy hat*. Who gives a crap? Anyway, the end result of this thrilling verbal tête-à-tête is a mixed tag match for later, continuing the traditional "blueblood snob versus good old southern boy" feud between Harvard and Bradshaw that harkens back to such epics as Henry Godwinn versus Hunter Hearst Helmsley and Ric Flair versus Dusty Rhodes. Not necessarily in that order, of course.

The Stipulations: Everyone in the match must sign a notarized document agreeing to never let this atrocity air again or to ever wrestle this particular tag match again.

The Overall Importance: Your winner of Worst Match of the Year, 2002. Which is quite the accomplishment since it happened on July 8 and people remembered it for so long. Some shit just don't wash off.

Trish Stratus and Bradshaw versus Jackie and Chris Nowinski. Chris ducks away from Bradshaw, so Jackie and Trish start. They slug it out and then try some kind of disastrous attempt at a drop toehold spot that goes horribly wrong and results in them tripping over each other and the crowd booing heartily. Hoo boy. Bradshaw kills Nowinski with a boot and slam, and Trish and Jackie come in for round two. This time, they head up and Jackie gets knocked off, allowing Trish to follow her down with what in theory should have been a bulldog but in actuality made no contact, and even worse ended up being shot from the front so as to completely expose the lack of contact, but by this point it's too late to save the match anyway and it gets the pin at 3:11. "Mercifully, it's over," sez JR. Easy Worst Match of the Year candidate. If Jackie is the winner of Tough Enough, I'd hate to see the losers. ★★★

Not all the newcomers during this period were quite this level of disaster, of course. One that worked out really well in the long term was the wrestler who dominated OVW for most of the preceding year, "Prototype" John Cena. Cena was always portrayed as a kind of "Sting for the new millennium," with the same spiky blond hair as the '80s version of Sting (the wrestler, not the singer) and the same athletic move-set. Lacking anything more interesting to do with him, they decided to go with this wacky idea for Smackdown, whereby Cena would wrestle against people who were really, REALLY excellent professional wrestlers, and thus look good in the process and become a bigger star as a result. If I'm losing you here with these crazy and complicated notions, be sure to let me know and I'll dumb it down a bit. He lost to

Kurt Angle in his debut match, answering an open challenge, and then lost to Chris Jericho, but both times they sold for him so well and gave him such a hell of a match that the actual result didn't matter, because fans (myself included) were buying into Cena as the next big thing. Soon enough, politics (i.e., HHH) conspired to kill his push, and the next big thing became the next big curtain-jerking jobber.

But someone who *was* the Next Big Thing was Brock Lesnar. As noted, Brock came in after Wrestlemania, throwing around Hardy Boyz for the most part and getting stuck in a feud with them. This showed real ineptitude on the part of the bookers, because a push of a guy like Brock is the easiest thing in the world to do: you throw out a jobber every week, let Brock turn him into creamed corn, and keep him from getting exposed until the fans catch onto his act and start cheering him. In fact, they knew he was going to be cheered eventually, because he was purposely brought in as a heel so that any negative reaction to a massive overpush would be interpreted by casual viewers as more heel heat, and from there they could turn him babyface when the need arose. The problem came because his first feud was with the Hardy Boyz, which in any sane universe would be perfectly natural and useful toward getting him over. Matt and Jeff Hardy are insane bumpers who were trained to be TV jobbers in the early '90s, so they knew exactly how to build things toward making Brock Lesnar look like the Incredible Hulk. But at the same time, Jeff Hardy was a heavily protected favorite of Vince McMahon, who was never really asked to go out and get destroyed in that sort of role, which kind of makes the whole thing counterproductive. At house shows, in fact, Lesnar would often lose matches by DQ to the Hardyz. He took a step upward from May through June, feuding with Bubba Dudley, but again they were so paranoid about protecting one of their new characters that Brock ended up selling far too much for someone in the position that Bubba was in. I mean, I'm all for guys helping others to get over, but there's big money to be made with natural freaks like Brock Lesnar, and taking suplexes from Bubba Dudley (who, as everyone predicted, was dead as a character by Survivor Series anyway) was only going to hurt the short-term drawing power of the guy who needed it the most. However, one of the wins that Brock got over Bubba qualified him for the King of the Ring, and he was shot to the finals against Rob Van Dam at the PPV of the same name.

The Background: This was the finals of the yearly King of the Ring tournament, as Brock Lesnar met Intercontinental champion Rob Van Dam, who was fresh off of regaining the title from Eddie Guerrero in the classic ladder match. Lesnar defeated Bubba Dudley, Booker T, and then Test to make it to the finals, and RVD went through Eddie Guerrero, X-Pac, and Chris Jericho. The match RVD had with Jericho was part of the PPV and opened the show, in fact, and while a good match, it wasn't a classic, which caused Jericho to explode in a rant against Internet fans in general on his Web site.

The Stipulations: The winner is King of the Ring 2002 and gets a title shot at the champion at Summerslam in August.

The Overall Importance: The tournament was scrapped after this, so Brock wound up as the final King of the Ring. While not an immediate effect, winning the tournament in his rookie year shot him to the top of the promotion in a very real way, setting him up for a big-money match

with Rock, who was the one person they could depend on to do the right thing.

King of the Ring 2002, June 23, 2002, Columbus, OH

King of the Ring: Brock Lesnar versus Rob Van Dam. Rob hammers away to start and goes for the knee, then gets a superkick. Monkeyflip is blocked with a powerbomb. Brock stomps away and tosses him around the ring. Powerslam gets two. Backbreaker sets up a bearhug. Brock keeps pounding in the corner, but misses a charge and hits the post. Rob goes back to the knee and gets a spinkick and a missile dropkick. Rolling Thunder gets two. Legdrop and frog splash get two. Brock no-sells and gets the F5 for the crown at 5:42. Yawn. ½★

Perhaps the biggest debut, and the one no one in their right mind thought they'd ever see, came at the end of July. To refresh your memory, Vince defeated Flair in a tossed-off main event of RAW to win 100 percent of the company back, but that left a pretty serious conflict of interest, storyline-wise. So to alleviate these concerns, he announced the hiring of two general managers, one for RAW and one for Smackdown. These GMs would have the same powers as the owner did, thus throwing the whole horribly complicated "Who books the matches in the WWE" argument into yet another round of maddening complexity.

On Smackdown, you had Stephanie McMahon, last seen losing a match where she had to leave the WWE forever. Well, forever is only six weeks in WWE speak, I guess, because she not only returned, but as a babyface and without heat with her father. And then you get back to

> The only truly effective figurehead was Jack Tunney in the '80s, and that's because he was never on screen and only ruled on important matters. He passed away in 2004.

the same issue as with her "purchase" of ECW in 2001—fan credibility. Now, I don't want to get off on a rant here, but here's the thing with Stephanie: It's not just that it's a girl running Smackdown that I think rubs people the wrong way, it's that it's a girl with absolutely no consistent character motivation. One segment she's a caring fan-friendly overlord of Smackdown, the next she's a calculating bitch who's only out to help herself, the next she's there seemingly only to have Eric Bischoff put her over as a great strategist. Do we cheer her? Boo her? Ignore her? What is her purpose to even be on the show? Furthermore, you never actually see, for instance, what she's doing to convince these guys to go from RAW to Smackdown. The guys are either self-motivated (like Benoit and Guerrero, seeking competition), or just sort of appearing there with no real indication given of what the negotiating process actually entailed (Brock Lesnar). When she tried to woo Scott Steiner away, at least there was the implicit offer of sex in exchange for the contract, even though it didn't work. Okay, that being said, there is a bigger issue with her and "taking people down a peg," which she did once she was in control of the Smackdown side.

Let's face it, there are many jobs where women deserve equal respect, pay, and treat-

ment because they can do the job just as well as men. Wrestling is not one of them. If you stick a 100-pound woman in the ring with a 300-pound behemoth, no matter how you finesse the storytelling there's no believable way to have her portrayed as a threat to the man. Within the women's division, sure, no problem, but there will never come a point where a male wrestler will be physically intimidated by a smaller woman without it killing the male's heat, right? Reference Jeff Jarrett versus Chyna and Jericho versus Chyna for examples.

Now then, having Stephanie out there using the power of her family connections to cause potential money-drawing wrestlers to cower in fear from her does no one any good. What's the practical purpose in having *any* wrestler back down from a girl? It doesn't matter that fans know that Stephanie is Vince's daughter—in fact, it's worse. Wrestling is about escapism, not watching the same fucked up nepotism we all see *every day* in our own lives extending to the supposed fantasy world, too. Do I *want* to see people getting verbally castrated by "Daddy's Little Girl"? Does this make me want to buy a ticket to see this person fight another person as a result? No. Thus, it's useless as a storytelling device and is only serving to let Stephanie put herself over the talent, as usual. More to the point, "General Managers" are just another recycled plot device for lazy bookers—the Evil Commissioner. It's a dead plot element and constantly trying to trick the fans into thinking that they're seeing something new is just going to insult them even more.

Finally, Steph was last seen losing her entire fortune and getting dragged off by security "for good"—why should we suddenly believe that Vince has forgiven her and restored her to power again? This is why they had so much trouble:

they completely skipped over huge logical potholes and then just expected the fans to fill in the gaps themselves, when it's much easier to just change the channel.

Over on the RAW side of things, the surprise announcement was that Eric Bischoff, late of WCW and Vince's biggest foe for six years, would be running things. The fanbase immediately thought of a dream match between Bischoff and Vince, but since Vince doesn't consider Bischoff to be at his level (he always thought of his "feud" as being with Ted Turner), it's immediately ruined by having them hug to begin Uncle Eric's WWE stint. Despite rumors to the contrary, Bischoff's role is merely that of on-air talent and he has no creative input, as he's instead content to play an on-air sleazeball and leave running the company to those who get paid for it. However, another major change on RAW coincides with Bischoff's hiring, as Sean "X-Pac" Waltman is fired (or quits, the truth was never truly clear) for missing shows and showing up at the airport in a dazed stupor at one point, leaving the nWo as Kevin Nash, Shawn Michaels, and Big Show. With this less-than-impressive lineup being all that's left of the group, Vince does the inevitable and announces the final destruction of the group to end that very sad and pathetic chapter in the history of the nWo name. Bischoff's main storyline goal then becomes wooing HHH away from Smackdown, a storyline substitution for the previous "Shawn Michaels wooing HHH away from Smackdown" plot point that had been set up a couple of weeks before that.

But no debut was both more shocking to the people who knew about it or more invisible to those who didn't than that of Vince Russo. Russo is, of course, the legendarily bad booker (discussed at length in my previous book) who helped bring the WWF out of the outhouse in 1997 and into the penthouse, and then jumped to WCW in 1999 for huge money and essentially sank the entire company single-handedly. Russo, however, either was a brilliant tactician or had one sending him messages through an earpiece, because he devised the most deviously brilliant end-run ever seen in July. You see, Russo had an iron-clad contract with Time-Warner as part of his WCW deal, and while he was collecting millions to sit on his ass at home, there was a clause in the deal that stated that as long as he was collecting money from Time-Warner's pockets, he wasn't able to negotiate with or actively work for another wrestling promotion. But he was friends with Jeff Jarrett, who was starting up an interesting little company called Total Nonstop Action (NWA-TNA), with the idea being live, weekly PPV shows in place of a regular TV show. Russo rather desperately wanted to work as the booker of that endeavor, but was prevented by his contract. Jarrett didn't have the kind of cash to simply buy out Russo's WCW contract and thus free him up, so they needed someone who did. Russo, knowing that the WWE was getting increasingly desperate for new ideas and directions, patched up his differences with the other Vince and found himself with a job offer as creative consultant. And as a pleasant side effect, McMahon *did* have the cash to buy out his deal, so he could then work elsewhere. McMahon simply presumed that it meant for him. However, on his first day of work, Russo proposed a preposterous storyline encompassing every idea that Vince McMahon hated: a restart of the WCW invasion, using the WCW name, with Bret Hart, Goldberg, Scott Steiner, and Mick Foley spearheading the WCW side of things, along with every other major name from WCW's dying days that happened to be available. It was ludicrous, outdated, would cost millions, and made no sense. McMahon fired Russo within a day of him getting the WWF job, and Russo calmly began ghostwriting NWA-TNA, having escaped his iron-clad contract and now free to work in the business again wherever he wanted. Russo got the last laugh, too, because an increasingly desperate Vince McMahon signed everyone on the above list (except for Bret Hart, but he's still trying) for millions of dollars each and used them far less effectively than even Russo's dumb idea might have been.

You can't make this stuff up.

Russo himself got a taste of his own medicine in 2003, when NWA-TNA tried to sign his longtime enemy Hulk Hogan, resulting in Russo temporarily being punted out of the promotion to keep Hogan happy. Much like an STD, Russo was back sooner than anyone wanted, however.

9.

Learning to Work

I think it is conceded that I generally do pretty big things as a manager, am audacious in my outlays and risks, give much for little money, and make my shows worthy the support of the moral and refined classes.
—P. T. Barnum, letter to Mark Twain, 1878

Apparently, with all the controversy surrounding the departure of Steve Austin, HHH thought people weren't paying enough attention to him. I can only speculate, of course, but with Austin gone and Linda McMahon spinning things in the quarterly investor's call in such a way that you'd think Brock Lesnar was the second coming of Stone Cold, the Rock, and Hulk Hogan all rolled into one, it was time to move up some new people, fast. Unfortunately, HHH and Undertaker stepped up and decided it should be *them*. Even worse, there was apparently a bigger scourge of the company that was bringing down ratings and buyrates and sinking things by the day—people who don't know how to work.

You see, before RAW at the end of July, the agents and writers all had a powwow session with the hoi polloi of the RAW brand, whereby they laid down a big lecture on behalf of Vince McMahon, talking about the need to slow things

down and tell a story in the ring. However, HHH was there (from Smackdown) on the side of management, adding his two cents by telling the guys there that they "didn't know how to work" (presumably like he did), and they have to "earn" their spot (like he did) and generally have better matches (like his main event at King of the Ring against Undertaker, presumably). Oh, and they should be backstage at night watching videotapes of better workers instead of playing video games. This was, of course, said with people like Chris Benoit, Eddie Guerrero, and Ric Flair standing right there in the room, who could probably improvise a ★★★★½ match together on five minutes' notice if need be.

Now, just for fun, let's take a quick look at that HHH-Undertaker title match, shall we?

The Background: Originally scheduled for the Backlash show in April, circumstances switched it here, because god knows the world would have imploded if we hadn't gotten our HHH versus Undertaker main event at some point in the

73

year. Even more perplexing, HHH was aware going into the match that he had a leg injury and would be missing a few weeks afterward, which led people to wonder why he was even in the title match in the first place.

The Stipulations: Nothing, just a regular title match.

The Overall Importance: It set up Rock's involvement in the title scene again, which in turn set up the three-way main event for the title at the following PPV. Other than being a valuable tool at the Clinic for Sleep Disorder, nothing else.

King of the Ring 2002, June 23, 2002, Columbus, OH

World title: Undertaker versus HHH. Slugfest to start, won by UT. Then HHH. Then UT. HHH comes back with the choke, but UT pulls him out and slugs away again. They keep punching each other on the floor. I guess this is what JR meant by "more old school" in his Ross Report. Okay, we've established the punch quite well for both guys now. Back in, Taker—you guessed it—keeps punching. HHH punches back. Taker hotshots him to escape all the punching, and mixes it up with a clothesline for two. That's enough mixing it up, he says, and goes back to punching. And hey, how about another punch for two? HHH punches back again, but walks into a sideslam for two. Well, at least it's not a punch. Taker chokes away as JR starts spin-doctoring the nonaction with his "Well, this isn't catch-as-catch-can" speech. Taker whips him around, but walks into an elbow. And guess what's next? Punching! There's a kick from UT for two. JR uses the old "deliberate methodical pace" line to say that it's boring as fuck.

On the floor, HHH suplexes him and both guys lay around for a bit. Back in, UT clotheslines him and drops the leg for two. They head to the top rope—very slowly—and Taker's superplex attempt is blocked. What a highspot. HHH—that's right—keeps punching. Taker clotheslines him for two. This match is slower than a French art film. Taker undoes the turnbuckle, but HHH keeps punching. Taker clotheslines him and they stand around again. I check to ensure that my stopwatch has not, in fact, run out of batteries. You know it's a bad match when you check your watch, but you know it's a truly horrible match when you check to make sure it's still working. HHH with the neckbreaker and he punches and gets a sad spinebuster for two. More punching. Taker gives him Snake Eyes on the exposed turnbuckle, but HHH no-sells and gets the high knee for two, and then does the AJPW delayed sell. But not for long.

Taker DDTs him for two. Taker punches away, HHH punches back, but the ref gets bumped, twice. Double KO and everyone is selling it like death, even though there's been like three minutes total of contact so far. Rock does a walk-in, complete with music, but is only there to do commentary. Damn, I thought maybe he might be there to save this shitty match. Taker and HHH lay around FOREVER and UT grabs a chair, but can't use it. Taker gets dumped and they brawl, and SHOCKINGLY Rock gets nailed by mistake, and then even more shockingly goes after UT and hits HHH by mistake. Can you guess what next month's main event will be? I guess in WWF-land Rock versus HHH versus UT is a fresh matchup because we've never seen that exact combination of the same three guys we've been seeing for four years now. Back in, Hebner is still unconscious, so the Last Ride only gets two, courtesy of Nick Patrick. Patrick gets bumped, too. Rock interjects himself and beats on Taker with a Rock Bottom, and HHH gets two from that after they lay around for twenty minutes to sell all the action we've seen. More laying around substitutes for actual drama. What have they actually done to justify all this selling? A kick wham pedigree gets nothing because Earl is still out. UT goes low and gets a rollup for the pin at 23:43. Nearly half an hour for THAT shitty finish? Blow me, biatch. —☆☆ Easy candidate for Worst Match of the Year to that point, although it would be topped (bottomed?) later by the Jackie-Bradshaw-Nowinski-Trish disaster. So glad we had HHH and UT to step forward and carry the slack left by Austin.

I apologize if I put anyone to sleep by recapping that match for you, but sometimes you need to feel the pain I suffer.

Amazingly, there was a drive among the agents to start working a more submission-based style into the main events, to accentuate the skills of "real" wrestlers like Kurt Angle and Brock Lesnar and set up their eventual match. This stemmed from people like Undertaker and Bradshaw being big fans of mixed martial events like the Ultimate Fighting Championship and Japan's Pride organization and that enthusiasm rubbing off on the agents and creative team. Bradshaw in particular is frequently in the front row at UFC events. Specifically, a match between Carlos Newton and Matt Hughes at a UFC event provided a finish for a WWE match, which was a strange occurrence that showed the rising influence of the MMA style within the more traditional pro wrestling circles. The finish in question saw Matt Hughes applying a submission move called a "triangle choke" to Newton.

Just to backtrack for those who aren't familiar with the rules of MMA, chokes are legal and frequently end matches, because the object isn't to force your opponent into unconsciousness, but merely make him submit on the *threat* of unconsciousness. At any rate, a triangle choke is applied by trapping your opponent's arm by wrapping your legs around it, and at the same time using the legs to cut off their airflow around the neck in a kind of headscissors. This generally leaves the victim in a hunched-over position, with the person doing the move laying on the mat and fighting from the bottom. Now, while this would normally be an automatic submission, if you can hold on long enough, you can actually power out of the move and lift the choker off the mat, and slam them down again, hopefully rendering them unconscious. Carlos Newton did exactly that, and the referee declared Matt Hughes (still holding the move) unconscious, while Newton could no longer take the pain and tapped out at the same time.

Well, you just knew that a finish that screwy couldn't go for long without migrating to pro wrestling, and indeed a match between Kurt Angle and Undertaker ended the exact same way, with Undertaker attempting a powerbomb on Angle, only to have Angle put him in a triangle choke while in the air. The move still hit and the referee counted the pin on Angle, but Undertaker tapped at the same time and the match was declared a draw. The funny thing about that match, however, is that it was on a taped Smackdown show and no one in the audience actually *understood* the finish because Undertaker isn't exactly a master of subtleties like that. So they reshot the finish from the same camera angle later in the evening, having to use production people as stand-in "fans" who then acted thrilled at the finish and presumably could express a wider range of emotional reaction to the match than the actual fans earlier in the show could. One then wonders why Vince doesn't just skip the middleman and hire professional actors as his audience for TV shows, but I'm sure that idea has already floated through his head anyway. One final weird note about this whole incident is that later in the year, Undertaker became Mr. Submission and started using the triangle choke himself, albeit a version so laughable that the submission is probably due more to boredom than pain.

Speaking of changing styles, they actually found a way to use Hogan that didn't annoy me, which is no small feat. Hogan shocked the hell out of me and many others by first putting over Kurt Angle clean at King of the Ring, and then moving down to the midcard as a tag wrestler.

The Background: No specific background to the match, although Edge was a lifelong Hulkamaniac (and was even featured in a WWE promo package for Wrestlemania 2000, with footage from Wrestlemania VI in 1990 of a young Edge sitting at ringside with a Hulk Hogan t-shirt on) and it was the Fourth of July (actually the show was filmed on July 2) so they decided to do something special with Hogan that night. Of course, Edge is Canadian, but that's a minor point, I suppose. Billy and Chuck weren't setting the world on fire as tag team champions anyway.

The Stipulations: This was for the WWE World tag team titles.

The Overall Importance: It marked a notable downshift in the usage of Hogan, as he dropped from main event player to "guy standing on the ring apron in a tag match" and foreshadowed his role in making Brock Lesnar a bigger star. It

was also, believe it or not, his only tag team title in his WWE career.

Smackdown, July 2, 2002, Boston, MA

WWE Tag team titles: Billy and Chuck versus Hulk Hogan and Edge. Hogan locks up with Chuck to start and overpowers him, but Chuck slugs him down. He pounds him in the corner, but Hogan pops up and returns fire to set up a clothesline and his elbowdrops. Billy comes in to try and gets pinballed by Edge and Hogan. Michael Cole notes that Billy may be the greatest tag wrestler in history. I can't even make a joke funnier than that line. Edge gets the Edge-O-Matic on Billy and slugs away on Chuck, but turns around and gets clotheslined by Billy. So he's YOUR face-in-peril. Chuck fires away in the corner, but Edge fights back, only to be suplexed for two. Billy comes in for some choking and a suplex that gets two. Chuck drops a knee for two. Edge fights back again, but gets tossed by Chuck. Rico's attempt at interference backfires, and Billy goes down after a superkick, but recovers and sends Edge into the stairs and back in for two. Billy grabs a facelock and Edge tries to move him to the face corner, but Billy brings him down with a sunset flip and gets two. Chuck is back in and gets faceplanted by Edge to set up the hot tag. Crowd goes crazy. The oldest tricks are still the best.

Hogan goes nuts on the champs and we get some noggin-knocker action and a big boot to Billy. Legdrop is interrupted by a superkick from Chuck, giving Billy two. They double-team Hogan, but he clotheslines them both and brings Edge back in. He comes in via the top with a double clothesline and fights everyone off, and the Im-

Trish Stratus: Fitness model, multiple-time women's champion, and most important, Canadian. Best of all, she's able to do talk show rounds in Canada and talk about the rigorous demands of the women's division while keeping a straight face.

All photos Darren Smith/Lincoln University

Ah, Stacy Keibler. It just wouldn't be a photo section without at least one gratuitous shot of her. I mean, come on, who are we kidding here? "Stacy stands there and looks attractive." There, those who need justification for this picture have it. For the rest, enjoy.

Molly Holly, back in her superhero days. They tried about five different identities for her before settling on "Molly Holly: Wrestler." I know, what a crazy idea.

Hey, look, it's Stacy again. Um, photo caption . . . okay, "Stacy gazes into the eyes of the referee, wondering if . . . " Oh, screw it, you know why this is here.

Weird but true: Lita was set to become a crossover star with acting appearances outside of the ring, but broke her neck while shooting *Dark Angel* and got left behind by the rest of the women's division.

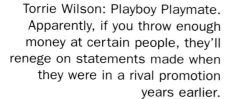

Torrie Wilson: Playboy Playmate. Apparently, if you throw enough money at certain people, they'll renege on statements made when they were in a rival promotion years earlier.

Sable *(right)* returned to the WWE in 2003 and posed naked for a third time, this time with Torrie Wilson *(left)*. They were portrayed as best friends on screen from that time on, presumably because posing naked in a men's magazine is some sort of bonding experience for women. Sadly, my girlfriend disagrees.

Rey Mysterio, who defied the odds against him by overcoming both a lack of height and a career associated with WCW to become a major star in the WWE.

Rob Van Dam begs Big Show for mercy, desperately trying to tell him for the last time that he doesn't want to see "the Big Show in his pants."

Bubba Dudley, obviously upset that his clever camouflage outfit failed to conceal him from his opponent.

Kurt Angle suffered what should have been career-ending spinal problems in late 2002, but underwent a somewhat miraculous neck surgery from Dr. Jho to go right back to throwing suplexes again in 2003. Sadly, Dr. Jho's attempts to cure male pattern baldness are still not up to the same levels.

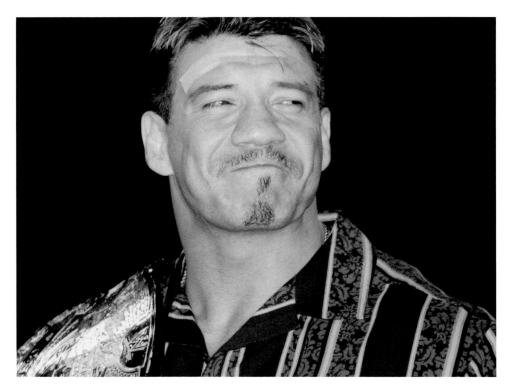

Eddie Guerrero, unlikely folk hero, with the WWE championship over his shoulder, is a sight that I would have sworn would never take place. It's all the more amazing since he's been fired multiple times for drug problems, and he's not seven feet tall or married to Vince's daughter.

Michael Cole & Tazz, who blossomed into the best commentary duo in wrestling, thanks to the wonders of postproduction and good chemistry.

This is Chuck Palumbo, who made perhaps the most drastic character change of 2002, going from half of an ambiguously gay tag team to half of a Mafia hood team. Sadly, we never got the Billy Gunn as jealous lover storyline.

Matt Hardy: Version 1.0. Luckily he's not a product of Microsoft, or he'd be Matt Hardy: Version 6.0 with a million bug fixes by now.

Kane, the Big Red Ratings Machine, who revived his career for about two weeks by finally unmasking, to reveal he was just wearing heavy mascara all those years. You just never know with some people. . . .

John Cena *(left)* tussles with Big Show, leading to their showdown for the U.S. title at Wrestlemania XX. At publication time, it wasn't known if Show ate the belt to prevent having to defend it.

Rob Van Dam finds innovative new ways to search for his lost contact lens.

Mike "Crash Holly" Lockwood, who died in 2003 only a couple of months removed from being fired by the WWE because of his substance abuse problems. They cared so much that his death was never mentioned once on any of their programs. Well, here ya go, Mike.

Booker T asks HHH *really* nicely if he can win, just this one time.

Brock Lesnar, who is not only a former NCAA champion, but can also defy gravity itself by doing pushups on the top rope. Even the laws of physics aren't dumb enough to mess with him.

D-Von Dudley, who in 2003 made a rare onscreen transformation, from born-again preacher back to wrestler. It's usually the other way around.

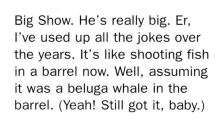

Big Show. He's really big. Er, I've used up all the jokes over the years. It's like shooting fish in a barrel now. Well, assuming it was a beluga whale in the barrel. (Yeah! Still got it, baby.)

Jeff Hardy. I have no idea why anyone would accuse him of doing drugs. Doesn't everyone fall asleep while standing on the top rope?

Kane shoots pyro out of the ringposts, which makes me wonder if he can shoot fire out of anywhere and if he rents himself out to college parties for a few extra bucks.

Brock Lesnar continues to justify his massive push and salary by beating Billy Gunn into a quivering mass of jelly. I don't ask for much, really.

The humorless Lance Storm, who was turned into a dancing fool by a storyline in 2003, with the payoff being that he's supposedly incredibly well endowed. And this is supposed to make the guys in the audience like him because . . . ?

Rob Van Dam, an open pot advocate and public critic of the promotion he works for. I have no idea why he's not pushed more.

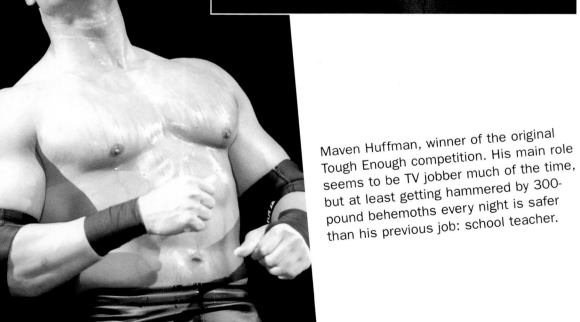

Maven Huffman, winner of the original Tough Enough competition. His main role seems to be TV jobber much of the time, but at least getting hammered by 300-pound behemoths every night is safer than his previous job: school teacher.

Goldust, who appeared to have his life together in 2003 and had turned himself into the comeback story of the year as a result, was released by the WWE in early 2004 for unspecified reasons. I just hope his story doesn't end the same way Crash Holly's did.

I don't know who this guy is, but he's on RAW for what seems like ninety minutes a week, so he must be married to the boss's daughter or something.

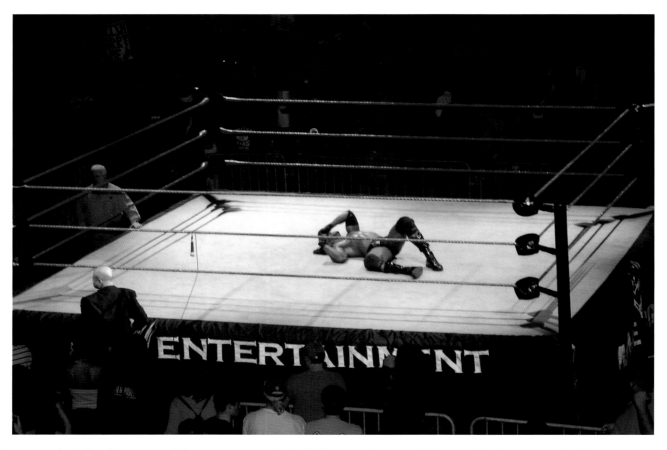

And finally, some nights your name is in lights, and some nights you're just counting 'em.

plant DDT on Chuck follows. Rico trips him up, so Hogan takes matters into his own hands. In the ring, Billy and Chuck the switcheroo, but Billy gets speared for two. It's BONZO GONZO (everyone in the ring at once) and they both hit Chuck with big boots and legdrops to win the tag titles at 10:01. Total old-school southern tag wrestling that made use of Hogan's greatest asset: his ability to stand there and get people chanting his name to build heat for the match. ★★★

Oddly enough, the very well-done Edge-Hogan tag team only lasted two weeks, as they dropped the tag titles to the team of Lance Storm and Christian at the Vengeance PPV in July to jumpstart the "Un-Americans" group that had been kicking around since January. This was a weird decision on several levels, not the least of which was that Storm and Christian just weren't that over as a team or as a concept. The heel gimmick ("We don't like America") was so pathetically generic that fans would boo them as a kneejerk jingoistic reaction and then fall asleep again during the matches. It also interrupted another feud ongoing, between Jericho and Edge, that would have put Edge over as an even bigger star and ended up going nowhere because their PPV match was changed to Edge-Hogan doing a meaningless job to Storm-Christian while Jericho dropped a match to John Cena in the opener.

This leads to a weird story about Cena, as he was being given a big babyface push as a plucky rookie following his entrance, but certain people (HHH) went to Vince McMahon and had a storyline (where Cena would stand up to Vince and get punished with a match against Jericho) quashed because Cena hadn't yet earned that

sort of push. This left the Cena-Jericho match with about a dozen different possible endings (since the buildup to the match was now destroyed) and it ended up helping no one. Cena was buried and nearly destroyed as a character by that, but he'd be back soon enough with a surprising twist.

Amidst all the booking chaos and last-minute decision making, they started tinkering with the main TV shows as well, in order to emphasize the split nature of the programs. With Bischoff running RAW in storyline terms, the show was given an oddly WCW-ish feel, as the announcing table was moved from ringside to the entrance ramp, whereas Smackdown continued to feature Tazz and Michael Cole at a table by the ring. This, however, had another advantage when it came to PPVs: they could have the announcing teams switch off on commentary between RAW and Smackdown matches without physically having to change positions each time. Tazz's resurgence as an announcer is also an interesting case, as he was essentially written off for dead after Jerry Lawler returned in November 2001 and took both the RAW and Smackdown color commentary jobs. The agents (and Vince specifically) often berated Tazz's commentary in the headsets they wear, but with the brand extension they obviously couldn't have Lawler doing both shows, so he got another shot at it. Since that point, Michael Cole and Tazz have been widely acknowledged as the better announcing duo, although much of that has to do with postproduction work.

Back over on RAW, the writers began a series of storylines for Rob Van Dam that showed a remarkable attention to actually trying to get someone over in the long term. Since RVD was the Intercontinental champion and Jeff Hardy was the European champion, the feeling was that there were still too many secondary titles cluttering up RAW, and thus they needed to be pared down with a unification match. Hey, why not, everyone loves unification matches. This was actually a long-term plan to make the Intercontinental title into a RAW-only World title for RVD, but things got changed around, which we'll discuss later. Suffice it to say, it was only fitting that these two would settle things in a ladder match. Unfortunately, the spotlight on that show would be stolen by HHH, who took up fifteen minutes of the PPV the night before to announce that he was jumping from Smackdown to RAW, bringing Chris Jericho, Test, Christian, and Lance Storm with him. In exchange, Brock Lesnar, Chris Benoit, and Eddie Guerrero moved to Smackdown, although it wasn't an actual trade as such. Vince McMahon declared open season previously, basically giving everyone carte blanche to go where they wanted for a limited amount of time. These new resulting rosters were closer to what the original intention for the split was all along, and it also allowed for the buildup to Brock's title shot at Rock (who won the belt in a three-way victory over Undertaker and Kurt Angle at Vengeance) to be on the Smackdown side of things, where postproduction work was essential to Brock's rookie promo skills getting the points across properly.

Now, back to HHH for a moment, as two months after Shawn Michaels throws out the initial challenge to HHH, the storyline is finally picked up on again. The nWo was dead, and Kevin Nash had set a new record for ineptitude by tagging into a six-man tag match (his first match in weeks) and immediately tearing his quad muscle ala HHH, except without the steroids. Because believe me, if you saw pictures of Nash's legs without the puffy leather

pants, you wouldn't accuse him of bulking them up. So now they have to find a reason for these two to be feuding, because god knows the world would stop turning if two Clique members weren't programmed against each other to the exclusion of everyone else on the roster. So then, here was the logic involved in what they came up with:

1. HHH arranges an interview on the Vengeance PPV, where he listens to deals from both Bischoff and Stephanie, and then Shawn Michaels interrupts and talks him into coming onto RAW so they can mess with Bischoff's mind and be hell-raisers again. So HHH signs with RAW.

2. The next night on RAW, Shawn talks HHH into reviving the D-Generation X gimmick from 1997, complete with entrances and t-shirts. It gets a huge pop and probably would have turned HHH into the monster babyface star that he had been trying to be for months, but now he wants to be a heel, so he turns on Michaels and lays him out with a Pedigree. They also, it should be noted, probably flushed a couple of million dollars worth of merchandising down the toilet in terms of D-X t-shirts, D-X DVDs and videos, and "Clique sign" foam fingers. It wouldn't have revolutionized the business again or anything, but given how desperate they were for something that could draw by then, throwing away a perfectly good angle that's over is just silly.

3. So the next week, they're good friends again for no particular reason, and we get a "mystery man" angle that ends with

Michaels having his head smashed through the windshield of the car and nearly killed. I wonder how this was supposed to make the attacker a heel . . . hell, I'd pay good money to see people smash Shawn's head into windshields every week, born again or no.

4. After an exhaustive one-week search for the real killer, HHH is revealed as the assailant and a match is signed for Summerslam between them, Shawn's first since returning from retirement.

All that for the one match, which already had backstory built in and didn't need the goofy whodunit twist or extended interviews from HHH about where he'd end up. Plus, you'd think that HHH's involvement would have been apparent, since he was the guy who turned on Shawn the week before and all. The match was at least good, so in the long run I can't complain too much. Well, actually I can. I've since mellowed to Shawn again, since he's back as a full-time performer, but I don't forsee the same leniency where HHH is concerned.

The Background: As noted above, HHH invited Shawn to reform D-X, turned on him, and then turned on him again just so we knew who the smartest guy really was. Shawn carried his end well, cutting killer promos from a wheelchair about how HHH would have to kill him to beat him and stuff.

The Stipulations: First guy to do a clean job to anyone other than a close friend *dies*. Oh, wait, that's real life, sorry. This was a nonsanctioned, no-DQ, no-countout lights-out match.

The Overall Importance: It reestablished (in the WWE's mind) Shawn as a main event player again, even though he wasn't, and allowed HHH

to brag about a great match, even though it was due to Shawn's timing and selling. Aren't politics wonderful?

Summerslam 2002, August 25, 2002, Uniondale, NY

Official WWE Non-Sanctioned Match: HHH versus Shawn Michaels. Shawn is sporting his 1995 Smoking Gunns attire tonight, with jeans probably concealing leg braces or the like. HHH also takes us back to the past, shaving for the first time in what seems like years. He looks kinda like Homer Simpson without the beard. And almost as bald—check out the Michael Bolton baldness denial going on here. Another couple of years of shooting steroids and he'll look like Kurt Angle. Say what you will about him "just working out," but you don't go from thick blond hair in 1997 to thin straggly hair and a bald spot in 2002 without some chemical assistance. Unless he's got cancer, I guess. Does it work the same way when you ARE a cancer?

They slug it out and Shawn takes him down and dumps him. He follows with a pescado and they head back in, and do a chase on the way. Shawn finds a garbage can, but gets dumped on the railing. Back in, Shawn gets a clothesline and goes up for a double axehandle. Superkick misses and HHH gets a sadistic backbreaker and another one to show that he really means business. The psychology here is a gimme in terms of getting it over: it's well known that Shawn has a crippling back injury, so any punishment at all to the back is amplified 100 times in the fans' minds. It's a great shortcut— you can skip ten minutes of working the body part because one move, in the minds of the fans, is enough to damage the back again. HHH whips him into the corner and slugs him down.

Elbow to the back gets two. I feel like singing "You always hurt the one you love." Good old Spike Jones.

HHH gets a chair and blasts Shawn in the back for two. Shawn reverses a suplex for two, but walks into a facebuster and gets DDTed on the chair for two. HHH uses Shawn's own belt for some S&M-styled foreplay. Then it's off under the ring, where he finds his trusty sledgehammer/phallic symbol, but Shawn fights him off. Man, this match works on so many levels, even the sick ones. HHH goes to an abdominal stretch instead, and that provokes an argument with Earl Hebner about using the ropes, which is, of course, completely ludicrous because the ref has no authority here. They head up and Shawn gets crotched and hung upside-down in position for either a chairshot to the ass or some spanking, depending on which level you're reading this recap. HHH sets up the chair and drops Shawn's back on it, which is just such a sick spot that I have to wonder about Shawn's sanity. Sideslam on the chair gets two. Ditto. Pedigree, but Shawn goes low to block. HHH stalks him with the chair, but Shawn superkicks it back in his face to reassert his manhood in the relationship. A bigtime bladejob for HHH results. Shawn's facial bleeding earlier in the match, by the way, was pretty much the first appearance of the legendary blood capsule in like ten years, but I can understand not wanting to mutilate yourself for a one-shot match.

Shawn fights back with the forearm and kip-up, and suddenly he's on fire again like a revivalist preacher. Chairshot and Shawn dumps HHH and batters him right back with the belt. He even uses Hugo Savinovich's boot, which might be a tip of the hat to his match with Diesel in 1997, but I doubt it. He finds a ladder and harpoons HHH with it. Catapult into the ladder gets two. HHH baseball slides the ladder back into him, and they head back in. Shawn superplexes him for two. Sunset flip gets two. HHH hits him with the high knee for two. He grabs the stairs, but that backfires and Shawn dumps him. A table gets set up and HHH ends up on it, and then through it via a splash. Ladder gets set up in the corner back in the ring, and Shawn drops the elbow and cues up the band. Superkick misses, but he reverses the Pedigree for the pin at 27:23. He probably should have just gone over clean with the superkick, but that's not important. ★★★★ HHH attacks him and Shawn does the stretcher job to close out the match.

This match actually received one of my lower end ratings though most others had it pegged in the ★★★★¼–★★★★¾ range. I felt that the garbage wrestling aspects hurt them and that they had a better match in them. And they did, hitting a more consistent plateau in December 2003 on RAW, with a ★★★★¼ TV classic.

Now then. Yes, it was a great match, but there's mitigating circumstances. First, the greatness of the match was based on two primary things: Shawn Michaels knowing the *exact* moments to make his babyface comebacks, and Shawn Michaels bumping like a man on enough painkillers to tranquilize Anna Nicole Smith with the knowledge that he is never going to wrestle a full-time schedule again. The match stood out in stark contrast to the mat-based wrestling surrounding it, and thus seemed different and edgy, even though it wasn't really. The booking was extremely protective of both guys, and the question you have to ask yourself is this: Who does it help? Does it help Shawn Michaels, retired for four years and back into semiretirement again? Does it help HHH, already a big star and no longer needing the rub given by Michaels? Does it help any of the guys below them who had to watch HHH sleepwalk through matches with people he should have been elevating and then lecture them about needing to work harder? Notice how HHH gets motivated: wrestling a Clique buddy who he is only all too willing to show ass and sell his ass off for. Does it help the people above them who have been trying for four years to get out from Shawn's shadow, only to have him try to steal the show again? What it comes down to is that sometimes a great match shouldn't necessarily *be* a great match, when a good one would have done just as well to show that Shawn could still have *any* match, period. I'm not saying that everyone should start deliberately dogging it so as not to show up the main eventers, but did we really need Shawn splashing HHH through a table and diving off a ladder? The story of the match—Shawn gets his back beaten to a pulp but comes back because he has heart and guts—was enough of a story without all the ga-ga on top of it. Sometimes less is more. And think about this: What if Shawn had done his comeback match against Brock Lesnar and sacrificed his bad back to the bearhug in the name of getting Brock over as a career killer? That

would be a worthwhile goal. This, as it is, was good, but at best served only as an egofuck for HHH and Shawn in terms of usefulness to the promotion. If HHH was really serious about doing what's right for business, he'd go out on RAW and make someone a star, no excuses, no self-serving bullshit nonfinishes, no inspirational speeches before and after. But who needs action when you've got words?

This sort of "protect yourself no matter who it hurts" attitude was also prevalent with Undertaker in July, as they did a storyline intended to get Jeff Hardy over as someone more than his usual weird undercard self. Hardy, by this point, was so far beyond a shell of his former self that people were actively wondering how he could still wrestle a regular schedule without falling apart. As yet another idea to get him motivated again, he was given a feud with Undertaker, whereby Undertaker would kick the crap out of him on several occasions, but Jeff would be foolish enough to keep coming back for more. This led to a ladder match for the WWE title that was heavily praised by many but overrated, in my opinion. That match ended up being an extended squash for the Undertaker, as he pounded Hardy from one side of the ring to the other before giving him a couple of hope spots and then claiming the title belt to win. He then beat up Jeff AGAIN, but shook his hand as though offering endorsement of him as a tough guy. Well, I don't think anyone who saw Jeff Hardy and his day-glo body paint and "cruising the streets of San Francisco" wardrobe would ever accuse him of being a tough guy, so that didn't work out too well, and thus the only guy who benefited was Undertaker. Undertaker later gave an interview where he talked about how much he would have loved to put over all these young guys, but no one was able to "step up" and take the spot from him. How someone "steps up" in a fixed sport is beyond me, but that was his explanation.

However, one guy who no one had any problem putting over huge, because they knew it was gonna happen to him sooner or later anyway, was Brock Lesnar.

10.

Brock, Brock, Till You Drop

Those who really desire to attain an independence, have only to set their minds upon it, and adopt the proper means, as they do in regard to any other object which they wish to accomplish, and the thing is easily done.
—P. T. Barnum

Whereas people like HHH and Undertaker were over on RAW protecting their own spots by any means necessary, Smackdown featured a new attitude toward the booking of Brock Lesnar as someone who was truly the next big thing, and he exploded like a bombshell onto that show.

Having won the King of the Ring tournament in June, Brock was in line for a shot at Rock's newly won WWE title at Summerslam in August, and the first order of business was to erase the crappy half-assed booking since his debut and have him start KILLING people. Preferably big people. After barreling through Mark Henry and Rikishi, and hitting them with his new F5 finisher (a fireman's carry into a slam, which looked pretty impressive on a pair of 400-pound guys), it was time for the bigger test, as Brock was fed Hulk Hogan on the August 8 Smackdown to build him up for the title shot.

The Background: Hogan defeated Kurt Angle by DQ the week before, due to Brock's interference, in a match to determine who got to face Lesnar. In the '80s, the dynamic for this match would be drastically different, as Brock would be the monster heel who plowed through midcarders and then faced Hogan thirty or forty shows in a row on the road at $20,000 a night. 2002, however, was long past the point where Hogan was going to draw that kind of money, so they had a different use in mind for him.

The Stipulations: Brock was goaded into putting his title shot on the line here, so the winner got Rock at Summerslam. This prompted a classic line from manager Paul Heyman, who objected because "that's his whole M.O.! He overcomes adversity!"

The Overall Importance: This was not only Brock's biggest win to date in terms of establishing him as a player, but it also marked the exit of Hogan from the WWE until Wrestlemania XIX, as he sold an injury angle and then threw a tantrum over his usage and "retired."

Smackdown, August 6, 2002, Richmond, VA

Brock Lesnar versus Hulk Hogan. Crowd heat for this is unreal. They do the staredown thing to start and Brock wins a lockup battle, which was traditionally Hogan's spot to win. Brock pounds him down and stomps away, but Hogan no-sells it and slugs back. He fires away in the corner, and Brock misses a charge to the other corner, giving Hogan a two-count off a clothesline. Hogan drops the elbows and clotheslines him out of the ring, and Brock takes a breather. Brock pulls him out and crotches him on the post, twice, and then drops his own elbows to return the favor. As always, I award extra points to people who hit Hogan in the nuts multiple times. Brock pounds him with shoulderblocks in the corner, and they head outside, where Brock pulls apart the table, but that gives Hogan a chance to recover and send Brock into the post. Back in, Hulk punches away in the corner, but Brock casually powerbombs him out of there and gets two. Hogan hulks up, three punches, big boot, but Brock no-sells, so Hogan tries the same series again, and a second big boot sets up the BIG FAT STINKY WART-INFESTED GIANT-KILLING LEGDROP OF DEATH, which only gets two. Crowd was kinda shocked at that. Hogan, out of moves, tries punching again and another big boot, but Heyman trips him up and allows Brock to hit the F5. Ah, but he's in a really bad mood, so he doesn't want the pin. Three big boots will do that to you. Brock opts for a bearhug instead, and although the crowd just takes it as a spot to cheer Hogan back to life, Hogan instead passes out at 10:06, shocking everyone. Good little power match that turned Brock into a major star and set up Summerslam and a showdown with the champ. ★★½ Hogan has Ken Shamrock Disease, causing internal bleeding from unspecified damages to the insides.

> I enjoyed this one *a lot* more on second viewing, going from a ★ rating to ★★½. Since the initial push, I've since become a huge fan of Brock Lesnar's work, and I can appreciate his earlier stuff a lot more.

The build to Rock versus Brock continued, with a hands-off approach to the feud, as they didn't touch until the show. To quote the Rock, he repeatedly asked Brock to "just bring it," and Brock brought nothing. However, that's Booking 101—makes the fans REALLY want to see it when it finally happens. Rock was kept busy as new Smackdown additions Chris Benoit and Eddie Guerrero attacked Rock week after week, leading to a diatribe by Stephanie against them for hurting "her" Smackdown main event. You know the difference between Bischoff and Stephanie? Bischoff not only talked the rhetoric, but his character backed it up with action. What does Stephanie ever do? Yell at the talent? Come out on stage and talk about how her show is superior? Run to her father for backup? It's astonishing that someone who has pretty much 100 percent control over her own character would write herself to be such an ineffective whiner. Furthermore, Brock had that title shot—which he EARNED himself, mind you—when he was still part of RAW. All Stephanie did, in storyline terms, was steal him away and take credit for someone else's work. Isn't that *exactly* the sort of thing that we were supposed to hate Bischoff for doing all those years ago? And meanwhile, what was Eric doing? Actively trying to create new stars (by giving the title shot to the hot team of Booker and Goldust, by making RVD his #1 guy, and by using 3 Minute Warning as his personal enforcers, which we'll get to in a little bit) and making the necessary changes to help the product, like changing around the layout of the arena. If it was Stephanie who was writing the Bischoff character, she had actually managed to create a more compelling character as her nemesis than she herself was. And once that happens, there's no way to get over as a babyface.

Speaking of Chris Benoit, this leads in a roundabout way to a discussion of Rob Van Dam. Hey, you take the segues you can get in the big bad world of publishing. Anyway, back when Benoit was still on RAW, way back in July, he won the Intercontinental title from RVD in a damn fine TV match, and then immediately buggered off to Smackdown because he had nothing better to do on RAW. From there, he spent the next four weeks basically fighting Rock in TV main event tag matches every week, before dropping the title back to RVD at Summerslam. Thus, the only reason Benoit even won the belt in the first place was to set up a loss to RVD at the PPV a month later, without ever defending the title. So, the whole point was to build up Van Dam as a top guy and establish the Intercontinental title at that level along with him. Toward that end, RVD had previously defeated Jeff Hardy to unify the belt with the European title, and then defeated Tommy Dreamer in a hardcore match to unify the belt with the Hardcore title. Thus, RVD's entire purpose for the months

of July and August was to create an uberbelt on RAW that would be considered the elite title for that show, and it was wholly intended for Rob Van Dam. Keep all that in mind, and we'll get back to it in a bit.

Now then, I believe I mentioned something about 3 Minute Warning, who were kind of the evil opposites of Brock Lesnar. A pair of Samoans stuck in developmental hell for years, they were formerly kicking around the indy leagues as the Samoan Gangsta Party among other names, and while not really possessing much in the way of marketable skills or talents, they were big and fat and could occasionally move, and thus got a shot at a tryout now and then. Finally, once creative had something to do with them, they were brought into the big leagues, despite reservations about their ability to keep up in the tag division. The solution to their usage was rather unique and a neat workaround that prevented them from getting exposed too early: they would serve as Eric Bischoff's personal bodyguards. Specifically, since Bischoff was notorious for having a short attention span when it came to things happening in the ring, a gimmick was built up where he'd get a pair of midcarders to do a meaningless wrestling match, and then come out and declare that it was "three minutes too long" and suddenly the Samoans would rush out and beat them to a pulp. Ironically, Vince himself would do the same thing at a house show in 2003, stopping a match between Rhyno and Tajiri for real, because it was boring him. This same philosophy was also applied to boring interviews and old people, as Mae Young soon took a beating from them, as well. Even Jimmy "Superfly" Snuka returned for an interview and got attacked, although he was allowed to hold his own for a bit.

However, the newly named "3 Minute Warning" was very quickly exposed as both sloppy in the ring and dangerous to opponents (with a series of injuries caused by their inattentive ringwork, most notably senior citizen Pat Patterson needing surgery after taking a splash from them), but in a move that shows either the pigheaded determination of Vince McMahon or the truly awesome intimidation power of the Samoan mafia (and don't discount that one as a joke, either), the team was consistently pushed for months before Eddie Fatu (by then known as "Jamal") ran into a legal problem that wouldn't go away (attacking cops will generally do that to you) and was fired, leaving his partner, Rosey, as a single, and amazingly still a pushed single.

But anyway, back to Brock Lesnar.

By Summerslam, they had done such an effective job of building him up as a main event caliber heel challenger that the show ended up doing a higher-than-usual buyrate, and the gods of good fortune struck twice, as even the traditionally dead crowds of Long Island, New York, were in full force that night, although not in the way the WWE expected.

The Background: As noted, Brock won King of the Ring to earn a shot at the title and beat the crap out of several big huge guys to put the fear of god into the rest of the roster. Rock did several clean jobs to people like Chris Benoit to make him look vulnerable. The coup de grace was a series of promotional videos to build up the match, which showed Brock's insane training methods and effectively created a sympathetic monster who people *liked*.

The Stipulations: Like every main event, this ended up being a no-DQ for the WWE Undisputed title.

The Overall Importance: This is the match that MADE Brock Lesnar. And also had an unexpected side effect, as you'll see. It's also the final appearance of the Undisputed title, as the title would become disputed the next night, thus ending eight months of having one, and only one, World champion. I think I had "four months" in the pool.

Summerslam 2002, August 25, 2002, Uniondale, NY

WWE Undisputed title: The Rock versus Brock Lesnar. Rock charges in for a slugfest to start and gets battered with backbreakers by Brock, for two. The crowd has immediately turned on the Rock. Brock batters him in the corner with shoulderblocks, working on the ribs, and knees him out of the ring. Heyman gets in his shot. Brock clotheslines him into the crowd and then presses him onto the railing, further hurting the ribs. Back to the floor via another clothesline, and back in for a huge overhead suplex that gets two for Lesnar. Rock fights back and gets tripped up by Heyman, and Brock drops elbows on the ribs, a spot that he took from Hulk Hogan and dropped once he turned babyface later in the year. Brock sets up for the bearhug, but Rock fights back, only to walk into a powerslam. That gets two. The crowd turns on Rock again with "Rocky sucks" chants. This was a combination of the fans thinking Rock "sold out" with his Hollywood career and was just doing a short run with the WWE again to make some extra cash, and also a general fascination in the Northeast United States with big powerful guys like Brock.

Rock suplexes Brock out of the corner after he misses a charge, and it's a double KO. Both guys kip up in a cool spot, and Rock tries a forearm, which Brock won't sell. Crowd eats it up. A third try finally works, and Rock DDTs him for two. Rock tries the Scorpion King Deathlock, pauses to chase Heyman, and then gets the move for real. Lesnar tries to power out, however, which was established by Lesnar's training videos. Rock finally releases to chase Heyman again, and Brock clubs him from behind. Brock gets a chair left by Heyman, and goes to the injured ribs with it, and then grabs the GOBLIN-KILLING BEARHUG OF DOOM. Rock fights back, so Brock suplexes him down to the mat and keeps the hold on. Rock fights out, however, which has now turned him fully heel. Rock slugs him down and goes low. Hey, if you're getting booed, you might as well go for the family jewels. Brock rams him back into the corner, however, while selling the ballshot, and keeps driving the shoulderblock into the ribs.

Rock comes out with a lariat and slugs away, and now the crowd is really on him. Rock slugs him out of the ring and dismantles the Spanish table for bad intentions, as they get into a brawl. He catapults Brock into the post (as Brock does an impressive leap at the post) and then Rock Bottoms Heyman through the table. Back in, Rock looks to finish with Rock Bottom, but it only gets two. Rock is left talking to himself in disbelief. Brock comes back with Brock Bottom, which gets two. This match has a real bigtime main event feel to it, and was probably the first one that Brock was holding his own in like that. Rock recovers first and gets the MAIN EVENT SPINEBUSTER to set up the People's Elbow, but Brock pops up and MURDERS Rock with a lariat, and the F5 is countered by Rock. They exchange counters, and the F5 finishes for Brock Lesnar, clean as a sheet, at 15:49 to

give him the WWE Undisputed title. Here comes the pain, indeed. ★★★★

Another case where Brock's past work won me over later—my original rating on this match was only ★★★, and I short-changed it a lot. It was a terrific power match, and it made Brock Lesnar into a breakout superstar.

However, in what was seemingly a neverending parade of "one step forward, ten steps back" booking goofiness, the next night on RAW saw HHH completely undermining Brock's big win right off the bat, cutting off his victory speech and bringing the focus of the show from Brock's win to his own #1 contender status. This led to Brock running in fear from a HHH-Undertaker brawl (well, I'd run in fear too, but for different reasons) and in fact running all the way to Smackdown, making him look like a cowardly heel. Now, just a small note about booking here: guys who are 6'5" and composed of solid granite instead of skin and bones don't really need to be cowardly. Brock could have been painted green and used as the Hulk in the movie, okay? I'm all for little guys playing cowards, but Brock should be fucking people up, not fleeing from fights. And just to make sure that both HHH and Undertaker's needs were served (but not Brock's), HHH defeated Undertaker in a dull-as-dishwater main event for the show, making HHH the #1 contender. However, since Brock was now on Smackdown and appearing there exclusively, Undertaker jumped there as well, went over Chris Benoit for the millionth time to make *himself* the #1 contender, and got the title shot for the next PPV, Unforgiven.

As for HHH, well, he had a different route to go.

You remember all that stuff about Rob Van Dam and unifying all the secondary titles into one big secondary title just for him? That was supposed to lead into a feud between Van Dam and HHH for that belt, which would then be RAW's version of the World title and elevate the Intercontinental title to the same level as the WWE title over on Smackdown. However, HHH didn't want to be feuding over the Intercontinental title because he felt it was beneath him. So, the slut of the wrestling belt world, the Big Gold Belt, was resurrected as the RAW title (called the "World Heavyweight title" within WWE canon, but everyone else calls it the RAW title, much like they call the WWE title "the Smackdown title") and a grueling, one-night tournament with the biggest and best of the RAW roster was set up.

The Background: In order to legitimize the new World title, a sixty-four-man, one-night tournament was arranged, featuring not only the thirty-two top stars of RAW present, but another twenty legends of WWE past and twelve international stars. The show had to be expanded to six hours in order to contain all the action. Every win was clean.

The Stipulations: One fall to a finish, winner gets the first World title, Lou Thesz is the special guest referee.

The Overall Importance: Okay, I just made this whole thing up.

In reality, there was no tournament, or even a match. It was just Eric Bischoff handing HHH the title belt because he's that damn good and deserves it more than anyone else on the roster. That's probably why no one considers the RAW version of the World title to be anywhere near the importance of the Smackdown version. There's no history to the belt—it shares the same physical title belt as the NWA World title and WCW World title, but that belt was merged with the WWF version when Chris Jericho defeated Steve Austin in the unification match. This was explicitly stated as a brand new title, which we were then supposed to just accept as a main event level belt, given to a guy who was rapidly becoming overexposed in his new role of carrying the show. And that wasn't even the end of his overexposure that night, as he beat idol Ric Flair with his usual "ref distracted, low blow, Pedigree" finish, and then wrestled *again* in the last match of the night, a tag match with Chris Jericho against Flair and Rob Van Dam. In this case, he did the clean job to Van Dam, but then he'd already been awarded a title and beaten the million-time World champion in the same night, so really he could afford the loss by that point.

This set up a feud with RVD leading to Unforgiven, where everyone assumed that Rob would win the title, but once again they SWERVED us. It was also very bizarre booking leading up to the show, as Rob was put into positions where his weaknesses would be deliberately exposed. For example, a lengthy interview debate with HHH where he made fun of HHH's water-spitting entrance, but then got verbally dismantled by HHH, who is much more well spoken (albeit rambling) than RVD is. The promotion knew full well what Rob's limitations as a talker were, and yet he was left out there to die in a twenty-minute interview regardless. Even stranger, mere days for the show, Rob was made to job to Chris Jericho by tapping cleanly to the Walls of Jericho, thus losing the Intercontinental title and going into the show cold. The plan, as best I can figure it, on HHH's part was to undermine his challenger (HHH books his own programs) to the point where he'd simply say "Oh, he's no longer worthy of getting the title" and thus get the win. And thus we get Unforgiven.

The Background: Rob pinned HHH clean in a tag match on RAW to earn a title shot and unified the Intercontinental, European, and Hardcore titles into one belt in order to set up a showdown over who was the real champion of RAW. He won a minibattle royale, pinning Chris Jericho to officially earn the title shot. However, he lost the Intercontinental title days before the PPV to negate that aspect, leaving people scratching their heads.

The Stipulations: The winner gets the World heavyweight title, a.k.a. RAW title.

The Overall Importance: This marked the end of RVD's relevance to the main event scene, as HHH finished him off and sent him into the midcard, which killed his drive to improve and left him wrestling sloppy, inattentive matches night after night, knowing that his advancement had been halted. Ric Flair's interference also marked the beginning of months of servitude to the Almighty Nose, as he basically became his bitch and a chance for HHH to dominate his boyhood idol and put himself over by proxy.

Unforgiven 2002, September 22, 2002, Los Angeles, CA

RAW World title: HHH versus Rob Van Dam. RVD grabs a headlock to start, HHH escapes. Another headlock, another escape. HHH blocks a third try by shoving him down via the hair, but RVD takes him down with another one. They work off that and trade slaps. HHH slugs him down and overpowers him, but Rob outsmarts him on a crisscross and grabs another headlock. It was later learned that HHH was deliberately calling a basic, mat-based match to throw RVD off his game and make himself look better. HHH bails, allowing Rob to imitate the water-spitting act. Crowd digs that, but Rob goes back to a headlock when HHH comes in, killing the momentum. The idea, which had been floating around all year, was to slow down the pace with more holds and mat-wrestling, but RVD isn't the guy to try that with. A rollup out of the corner gets two. They do a sloppy Flair-Steamboat pinfall-reversal sequence into a backslide, and Rob legsweeps HHH for two. Back to the headlock.

A spinkick puts HHH on the floor, and Rob follows with a somersault dive, but HHH casually sidesteps him and allows him to splat on the floor like an idiot. He didn't even make it look like Rob had a shot of hitting him. That's the kind of stuff that really annoys me about him. Rob beats the count back in, but HHH stomps him and brings him out for a meet-and-greet with the steps. Back in, that gets two. He hammers away and slingshots Rob under the ropes, which gets two. Rob escapes a suplex and gets a rollup for two. HHH hits him with a neckbreaker for two. Rob gets tossed and they walk around outside the ring and ram each other into the table, and head back in where RVD slugs away.

HHH catches him with a high knee for two. He heads up, but Rob catches him with a kick and slams him off. That's a very Ric Flair spot. HHH, however, comes back with the MAIN EVENT SLEEPER, a move that put away such luminaries as Jeff Hardy and Spike Dudley in the weeks leading up to this match. Rob counters him into the corner, but misses a charge before recovering with a spinkick. They slug it out and Rob spinkicks him again and dropkicks him to set up a running moonsault for two. Monkey-flip out of the corner and Rob works him with shoulderblocks to set up a missile dropkick, and Rolling Thunder gets two. HHH takes a breather, so Rob follows with a pescado and hammers away.

Back in, Rob goes up with another missile dropkick for two. HHH comes back with a face-crusher, but the ref is bumped. Rob spinkicks him down again, and gets the visual pinfall with no ref. A visual pinfall is where the babyface pins the heel for the benefit of making the fans think that he can beat the heel, but without a ref to count anything so that the heel can go on to win later. Rob catapults him into the corner to block the Pedigree, and heads up for the frog splash and another visual pinfall. HHH was apparently in a generous mood on this night. Rob checks on the ref, allowing HHH to go low and retrieve his trusty phallic sledgehammer. Rob kicks it out of his hands, but Flair does the run-in and we get the Vince Russo swerve finish, as he teases hitting one guy (HHH) and then hits the other (RVD). A KICK WHAM PEDIGREE finishes at 18:16, as Rob has to lay there for about twenty seconds while the ref recovers enough to count the pin. The Pedigree is very devastating, you see. Match was technically fine, but too slow-paced and mat-based to benefit RVD, which was kinda the point. ★★★

> **Rob Van Dam was originally booked to win this match, but HHH changed the decision, because that's what he does. I actually liked the match better the second time around (original rating: ★★¼), but it still wasn't great or anything.**

The anti-HHH bandwagon was starting to grow larger backstage at this point, but at the same time HHH was becoming Vince McMahon's right-hand man, ingrained so far into the booking sessions and trusted so implicitly by the boss that saying anything in public would be tantamount to career suicide. The sad thing is, it'd get much worse as his title reign wore on. And on.

But I don't think anything could have prepared us for what would happen to the company once Kevin Dunn spoke up at a production meeting and opined that the shows should feature more "soap opera."

11.

Creative Bankruptcy

The Mermaid, Woolly Horse, Ploughing Elephants, etc., were merely used by me as skyrockets or advertisements, to attract attention and give notoriety to the Museum and such other really valuable attractions as I provided for the public. I believe hugely in advertising and blowing my own trumpet, beating the gongs, drums, etc., to attract attention to a show; but I never believed that any amount of advertising or energy would make a spurious article permanently successful.
—P. T. Barnum, private letter, 1860

While the subject matter is sensitive, on balance this was an attempt at dark humor, capitalizing on the popularity of programs such as *CSI*, *Six Feet Under* and *X-Files*.
—Kevin Dunn, press release, 2002

In September 2002, Vince McMahon and trusted advisor Kevin Dunn decided that the WWE was in need of a new direction to "push the envelope" and "max the extreme" and all that junk.

Kevin Dunn, who is basically in charge of all the production duties for the WWE and is pretty close to running the company at times, got it into his head that what the promotion was lacking was soap opera. That right there should tell you how desperately out of touch with their target audience that this company was getting at the time. But since Vince McMahon has the kind of attention span that allows him to change the entire direction of the company on a whim, suddenly he got it into his head to start doing this as "event TV"—funerals, weddings, controversy, shock TV. Hell, if it worked back when they could shovel whatever shit onto the shows they wanted and hide behind their bulletproof defense of "Get it?" via a million-dollar Superbowl ad like they were the modern version of Andy Kaufman, misunderstood genius, then why shouldn't it work in 2002? Since we're talking about a company that has spent the past twenty years educating its fans to never call anyone a "wrestler" because it's a dirty word, it only made sense (in the twisted mind of Vince McMahon) that by emphasizing the stuff that makes *him* laugh, then obviously ratings would skyrocket if the entire show was built around lowbrow humor and misguided attempts to ride the coattails of better-written shows.

Case in point: only a few weeks removed from getting their ass handed to them in court by the World Wildlife Fund over the issue of confusing their version of "WWF" with the fund's, they began doing a series of subway ads for RAW and Smackdown, using the McMahon family to parody the *Sopranos* and other popular TV shows. It was this sort of inferiority complex, where Vince insisted on comparing his programming to sitcoms and other mainstream shows to avoid being lumped in with "rasslin," that keeps wrestling fans stuck in the dark ages and hiding their shirts in their closets again. Ironically, months later the WWE would lose a lawsuit against a t-shirt company who did exactly the same sort of parody of WWE stars, as this time they were claiming marketplace confusion because of a cartoon dog doing the Rock's catchphrases. This was not only ironic due to the nature of the fund's lawsuit, but incredibly hypocritical due to the WWE's own advertising campaign!

So anyway, Kevin Dunn suggested to Vince that they should try soap opera, and Vince was all for it because it doesn't take much to talk him into sleazing up the shows. This ended up falling under four major storylines, in order of increasing stupidity:

1. The gay wedding
2. HLA
3. Katie Vick
4. Al Wilson

First up, the gay wedding. Jokes about Pat Patterson set aside, the WWE had never really touched on the sensitive issue of same-sex marriage and the emotional and legal ramifications therein. And you know why? BECAUSE NO ONE FUCKING CARES. Well, at least no one watching the shows. However, Vince McMahon disagreed with this view, and moving on the assumption that the only bad publicity is no publicity, the decision was made to have latently homo tag team Billy and Chuck act even more overtly gay, leading up to Chuck proposing to Billy on Smackdown.

Now, let's stop and think about this for a second.

As I believe I may have mentioned before, wrestling fans in general aren't what you'd call really tolerant of storylines that positively promote the gay lifestyle. As a rule, the feeling is that two people of the same sex expressing their love for one another is a beautiful thing, as long as it's two women. Other than that, forget it. And Vince McMahon is the last person in the world with the kind of sensitively written material to change that perception. Because, let's face it, wrestling comes down to two sweaty guys rolling around on the mat and trying to get on top of each other as it is. Wrestling fans are already bugged enough about that sort of homoerotic undertone as it is, without having to go to an arena and be told that their homophobia is wrong by a guy who makes sure to involve himself in storylines where he publicly cheats on his wife with twenty-year-old blondes. Every week. Because we sure know that, by god, Vince McMahon is all man. And so is HHH, because he tells us so every week, just in case we forgot.

The idea was to push the envelope, but it wasn't even the first gay-themed storyline in the

WWE-WWF alone, let alone TV. In 1996, you had Goldust out there fondling himself and others to "play mindgames." That went farther than the Billy and Chuck storyline possibly could, because that was cable TV and Smackdown was on network TV, with much tighter standards. It's doubtful you'd see Billy Gunn trying to "resuscitate" Booker T by kissing him, for instance, whereas Goldust did exactly that to Ahmed Johnson in 1996. If you want to go even further back, Gorgeous George and Ricky Starr, characters from the "golden age of wrestling" in the '50s and '60s, were even more overtly gay. And in the '80s, Adrian Adonis went from a tough-guy biker to a flower-throwing fop as a punishment for his weight. Although his sexuality was never explicitly mentioned or dealt with in the storylines, the fans were encouraged to make their own judgments, which they did.

And that's not even getting into all the gay storylines done on other TV shows beforehand. The *Ellen Show* had years before featured Ellen Degeneres publicly dealing with her homosexuality, and shows like *Will & Grace* made it into a sitcom. The prison drama *Oz*, on HBO, not only featured several openly gay characters, but a love story between two male inmates named Beecher and Keller that became more compelling than most heterosexual relationships on TV. And the TV show *Queer as Folk* was out long before Billy and Chuck scheduled their wedding. Point being, thinking that doing a stunt like a gay wedding would somehow draw positive press and increase ratings because it was "edgy" was silly, because it had been done, and done better, many times previous.

Then came the mainstream press coverage.

Billy and Chuck were all over the radio and TV the morning of the show's airing (which was two days after the taping of the "wedding," it should

be noted, so the results were readily available), making it known that they weren't really gay, and it was basically a publicity stunt to "develop characters." It should be noted that a few months later their characters had developed into Mr. Ass (Mark 2) and an Italian hood, respectively. Anyway, the only really notable piece of positive press they got was from GLAAD, when a spokesman gave them a wedding present on the *Today Show* (a gravy boat) because of the positive role models they represented, and, of course, Stephanie McMahon was all too happy to take all the credit for writing those roles, and was nowhere to be found when the blame came later. Truly a McMahon to the end. GLAAD was later shocked and appalled (not sure if they demanded their gravy boat back, but you never know) at the way that the storyline turned out. Not that anyone should have really been surprised, least of all the wrestling fans who had seen it coming from the start.

This was, really, one final chance to get Billy and Chuck over as something special, since they had been largely abandoned by the product since July after losing the tag titles to Hogan and Edge and getting left behind. The WWE, in their buildup in the mainstream press, made it seem like they were the top heels in the promotion or something (although, they made sure to note, fans booed them because they were evil people, not because they enjoyed tossed salad for dinner, and even then deep down people *liked* them) and they were going to be pushing them as such as a result of the wedding.

This then, was the wedding.

Rico hosted the proceedings and we got a live rendition of "It's Raining Men." Billy and Chuck (with personalized cummerbunds) used that as entrance music. Chuck gave a badly acted vow recital, and Billy gave him a ring. Rico introduced a "Love Story" themed video, with all the highlights of their career as a team. Well, really there wasn't many, since they'd only been a team for six months. The objection process caused the entire audience to object, and then Godfather did the formal objecting, in what would amount to his final angle with the company. Godfather outted them as being straight, but the justice just skipped right to the end, as Billy suddenly looked very nervous. Wow, acting. Chuck got cold feet, but Rico reassured him and they're officially married. Chuck and Billy freaked out and revealed that it was all a publicity stunt and they're not actually gay. So really, it was type of another marriage: Bait and switch. The justice declared that tough shit, they said the vows, they're married. And by the way . . . it's not actually an old justice of the peace, it's Eric Bischoff under a rather impressive makeup job.

Rico turns on Billy, and 3 Minute Warning run in for some destruction, including a Samoan drop on Stephanie that draws a huge face pop. All the Smackdown workers united to save Stephanie, but the angle never ended up going anywhere outside of a throwaway tag match at the Unforgiven PPV between Billy and Chuck and 3 Minute Warning, which saw the supposed new top stars doing a quick job to get the Samoan faction over. Fans booed throughout the segment and made gay slurs toward the performers, which showed just how enlightened the fanbase was and how popular the team was. The difference, of course, was that fans weren't booing because they were gay, they were booing because they were being fed a segment that they didn't want to see.

And then the backlash started.

GLAAD, who now looked like fools for believing in this silly angle (which most wrestling fans had already figured out as a swerve weeks earlier and were just waiting to see the payoff), put out press releases decrying the WWE for playing them as fools and mocking gays. Mainstream sports shows jumped all over the skit, taking McMahon to task for launching a sleazy bait-and-switch angle for the sake of ratings (what, hadn't they been watching wrestling in the past, oh, HUNDRED YEARS?) and any positive press that might have come from the bit was flushed down the commode. The funny thing is that the segment was done the way it was because it was felt that fans wouldn't cheer Billy and Chuck if they were "really" gay, so in order to be babyfaces they had to be straight. Talk about a catch-22: they were given the gimmick to garner mainstream attention, but once they got mainstream attention, they had to give up the gimmick. Another funny thing is that afterward, in an attempt to be "straight," they went so over the top professing their manhood (while still hanging out together and dressing like they were cruising for guys) that they came off far more gay than in the days when they would do "groin stretches" together backstage.

Amazingly, the WWE *still* didn't learn their lesson about failing to deliver what they promised,

Since the tumultuous breakup of Billy & Chuck, Billy went into semi-retirement due to a hand injury, and then returned—twice—to diminishing returns as a singles "star." Maybe he should ask for the gay gimmick back again.

and the result was a match at the PPV between the two teams involved.

The Background: Rosey and Jamal, a.k.a. 3 Minute Warning, attacked Billy and Chuck to conclude the disastrous "gay wedding" and revealed that stylist Rico was in fact managing them now. This was the first interpromotional match in the long and storied history of the brand extension since way back in the days of . . . uh . . . three months before, when King of the Ring featured two of them.

The Stipulations: If Billy and Chuck win the match, then Eric Bischoff has to kiss Stephanie McMahon's ass live on PPV. If 3MW win, then Stephanie has to engage in lesbian sex with a woman of Bischoff's choosing. Most figured on the former coming to pass because (a) it could be paid off, (b) it involved a McMahon getting worshipped, and (c) it humiliated Eric Bischoff.

The Overall Importance: It marked the very last time that Billy and Chuck wrestled as a team on PPV and the end of their horrible "ambiguously gay duo" act. It was also 3 Minute Warning's PPV debut and the start of a terrible run as a supposedly top team. Other than that, nothing.

Unforgiven 2002, September 22, 2002, Los Angeles, CA

Billy and Chuck versus 3 Minute Warning. Billy and Chuck are supposed to be top babyfaces now, but barely even got a reaction coming out. In more ways than one. Big brawl to start and Billy heads out with Jamal, while Chuck gets nailed by Rico and Rosey hits him with a backdrop suplex. He pounds away but runs into a boot in the corner. Jamal comes in and kicks Chuck down for two. Michael Cole notes that 3MW are from the "hood" of Sunnyvale, Cali-

fornia. Rosey keeps beating on Chuck as fans leave, perhaps for a gay wedding in another arena. We hit the chinlock and Rosey headbutts Chuck down again. A double headbutt really changes up the moveset and that gets two. Billy accidentally distracts the referee and 3MW stomp away on Chuck in the corner. Rosey misses a moonsault while Cole asserts that playing against Emmitt Smith in college means that Rosey was a great athlete. Geez, William Perry played against Smith, too, I don't think anyone thinks he's a great athlete. Billy gets the hot tag and cleans house to no reaction, but makes the fatal mistake of ramming two samoans' heads together. You never do that. Jamal goes up, but Chuck slams him off. Rosey slams Billy with . . . something . . . but gets caught by a superkick from Chuck. Jamal superkicks Chuck in turn, and Billy catches Jamal with the fameasser. He goes after Rico, however, and gets finished with a samoan drop at 6:38. ½★

> **This match sucked even worse the second time through. I dropped the rating from ★ to ½★, mainly out of spite toward everyone involved.**

Now, as a result of this, Stephanie had to engage in a lesbian scene with a woman of Bischoff's choosing later in the evening. Now, since Stephanie considers herself to be a sex symbol (seriously) the idea was that fans would be excited to see this, and surprised because they thought it was going to be Bischoff getting humiliated. Of course, fans don't actually respond to Stephanie as a babyface, so this was a problem. The ironic thing is that had she actually gone through with making out with a woman on PPV, she'd be a bigger babyface than at any point in her career. But instead, Bischoff brought out Rikishi dressed as a woman in order to humiliate Stephanie (presumably he was so dumb that he actually believed that the 400-pound-Samoan and obviously male Rikishi was actually a big fat ugly woman whom he had never met before), and Rikishi then revealed his cunning disguise and ended up humiliating Bischoff with a stinkface after all. Thus, they get the match result they want (Rosey and Jamal going over Billy and Chuck) and they can duck out of their own stipulation by supposedly giving the fans "what they want." But they wanted to see Stephanie getting nasty with a pair of chicks, not Bischoff having his face shoved in a fat guy's butt crack. In fact, I can pretty much guarantee that any male in the audience would have taken the former over what they got. But Stephanie, as head writer, makes sure that she never shows weakness, never lets people forget that she's a McMahon and therefore is in control, and never does anything more degrading and/or humiliating than having her blouse pulled off by Steve Austin once, and even then it was just to show off her new boobs. And she certainly doesn't engage in HLA.

Which leads me to the second desperate attempt at ratings in September.

The week after the wedding was announced, Eric Bischoff went on RAW and announced that Stephanie was just arranging it for the sake of ratings and that it was desperation for ratings on her part. This was of course truer than the WWE would let on. However, in real life Brian Gewirtz had an even better idea for cheap rat-

ings pops: Hot Lesbian Action. They had t-shirts ready for production and everything. The concept was simple: Bischoff brings out two supposed lesbians, has them grope each other, and then interrupts it by having 3 Minute Warning come out and destroy them, thus pissing off the fans and turning 3MW into the monster heels of the year.

Well, the first part was right—the fans *were* pissed off. In fact, they were so pissed off that they wrote letters to TNN by the hundreds talking about how offended they were that garbage like that would ever be aired on a show where kids would be watching. TNN, reeling from the negative publicity, immediately issued an apology, slapped the WWE on the wrist, and basically told them to never go that far again. Vince McMahon then went on *Confidential* and made himself out to be the modern equivalent of P. T. Barnum, a misunderstood genius who was being held down by the censors and was just trying to do what was best for the fanbase. This disregarded the huge ratings drop for the HLA segment, but that was the least of his problems. He promised to keep delivering edgy content like HLA.

Those proved to be famous last words.

Don't even *ask* about the proposed T-shirts.

By October, ratings for RAW were still slipping, and the creative team pretty much bottomed out in a desperate attempt to create more mainstream interest in their shitty product by crafting one of the most famously terrible storylines ever.

It started with the team of Kane and new RAW member Hurricane winning the RAW version of the tag team titles from Lance Storm and Christian. He was clearly positioned as the star of the team, getting him in line to be the next victim, er, I mean, challenger for HHH. Soon after, he added the Intercontinental title to his collection by beating Chris Jericho in a match that made people wonder why the hell they had put the title on Jericho in the first place instead of leaving it on RVD (so at least he'd have *something* to take out of his loss to HHH), but all those questions would quickly be buried under the shit of a bigger dungpile.

With Kane positioned as the next challenger and Vince on a soap-opera kick that he believed would turn the company around (seriously), you just knew something bad was going to result. And so, on the October 7 RAW, Kane single-handedly won a TLC match to retain the tag team titles over three other teams, and then HHH came out and accused him of being a murderer.

Longtime fans and/or previous readers might be saying to themselves right about now, "Well, duh, of course he's a murderer, he killed his parents and set the fire that burned his face," but (setting aside that Undertaker later confessed to those deeds, which no one really remembers, and anyway let's not go *there* again) they had something even better in mind. In fact, the idea was that Kane killed Katie Vick.

Now, you're probably saying to yourself "Who the fuck is Katie Vick and why should I care?" and I can't disagree. But don't worry, Kane explained it all in a boring interview, and here's what the story boiled down to after what seemed like forty-five minutes of talking:

Katie Vick is indeed dead, but he didn't kill her. They were friends ten years before when

Kane was first wrestling, which makes absolutely no sense because in storyline terms he didn't debut until 1997. Kane drove her home one night, and not being familiar with a stick shift, got into a car accident and broke his arm. Not familiar with a stick shift? Forget that, wasn't he in a mental institution at the time? The crowd was so moved that they chanted "What" during the dramatic pauses. He said he was sorry to her parents, even though he didn't learn to speak until 1999. Oh, and he was also driving drunk, according to HHH. Oh, and the autopsy revealed that Kane was banging Katie at the time, thus giving us our first brush with the word "semen" on a nationally televised wrestling program. The question is whether he's a rapist or a necrophiliac. I thought Tori took his virginity in 1999? So the question then became, is he Kane, half-brother of the Undertaker, or Glen Jacobs, a guy playing a character? How the hell are you supposed to suspend your disbelief even a little bit when they can't even decide if Kane is a hideously scarred freak or just a guy playing a role? And don't *kids* watch this stuff? It kinda made me long for the well-thought out and sensible storylines of Vince Russo. And how was this supposed to make me want to see the match?

Obvious questions aside, this was just a terrible storyline that offended everyone. Oh, I'm sure there were a fairly sizable chunk of, uh, necrophiliac drunk drivers who were watching the show and going, "You know, it's about time a wrestling show spoke to *my* needs," but the rest of us were pretty disgusted with it.

And then it got better.

Having not quite pushed the envelope far enough, the WWE produced a videotaped segment featuring HHH in a funeral parlor, dressed as Kane, and sexually violating a mannequin that was supposed to be representing the dead body of Katie Vick. It finished with him throwing a handful of "brains" at the camera and proclaiming "I just screwed her brains out," which I guess is what passes for wit these days. The move was a desperate ploy for mainstream attention, as Vince basically instructed Jim Ross and Jerry Lawler to act like mainstream media would attacking the piece and thus go on the defensive by accusing all the critics of being fuddy-duddies who didn't get the joke. In fact, the joke was on them—burned by the gay wedding fiasco, there was not only no moral outrage from protestors, there was barely even a blip in the ratings or a mention of the stunt in the press. The angle continued to go wrong to end the evening, as Kane kidnapped HHH and locked him in the trunk of his car (hopefully it wasn't a stick shift), which then popped open as Kane drove away. Letters now poured into TNN by the *thousands*, the largest outpouring of negative reaction to a show in the history of RAW, and they were skating on very thin ice with Viacom by that point.

The next week, they tried to blow off the whole thing by having HHH make fun of critics and beat up a mannequin, but the damage was done and Kane's career as a main event threat was shot. And they still had a match to go through with!

The Background: As noted, Kane is a murderer, yadda, yadda, yadda.

The Stipulations: In a stipulation that got completely forgotten amid all the bullshit surrounding the match, this was actually a unification match between the World champion (HHH) and the Intercontinental champion (Kane), as it was decided that one major singles title on RAW was enough. In the week leading up to the PPV, they concentrated on that stipulation rather than

the rape and necrophilia and stuff, but that was the proverbial closing of the barn doors after the horse has not only escaped, but been killed in a drunk driving accident and raped by Kane.

The Overall Importance: Just another win by HHH, and the Intercontinental title ceased to exist forever. Forever, of course, in wrestling terms being a period of time defined as "not less than two weeks" and "not more than a year." In this case, a little over six months.

No Mercy 2002, October 20, 2002, Little Rock, AR

RAW World title: HHH versus Kane. Quick note on the origins of the "Katie Vick" character: originally a wrestler named Scott Vick (a.k.a. Sick Boy in WCW) was going to enter the WWE as a member of HHH's "New Horsemen" faction and would have been revealed as Katie's brother out for revenge on Kane. That idea was shot down when the angle subsequently bombed. Kane powers HHH into the corner to start, but gets nailed by HHH. He returns fire and HHH bails to the corner. HHH hammers away, but Kane powers him into the corner again and slugs away. Bad backdrop sends HHH out of the ring to recover, and he gets shoved into the railing while trying to pull Kane out. Back in, Kane keeps hammering and gets a clothesline for two. Corner clothesline and Kane slugs away, but misses a blind charge and falls prey to a neckbreaker. He no-sells with the zombie situp, and gets a powerslam for two. He puts his head down and HHH gets a facecrusher and dumps him to the floor with a clothesline. High knee sends Kane into the post. Back in, they slug it out in the corner and HHH gets another neckbreaker for two. Yet another neckbreaker sets up (you guessed it) a neckbreaker, which gets two. A little variation would be nice, guys.

HHH slugs away in the corner, but runs into an elbow. He comes back with the MAIN EVENT SPINEBUSTER and gets two, however. He guillotines Kane under the ropes, but Kane fights back. HHH goes to the MAIN EVENT SLEEPER, still at this point desperately trying to get it over as his #2 finisher, but Kane suplexes out. An elbowdrop misses by a mile, but Kane gets a big boot and slugs away in the corner. Corner clothesline and sideslam set up the flying clothesline, but Ric Flair runs in to run interference. Flair necksnaps Kane to allow HHH to fight back, but Kane boots him down again. HHH uses the belt instead, and gets two. Hurricane runs out to even the odds, but gets absolutely flattened by HHH as an afterthought and ceases to be a factor in the match.

Back in, Kane makes the comeback and pounds away in the corner to set up a power-slam for two. HHH goes up and gets caught by Kane, who tries to bring him down with a superplex, but HHH blocks. HHH follows him down, but lands on Kane's foot. Kane's chokeslam is blocked, and the ref is bumped, as HHH dumps Kane. Chokeslam through the table follows as Kane makes his comeback and no-sells some offense from Flair, and they head back in, where Kane fights off Flair again and steals HHH's phallic sledgehammer. But as you'd expect, HHH goes low and hits him with the sledgehammer. Kane comes back with another chokeslam for two, as a second ref runs in, counts, and gets bumped, and then stops to go after Flair again, which allows the KICK WHAM PEDIGREE to finish at 16:14. No shock there. Match was having a tough time getting going, and got to be all sorts of overbooked at the end. ★★

Not much change here, either, as I went from an original rating of ★½ to a little more generous ★★ because time heals all wounds—except for HHH's quad injury. Or something like that.

And from there, Kane was shunted down the card into a tag team with RVD and no longer treated as a serious challenger. Ironic considering he was scheduled to win the title before HHH changed it.

The final bit of soap opera, and the one that marked the blessed end of Vince's fascination with shock TV, was also the dumbest.

It began with a cunning plan from Paul Heyman, head writer of Smackdown. Indeed, this was a plan so cunning that Professor Fox of Cunning University, who teaches "How to Be Cunning 101," would probably look at it and go "Damn, that's one cunning plan." Heyman and his supporters on the writing team—David Lagana and Seth Mates—knew that this new focus on shock TV was going to sink the show, but at the same time Vince wouldn't shut up about the soap opera stuff, so what they needed was a diversion to make Vince THINK that they were following the new company line, while simply using up the time with storylines that weren't going to make a difference to anyone important anyway.

The result was the introduction of Torrie Wilson's father, Al, to the WWE world one week, as he met and fell in love with Torrie's nemesis Dawn Marie. Now, you have to understand that

Al was about as charismatic an actor as the mannequin playing Katie Vick's dead body on RAW, without the interesting backstory. And he had a voice like a stoned Kermit the Frog. So you can imagine how electrifying the segments were. However, perhaps because they were SO oddly bad, the cheesy storyline began garnering good ratings, necessitating that it continue. Soon, what was slotted as a one-month storyline was dragging on for the rest of year, encompassing Al's proposal to Dawn, various matches between Dawn and Torrie, an indecent proposal by Dawn to Torrie that led to a tease of a lesbian affair that Stephanie somehow considered her crowning achievement as a producer (and that was heavily edited by UPN), and a honeymoon gone horribly wrong, as the Al Wilson character was "killed off" by a heart attack due to the sex and a brawl between Torrie and

Dawn at the funeral pretty much ended the feud. It was also supposed to feature the debut of developmental wrestler Nikita as Torrie's illegitimate sister, seeking money from the will, but that plan was never developed further and in fact Nikita herself was never even told about it. The whole thing was intended as kitsch, and it certainly fulfilled that goal well enough, but at the expense of TV time that could have gone to something useful. Kevin Dunn often defended the segments by predicting correctly that they would be the second-highest rated (after the main event) for a given show, but that leads to the question: If they know what draws ratings, then why aren't they producing it?

Anyway, further discussion of this will cause me to need to shower to get rid of the stench of idiocy, so let's move on and get back to wrestling. Great wrestling, in fact.

12.

The Smackdown Six

Engage in one kind of business only, and stick to it faithfully until you succeed, or until you conclude to abandon it. A constant hammering on one nail will generally drive it home at last, so that it can be clinched.
—P. T. Barnum, 1852

From September until December, Smackdown became known as the show that was all about the wrestling. And hey, since I'm all about the wrestling, that was fine with me. It also gave some face time to guys who normally wouldn't get as much TV time as the main eventers.

The overriding theme of wrestling as the centerpiece for the show (what a crazy concept, I know) began in September, as Kurt Angle and Chris Benoit were in an argument over who had the better submissions. This naturally led to a match at Unforgiven, where the finish was Benoit pinning Angle with a rollup instead of, say, getting submission victory. But the people booking it were *trying*, I'll give them that. Plus it was a contender for Match of the Year.

To follow up on this, Paul Heyman began a storyline that was a favorite in ECW: partners who hate each other are forced to work togeth-

er by an authority figure for the greater good. In this case, Smackdown overtly became about having great matches for the sake of the show, which fell in line with a speech given by Vince McMahon earlier in the year about using "Ruthless Aggression" to impress him. Apparently, he thought this was going to be the next "Attitude" in terms of a marketable catchphrase, but besides a spoof on Benoit's t-shirt ("Toothless Aggression"), it didn't really take off the way he planned.

So now the title situation was getting even more muddied, as Smackdown's version of the tag team titles were created, since the tag belts had previously migrated to RAW and thus couldn't be defended on both shows. So in keeping in line with the naming conventions established by the split World titles, RAW got the "World tag team titles" and Smackdown got the "WWE tag team titles." In terms of lineage, RAW's tag belts were the ones that are directly connected to the classic WWF tag team titles, whereas the Smackdown version was a creation out of whole cloth and largely meaningless outside of the context of who holds it. That being said, I have no doubt they will end up reunified and deunified a million times anyway, thus rendering the whole argument moot.

Anyway, as mentioned the storyline was that the wrestlers were supposed to care about the quality of the show in terms of athletic performance, so GM Stephanie McMahon put together Chris Benoit and Kurt Angle as a team and forced them to work through their differences, toward the goal of increasing the excitement of the show. This was a rather high concept and slightly communistic approach for what was essentially a low-brow show, but we got great matches out of it, so what the hell, right? The tournament itself was built around three teams: Benoit and Angle, Eddie Guerrero and his criminally underused nephew Chavo, and the makeshift team of Edge and Rey Mysterio.

A word on Rey Mysterio, if I may.

Rey was something of an interesting case, as he was signed to the promotion in June 2002, ostensibly to carry the cruiserweight division, since he's 200 pounds, maybe, while carrying a 50-pound weight. However, never underestimate the power of advanced hype, as videos making his debut seem like a big deal had convinced the fans that this little guy with freaky tattoos and a mask was, amazingly, actually to be respected as an athlete, even though he wasn't 300 pounds and roided up. Well, to be fair, he was roided up, but he wasn't 300 pounds at least. Added to that the position of power that Rey fan Paul Heyman was in on Smackdown, and soon Mysterio was added to the main event mix, having a super-hot opening match with Kurt Angle where he got tons of

offense and was allowed to look like a superstar. He was paired with Edge (and briefly with newcomer John Cena before his push fell apart) as the "future superstars of Smackdown," but that gig only lasted for a couple of weeks before they forgot about it again. But the point was made: in a show filled with giants, someone as small as Rey could hang in a bigger position based on his amazing athletic gifts and the fans' response to him. Of course, by the next year he would be buried in the undercard again, but it's not like that was gonna be any big surprise anyway.

But I digress.

The tournament featured a series of ridiculously hot matches leading up to Mysterio and Edge going over D-Von Dudley and Ron Simmons in one semifinal, and the Benoit and Angle team (still feuding on the side, with a caveat that should they break up, both will be suspended) going over the Guerreros in a great match to set up the finals at No Mercy in October.

The Background: As noted, this was the finals of a tournament to crown the first Smackdown tag champions. Benoit and Angle had been teasing dissention all through the tournament.

The Stipulations: The winner gets the first ever tag titles on Smackdown, and if Benoit and Angle don't cooperate and try to screw each other over, both are suspended for a year. I never liked this aspect because it once again makes them look subservient to Stephanie, but it did add some drama to things because it was well known that Angle was considering going to the Olympics again, and could conceivably need a year off.

The Overall Importance: The consensus choice for Match of the Year, 2002, with the *Observer* and *Torch* newsletters, and most online sources. The only dissenting opinion was

Pro Wrestling Illustrated, which rarely based choices on merit and used a rigged vote that catered to a mark fanbase.

PWI's winner was Rock v. Hulk Hogan, which is pretty laughable, to say the least. Anyway, this is also from No Mercy 2002, October 20, 2002, from Little Rock, Arkansas.

Chris Benoit and Kurt Angle versus Rey Mysterio and Edge. Angle takes Rey down with an armdrag to start, and gives him a bit of humiliation on the mat. He casually takes him down with a double-leg, and he wants Edge. Rey, however, is full of machismo and wants to keep going with Angle. Angle goes behind, so Rey stomps on his foot and takes him down, then dropkicks him down there. Blind charge hits boot and Rey takes him down with a head-scissors, and gives Angle some humiliation of his own. Edge comes in and takes Angle down, and they switch off a hammerlock into a headlock, and Angle overpowers him. Edge controls with armdrags and a dropkick, so Angle brings in Benoit. Benoit takes him down off a headlock, and they work off a wristlock. Benoit hammers away in the corner and grabs a headlock, and they work off that, as Benoit overpowers him until running into a knee. Gutbuster from Edge gets two. Edge starts working on the ribs to go with the previous moves, and a backbreaker gets two. Edge works him over in the corner, but tries chopping and gets schooled. Don't ever trade chops with Benoit. Edge comes

back with a flapjack and an Oklahoma roll for two. Angle gets a cheapshot from the outside, however, and that prompts Edge to spear him off the apron. Benoit attacks from behind, but Edge rolls him up for two. Another cheapshot from Angle turns the tide, as Benoit drops an elbow to take over. Neckbreaker and Angle comes in to stomp on Edge and choke him out. That's an Olympic choke, mind you. They slug it out and Angle knees him in the gut for two. Angle goes to the chinlock and gets the hooks in (wrapping the legs around Edge's body, a UFC strategy), but Edge brings him to the corner and slugs out. Angle hits him with an overhead suplex to end that rally, however.

Benoit comes back in and starts working Edge over with chops again, and pounding the gut with knees. This sets up the rolling german suplexes, and Benoit gets off three of them cleanly to set up the diving headbutt. Edge catches him on the top rope, however, and gets a superplex. Hot tag Mysterio, who immediately knocks Angle off the apron and brings Benoit into the corner with a drop-toehold to set up a dropkick to the face. Ouch. He sets up Benoit on the middle rope and guillotines him with a legdrop, for two. Edge dumps Angle with a clothesline, leaving Rey to try a bulldog on Benoit, but Chris counters into the Crippler crossface. Edge makes the save. Angle yanks him out again to continue the brawl, as Rey dropkicks Benoit into position for the 619, but he catches him. Edge then dropkicks them over, giving Rey two. Benoit is still out, so Rey heads up to the top, but gets superplexed off by Angle with the Pop-Up Superplex. That gets two for Benoit. Benoit sends Rey into the corner and the heels work him over as Rey has become face-in-peril #2. That's the extended version of the classic tag team formula, as there's multiple hot tags and both babyface partners get beaten on for an extended period of time. Angle gets a backbreaker for two. Suplex gets two. Rey reverses another suplex, but can't reverse an overhead suplex, which gets two for Angle. Benoit comes in with a backdrop that has the proverbial icicles on it (i.e., Rey went so high that he went into another layer of the atmosphere), and that gets two. Benoit unloads the CANADIAN VIOLENCE and pounds the crap out of Rey in the corner, but a charge hits boot and Rey sends him into the post with a headscissors. Everyone tags out, as Edge cleans house on Benoit and Angle and backdrops Angle. Faceplant for Benoit, Edge-O-Matic for Angle. Edge spears Benoit into the corner, setting up a broncobuster from Rey, and they set up Angle for another double-team—Edge alley-oops Rey onto Angle, who brings him down with a rana from the top. That gets two, but Benoit saves with the diving headbutt. However, Edge moves and Benoit hits his partner by mistake, giving Edge two.

Angle comes back with a german suplex on Edge, but Edge suplexes his own partner INTO Angle, in a brilliant move. Edge sets up for the spear, but Benoit takes him down from behind and puts him in the crossface. Edge makes the ropes, but Benoit pushes him off again. Rey breaks it up with the 619, but falls victim to the Angle Slam. Angle puts Edge into the anklelock, but he counters with a small package for two. Spear gets two, but Benoit saves. Rey dropkicks Benoit to the floor, and Edge launches Rey onto Benoit. Edge gets caught in the anklelock again, however, and can't make the ropes, so he counters to his own anklelock! Angle reverses that (it is his finisher) and Edge is forced to tap at 22:12. This was a crazy match, filled with great wrestling, great spots, unpredictable book-

ing, and a clean submission victory for the new champions with no need for cheating or screwy booking. That was the theme of Heyman's Smackdown—the better WRESTLERS won. ★★★★★

> **Yeah, I boosted this one from ★★★¾ to the full monty for wrestling matches, ★★★★★, because frankly, I couldn't find any flaws with it no matter how much I tried. Plus I'm horribly biased towards all four guys. So there.**

With the titles established, a three-way feud for them was set up, with the new champions defending against both Edge and Mysterio and the Guerreros. Eventually, Edge and Mysterio won the belts in a two out of three falls match on Smackdown (another classic match), and the titles ended up with the Guerreros, who won them in a disappointing match at Survivor Series in November. But for about two months, you could be guaranteed a great match seemingly every week as a result of some combination of Benoit, Angle, Edge, Mysterio, Eddie, and Chavo.

More new stars were being made on Smackdown as well, in very different ways.

First up, Matt Hardy. After jumping from RAW to turn heel and escape the "pretty boy" stigma of the Hardy Boyz team, Matt came up with a unique gimmick change: Matt Hardy Version 1.0. The idea was that he was deluded enough to think that he was a superstar heel, the ultimate egoist who had "Matt facts" added to his entrance video and an army of Mattitude Followers (MFers) who obeyed his every command. Of course, the only one who actually ended up in his army was Velocity jobber Shannon Moore, who was trained by the Hardy Boyz in their North Carolina OMEGA promotion years earlier. It was a terrific gimmick that seemed to be perfect to launch him into the heavyweight midcard rather than the bowels of opening matches, but Matt is a smart guy who says what he feels, and often that resulted in arguments with the agents (like John Laurinaitis), which stalled his push significantly. I think he's talented enough and smart enough to end up doing okay for himself, though, and he has serious potential as a Randy Savage–type intellectual heel who plays mindgames with his opponents. Sadly, a move back to RAW to be with real-life girlfriend Lita seems to have stalled his career again.

Next on the character makeover list was John Cena, in the most unlikely of ways. Specifically, a Halloween party on Smackdown, where all the wrestlers were showing up dressed in increasingly goofy costumes. Cena, a fan of hip-hop, showed up dressed as '80s "icon" Vanilla Ice and launched into a goofy rap. It was both funny and instantly gave Cena a new character to latch onto: a clueless white rapper. When he started, he was closer to Vanilla Ice than Eminem, but really all the character needed was some tweaking. He was given the standard accoutrement for a new heel—a bodyguard—in the form of Bull Buchanan, who wasn't really doing anything anyway. My initial fear was that the team would only serve to turn Buchanan into the "star" of the team and leave Cena by the wayside once the bookers remembered that Buchanan was a big tall guy and Cena was

fairly short compared to him, but thankfully Buchanan's standing in the company wasn't quite that good by that point. They actually made a pretty funny team, as Buchanan seemed to find his groove in the promotion for the first time, well, ever, alternating idiotic rap names like "B Squared" and my personal favorite, "Bling Bling Buchanan." The problem became, however, that they were an undercard team stuck in dead-end feuds with anchors like Rikishi, whereas the plans for Cena seemed to indicate something larger. By the end of the year, Buchanan was gone and Cena was taking on a harder edge, and streamlining his raps into a more hard-edged heel character. Whether it works in the long run is still to be decided.

Another guy seemingly in need of a character makeover was Brock Lesnar, although for different reasons. By this time, Lesnar (the WWE champion) was firmly entrenched in the main event, but he wasn't drawing any money. Two PPV main events against Undertaker, one resulting in a double-DQ and the other waged inside the Hell in a Cell, failed to draw any kind of significant interest from the audience. Even worse, there was backstage politics threatening to undermine Brock's meteoric rise to the top every stop of the way. First up, in September Brock was scheduled to meet Undertaker at the Unforgiven PPV and go over in a cheap win to both cement him as a main eventer and set up a rematch at the next PPV. That's pretty standard wrestling booking. However, while the match was in preparation stages, Undertaker declared that he "wasn't feeling it" (i.e., didn't agree with the finish) and therefore wouldn't do the job for Lesnar that night. This left the bookers with a rather major problem, as they needed to set up a rematch for the next show and find a way to not have Undertaker win the title. The result was a finish that made everyone mad, as they battled in a weak brawl until the referee disqualified both guys. It was somewhat understandable since they couldn't put the belt on Undertaker and thus destroy Brock's push, but to the live crowd and paying customer, this felt like a major rip-off.

So the next month, the WWE decided to make it up to the fans by booking them in the most famously violent and brutal match they could: Hell in a Cell. It was actually the second such match that year, as HHH had defeated Chris Jericho in a forgettable Wrestlemania rematch in May, but the hope was that two a year was enough to keep from killing off the appeal of the gimmick. However, now there was another snag, as HHH considered the match "his" and wanted to use the gimmick for his match against Kane. He even went so far as to suggest a Texas Death match for the Brock-UT rematch instead, which got pretty far up the drawing board before various members of the creative team argued Vince down and got their way. The problem with a Texas Death match is that, by nature, it is another rip off to the fans, since there's no pinfall, just whoever can beat a ten-count first. The result is generally a screwy finish with the ref being knocked out and not seeing one guy down or whatever, so that wasn't gonna fly. Finally, the Hell in a Cell match went through, and the result was Brock's most intense, and one of his best, matches.

The Background: Undertaker won a #1 contender's match in September and fought Lesnar to a double DQ in their first match. There was a bizarre storyline thrown in about Undertaker cheating on his pregnant wife to play up the soap-opera stuff Vince loved so much at that point, but it was dropped when it was apparent how stupid it was coming across.

The Stipulations: The winner gets the WWE title. No disqualifications, no countouts, one fall to a finish.

The Overall Importance: Undertaker sold *huge* for Lesnar, really establishing him as a badass monster and marking one of the few times where he let someone else truly dominate him and pin him cleanly. I feel it was too little, too late as far as getting the rub from Undertaker was concerned, but others disagree. This put Lesnar on the map as a main eventer, but something was still missing.

No Mercy 2002, October 20, 2002, Little Rock, AR

WWE title, Hell in a Cell: Brock Lesnar versus Undertaker. Brock gets a powerslam to start, for two. Undertaker uses the cast to come back, however. Brock bails, but pounds away on Taker. He goes after the hand and goes to an armbar, but gets nailed with the cast again. Brock bleeds as a result. They head out and Taker sends him into the cage and jumps on his head. Taker gets two on the floor and keeps introducing Brock to the cage. Paul tries to reach through the cage and help, but Taker sends him into the railing, and HE blades, too. Brock meets the stairs, but comes back to send Taker into the cage and take over. More brawling out there. He pounds away with a STEEL chair, and works on the hand with it, although you can pretty clearly see that the actual hand was out of the cast. He tries to pull the cast off, but Taker fights him off. He finally gets it off and works on the hand, but can't get a superplex. Taker walks the ropes and drops an elbow (falling on the "broken" hand) for two. Whatever was in the needle that Undertaker got in a prematch vignette, they should sell on the open market. They'd make millions.

Brock heads to the apron, but gets sent into

the cage, and Taker follows with a dive. Brock hits him in the face with the stairs a couple of times, and Taker does a GORY bladejob off that, hitting 0.9 Muta within seconds. Back in, Brock gets a Main Event Spinebuster for two. Brock slugs away, but Taker fights back with his "broken" hand (I guess you could call that reverse psychology), showing no ill effects. Man, can't you at least punch the guy with your other hand? He starts stomping on Brock's hand, but Brock pulls him down to block the ropewalk. Taker is gushing blood all over the mat, and Brock goes for the F5, which Taker reverses to the chokeslam (again, with the broken hand) for two. Taker charges and hits boot, but Brock's attempt at a powerbomb is reversed. DDT gets two for UT. Brock stupidly pounds away in the corner, and UT powerbombs him for two. Taker drips blood by Brock's mouth while covering, giving us our yucky spot of the night. I believe dripping blood in your opponent's mouth officially makes it 1.2 Muta and sets a new standard. Tombstone is reversed to the F5 for the pin at 27:14.

I think a lot of people are being pretty liberal with the praise for this match because of the blood, but I'm personally sick of the NCAA champion wrestler being used in these stand-up slugfests that even Sid Vicious could do with the right booking in order to disguise other people's weaknesses. For what it was, it was good, but it's time to find someone who can hang with Brock in a wrestling match and let him expand past the kick-punch mentality of the "WWE Main Event Style." Plus Undertaker's magically healing hand injury was pretty annoying, too. And don't give me this "You have to give the Undertaker credit for doing the right thing" garbage, either—he should have done "the right thing" the month before and for about a dozen other people before this. Doing one job with a broken

hand and a blackmail threat hanging over you isn't exactly Ric Flair making Sting into a superstar at the first Clash, ya know? ★★★

So with Brock still not carrying the load for the promotion as a heel, the next step was to turn to him babyface. To that end, Big Show was traded from RAW to Smackdown (the only such trade ever made—final deal: Big Show to Smackdown for D-Von Dudley, Dave Batista, Randy Orton, and Ivory) to act as the foil for Show's turn.

This was actually not the original intention. For the longest time, the intention was to bring Hulk Hogan back from exile and have him put Lesnar over a second time, but Hogan's contention was that he should win the title from Lesnar and set up a rematch. Having been burned once already that year, there was no way that Vince was going to put the belt on Hogan AGAIN, and negotiations fell apart rather quickly. With the PPV rapidly approaching, this left two options for matches with Brock: Big Show or Chris Benoit. Very heated arguments from both sides of the issues lasted for days, but in the end it came down to "Chris Benoit is probably the best professional wrestler in the promotion, can give Brock the match of a lifetime and make him look like a million bucks, won't ever complain about doing a job, can do the same ★★★★½ classic every night at house shows, and can hang with him on the mat as a wrestler" on one side, and "Big Show is really, really big" on the other. I'm sure by now you can guess who was more persuasive to Vince's way of thinking.

The storyline, however, was intended more as a backdrop for Paul Heyman to turn on Lesnar, with the idea being that Heyman was growing jealous of Lesnar's independence and wanted to prove that he was still needed. Heyman was also supposed to be losing confidence in Brock's ability to beat someone as big as Big Show, due to injuries suffered at the hands of Undertaker in the Hell in a Cell match. Most people were skeptical about Big Show's ability to make it back to the main event again, but to the WWE's credit they kept them apart leading up to the PPV while Show steamrolled over mid-card opposition to build him up as a legitimate threat, and most people assumed that Brock would squash Show in a quick match to really show what a superstrong freak he was, as the "Will Brock be able to give Show an F5?" issue was the big one teased leading up to the match.

Then, seeming disaster struck.

While they were rehearsing the match at a house show in the week prior to the match (and not having a very good match, either), Show messed up and accidentally broke one of Lesnar's ribs, casting doubt about Brock's ability to work the match at the PPV or even continue wrestling that year. Now, with anyone else, injuring the #1 project of Vince McMahon would be a one-way ticket to OVW, but Show was 500 pounds and had a 10-year guaranteed contract, so he was bulletproof. Agents scrambled to come up with a plan to compensate, and people began to fear the worst—that Big Show would get the title again. And he did, beating Brock in a quick match as Heyman turned on the next big thing, so that Lesnar could take time off and heal the ribs. The idea was now that Heyman could take any piece of shit like Big Show and use his brilliant managerial skills to beat Lesnar. Brock was instantly turned face by his awesome, gutty performance with broken ribs, but then he didn't take time off. In fact, he didn't even miss a show. This left people wondering why the hell they didn't just keep the title on their biggest star, then, but you always have to keep in mind the Big Show factor. Given a choice, Vince will always push Big Show to justify his contract.

And speaking of people who always get pushed, back on RAW, HHH was getting out of control again.

13.

HHH Is God (or So He Claims)

> An honest man who arrests public attention will be called a "humbug,"
> but he is not a swindler or an impostor. If, however, after attracting
> crowds of customers by his unique displays, a man foolishly fails to give
> them a full equivalent for their money, they never patronize him a second
> time, but they very properly denounce him as a swindler, a cheat, an
> impostor; they do not, however, call him a "humbug." He fails, not
> because he advertises his wares in an outre manner, but because, after
> attracting crowds of patrons, he stupidly and wickedly cheats them.
>
> —P. T. Barnum, "Humbugs of the World"

By November 2002, things were getting bad on RAW.

HHH, purveyor of the long-standing tradition of advancing up the ranks by banging the boss's daughter, was now so firmly entrenched into the main event picture that you'd probably have to kill him to get rid of him. Not that the various fates didn't try, hitting him with quad tears, hematomas, deep bruising, knee problems, and Rob Van Dam. But, like any good cancer, he was now there for good and was taking down the rest of the body with him. Hey, with Hulk Hogan gone again, SOMEONE had to pick up the slack. Rob Van Dam? Fallen to the power of HHH and shunted down the card into a nothing feud with Ric Flair. Kane? Beaten by the mighty wind of the sledgehammer and left tumbling into a secondary role against new HHH flunky Batista. In fact, with the WWE so desperate to find competition for HHH that they'd sign *anyone*, Scott Steiner was brought into the promotion in November as the next person to step up and face the demon. He wouldn't be ready to go for another couple of months, so they needed yet another stopgap until it was time for HHH to crush another challenger.

To this end, Eric Bischoff introduced the first new idea for a gimmick match in quite a while: the Elimination Chamber. Okay, sure it sounds like a polite name for a British toilet, but it's the thought that counts. And hey, since this was probably going to be the closest thing we got to WCW's Wargames match, most of us counted ourselves lucky. The setup was pretty random, though: it was a giant cage and Eric Bischoff announced that the top five contenders would challenge HHH for the title. Not exactly Shakespeare, but it got the job done. The participants would be HHH (duh), RVD, Kane, Booker T, Chris Jericho, . . . and Shawn Michaels.

Now, one of these was not like the others. I'd forgo the suspense and just come right out and say that only a couple of months earlier, they had spent a great deal of time and effort making it known that Summerslam was Shawn Michaels's one and only comeback match, period. But hey, there'd be no way that they'd do something silly like a sustained push of a guy who couldn't work house shows and was liable to fall into pieces after a simple bump, right? I mean, here you had great alternatives like foiled challenger Rob Van Dam, possible necrophiliac murderer Kane, perennial upper-card heel Chris Jericho, main event mainstay Booker T, or even keeping the title on HHH. And if nothing else, beating Shawn Michaels gives one of those other guys the kind of rub they need to break through to the next level. Ah, but then we'd be robbed of another two months of best friends Shawn and HHH working together again while screwing over everyone else on the roster, so you can see how that might be construed as counterproductive.

See, here's the thing with Shawn Michaels: call me a skeptic (and most do), but I just don't buy into this "finding Jesus" crap that he started spewing in early 2002 as a catchall way to excuse his behavior for the ten previous years. Without turning this into a debate about the merits of religion in his life one way or another, people like Michaels, who stepped on the little people on the way up and then left the promotion before he could go down again, don't just change overnight. Shawn demonstrated in the past that he's a selfish primadonna and a pathological liar, and just because he goes to church on Sundays now and wears a Jesus-themed t-shirt I'm not going to immediately forgive his past sins. Even after he was born again, he went on national TV (well, *Confidential*, which is only watched by a few hundred thousand people, but it's national) and admitted that he had been lying about his involvement in the Bret Hart incident in Montreal, and had been lying on orders of the office for five years! He never apologized to Bret for his involvement even afterward, he contradicted his own stance within the same interview on more than one occasion (on one hand he'll say that he regretted doing it, and then on the other he'll say he would it again), and he basically did nothing to demonstrate himself as a better person, outside of possibly giving up his drug-laced lifestyle. But even then that's how you qualify to be a normal functioning human being, not a saint.

But most annoying about Michaels's comeback is his return to his exact same behavior within the context of the political games and willingness to screw everyone else over to make sure his spot is intact. Here's a guy who just came out of retirement, could be going back there at any time, doesn't even work house shows, and used up his last Cool Points in

1998, at which point the general public promptly forgot him. He barely even has a place on the card in that kind of role, let alone winning most of his matches. And yet that's what always happened in 2002—given every chance to make a new star out of someone, he seemingly hid behind HHH's political power and made sure he was always coming out looking strong in the end. Now, you can argue, "Oh, he's just doing what Vince McMahon tells him," but that was the same excuse he gave for years. Maybe if he had really grown up and changed his ways as a result of being born again, he'd stand up and offer to use his legacy to make someone like Rob Van Dam into the next HBK. That's always been the argument that has baffled me: people think that if some of these veterans ever stood up and offered to make a star, that Vince would refuse and have them fired for even suggesting it or something. Vince is a smart guy and a shrewd businessman, and the best way to his heart is money. And Vince knows that the best way to keep making money is to constantly create new stars. And certainly he's aware that the shelf life on a Shawn Michaels could be ready to expire at any moment due to another back injury, so he would, I'd imagine, be more than happy to let Shawn use his name to elevate someone else. And yet, in his entire run to date, Shawn has only lost two matches: one to HHH, and one to Ric Flair. Not exactly the two names that the legacy of Shawn Michaels can help. Furthermore, he's beaten several stars further down the totem pole than himself, like RVD and Chris Jericho.

Even worse than that, of course, is HHH himself. Building up to the Elimination Chamber title defense at Survivor Series, HHH interrupted a Shawn Michaels interview segment and declared himself to be God. And most people were won-

The standard cynical answer as to why Shawn lost a match to Ric Flair in 2003: He was maneuvering himself into better position to be elected to the *Wrestling Observer Newsletter* Hall of Fame. It worked.

dering if that was a shoot comment or not. And hey, let's take a look at HHH's record on RAW while we're at it.

Since the very beginning of 2000 until June 2003, HHH's RAW record is 44-29-9. Ah, but out of those twenty-nine losses, only eight of them were singles matches. Out of those eight singles losses, four were by disqualification. So now we're down to four singles matches where he lost cleanly. Those four are:

10/2/00: Kurt Angle beat HHH via pinfall

1/28/02: Booker T beat HHH via pinfall

3/4/02: Kurt Angle beat HHH in a cage match by escaping the cage

10/28/02: Kane beat HHH in a casket match by putting him in the casket

So now we're down to HHH being pinned in singles matches only *twice* in two years. So how exactly did he lose these four matches?

10/2/00: HHH versus Kurt Angle. Brawl outside to start. Into the ring, Angle works the ribs, but HHH faking it and he chokes out Angle with the bandages. Out to the floor where Angle gets a belly-to-belly, and back in for two. Angle suplex

gets two. Another gets two. And right on cue, here's Stephanie. HHH goes for the Pedigree but a lowblow stops that. Backdrop suplex gets two. HHH comes back with the neckbreaker and some Knee-Fu. HHH dumps Angle and elbows him through the Spanish table. Ref is bumped, cue Benoit. You can almost see the numbers on the people involved and Pat Patterson dabbing the paint on the screen. Benoit goes after Steph, and HHH attacks. Angle grabs a chair, but Steph stops him, Benoit hits HHH, Angle Slam, and Angle is your #1 contender at 9:14. ★★★½

1/28/02: Booker T versus HHH. Wristlock sequence to start, and HHH takes him down and pounds him. Steinerline and he pummels Booker, but gets sidekicked. Elbow gets two. HHH catches a spinebuster and and hammers away, then USES THE KNEE! Neckbreaker gets two. He dumps Booker and clotheslines him on the floor, but Christian attacks him from behind and allows Booker to get two. Axe kick misses, but Steph runs out to deal with Christian. HHH goes over to talk her down off the apron, and next thing you know, Booker gets a rollup for the pin at 5:04. This was mostly an exhibition of HHH's newer and slower move-set. Match was okay, despite the lack of offense for Booker. ★★

3/4/02: Cage match: HHH versus Kurt Angle. We'll skip to the finish, as Steph gets involved again, tossing a chair into the ring, and they clothesline each other. HHH climbs, but Steph charges in, chairshots him, crotches him, and thus ties him up in the ropes before single-handedly dragging Angle out for the win at 15:36. She's gonna end up with the WWF title before the year is out, I can feel it. Match was good for a ten-minute TV main, but unfortunately it wasn't ten minutes long. ★★½

10/28/02: Casket match: HHH versus Kane. Again, skip to the ending, as Kane makes the comeback and wins a slugfest. To the top for the flying lariat, but HHH hits him with a chair, and indeed Shawn Michaels appears out of the casket and attacks HHH. Sweet Chin Music wakes up the crowd as Kane revives, choke-slams HHH, and closes the lid at 11:14. Major yawner. ★★

So, out of four "clean" losses on RAW, two were by HHH getting distracted and two were by outside interference. Three of these involved Hunter's then-fiancée Stephanie McMahon, and one involved Hunter's best friend Shawn Michaels. That should show you what kind of a fair, apolitical, and vulnerable heel champion HHH really is. The question is, when Shawn gave his soul to God, was he referring to the one in Heaven or the one in Stamford?

Well, we found out the answer to that question, partially, at Survivor Series.

The Background: As a way to boost interest in the Survivor Series PPV, Eric Bischoff introduced a new title defense for HHH: the Elimination Chamber. Various generic brawls between the participants led up to the match, with the only storyline of any importance being Shawn Michaels versus HHH and how Shawn wants to prove that he can still hang with the best in the business (i.e., HHH). Everything else was secondary.

The Stipulations: It's a giant circular cage, with four smaller cages inside it. Two people start the match, and every five minutes, another person is let out of a smaller cage. Pinfall or submission eliminates you from the match, winner is the RAW World champion.

The Overall Importance: Nothing, really, as Michaels won the belt and then proceeded to defend it a grand total of one time in the course of the following month before dropping it back to HHH again. The original booking of the match had Edge making a surprise jump to RAW and replacing Michaels in the match to get the victory and create a fresh program for HHH, but you can see why both guys would feel threatened by something like that, and thus it didn't happen.

Survivor Series 2002, November 17, 2002, New York, NY

RAW World title, Elimination Chamber: HHH versus Chris Jericho versus Shawn Michaels versus Booker T versus Kane versus Rob Van Dam. Saliva sings Jericho's alternate theme music live from The World in New York. Quick note about the failed nightclub: In November 2002, it was discovered that manager Kelton Jenkins had embezzled nearly $500,000 from the restaurant complex during his tenure. Shock and surprise quickly spread through the business world, not because of the crime, but because no one thought $500,000 had ever passed through that place. It would close down not long after, amid much spin-doctoring from Linda McMahon. Oddly enough, the Elimination Chamber itself cost in the neighborhood of $500,000 to build. No truth to the rumor that Jenkins embezzled it right after the show and set it up in his backyard.

Your bit of JR silliness for the match has him claiming that Kane would be the first masked man to hold the World title if he wins. This can either have two interpretations: (1) Kane is the first masked man to hold this particular title, which is silly because to that point there had only been one champion ever: HHH. (2) Kane is the first masked man to hold the WWE title in general, which is again silly because Kane already held the title in 1998.

The match starts out with RVD against HHH in a rematch from Unforgiven. Rob hammers away in the corner and gets a leg lariat and a mule kick. HHH comes back with a facecrusher and goes for the Pedigree, but Rob backdrops him onto the steel apron extension. Rob stomps away out there and rams HHH into the cage itself a few times, and the door actually pops open. Ah, good old American construction. HHH starts bleeding early as Rob monkey-flips him onto the grating again. Back in, Rob hits him with a Rolling Thunder over the top and onto the grating. I pity the poor guys taking bumps on that stuff. Rob clotheslines him back in and heads up to the top of Jericho's cage, but gets tripped up as a result and slugs it out with HHH. Rob heads down again with a sloppy somersault senton off the top, onto HHH. This didn't prove to be an encouraging start. HHH eats more cage and they head in again for more abuse from RVD, and the first period expires, as Jericho is the next into the match. Jericho goes after RVD, but falls prey to a standing moonsault that gets two. Jericho charges and hits elbow, and Rob hits him with a missile dropkick and clotheslines him out to the grating. Rob dives off the top and misses, but grabs onto the chain-link cage like Spider-Man, and springs onto Jericho again.

Back into the ring, Jericho stomps him down and gets a backdrop suplex. RVD slugs it out with both heels, but gets hit with a high knee from HHH and a senton from Jericho. That gets two. Jericho and HHH team up for some more pain and agony on RVD, as HHH tosses him back to the grating and they whip him back-first into the cage. They keep doing that to weaken the back of RVD, and Jericho starts chopping. HHH whips Jericho at Van Dam, but it misses and Rob comes back with high kicks. HHH DDTs RVD, however, and next in is Booker T. He cleans house for Rob and pounds on Jericho, and clotheslines both heels to the grating, before stopping to Spinarooni. Rob then attacks him and they slug it out and crisscross until Booker gets a spin kick for two. Booker chops him, but Rob returns the spin kick for two. Booker gets a sidekick for two. HHH heads back in and slugs away on Booker, but gets axe kicked. Jericho makes the save on HHH's behalf, but RVD drop-kicks him in turn. Rob goes up to the top of one of the small cages for a frog splash on HHH, but he hits it wrong and ends up driving his knee into HHH's throat and hurting his own knee. Sadly, HHH would return to do more boring interviews the next week with a voice that was still fine. Booker hits RVD with a missile dropkick and gets the pin at 13:40, which the crowd is not happy about.

Booker also covers the injured HHH, but only gets two. I personally felt HHH should have also bowed out here, as his involvement in the match from there was minimal due to the injury. Jericho hammers on Booker and gets a bulldog, but the Lionsault misses and Booker whiplash-slams him. That gets two. Next into the match is Kane, and he slugs everyone left standing and backdrops Jericho. He pounds Booker in the corner and tosses Jericho, then javelins him into the cage. He follows up by tossing Jericho through one of the Plexiglas minicages (which was supposed to be "bullet-proof") and pounds on Booker in the corner. A pumphandle slam is reversed by Booker, but he falls prey to the chokeslam and he's gone at 17:40 via a lionsault from Jericho. Jericho is doing a mild bladejob at this point.

Kane keeps attacking Jericho, who climbs up the cage to escape, but Kane batters him into the cage to get him off and then slams him into the ring. HHH finally emerges from hiber-

nation but gets slugged down again, and Kane suplexes Jericho, for two. Elbowdrop misses and Jericho kicks him out onto the grating, but he chooses to go after HHH and slams him off the top rope. Why HHH was even on the top rope I choose not to explore further. Jericho gets a missile dropkick as we actually passed the five-minute mark thirty seconds ago, but Shawn indeed comes in last and now everyone is in that's gonna be in. Kane hammers him down, but Shawn comes back with a forearm. Kane sends Shawn into the corner, and then chokes out Jericho. Chokeslam for Michaels, and HHH, and Jericho. Well, you might as well complete the set. HHH reverses a piledriver attempt, however, and Shawn superkicks Kane into a KICK WHAM PEDIGREE to dispose of Kane at 22:53 via another lionsault from Jericho. That's what you call a receipt, kids.

Jericho clotheslines Shawn to the grating and rams him into the cage a few times, allowing HHH to continue the punishment. Jericho pounds on Michaels until he starts bleeding, and HHH tosses him and grates his face on the cage like a cheese grater. Well, a pretty ineffective cheese grater since there's about eight inches of space between each link, but that's pretty much the standard analogy you have to make in those situations to earn your PPV Reviewer's Club membership. Anyway, back in the ring, Jericho works on the cut, but Shawn fights off both guys and tries to piledrive Jericho on the grating. Jericho reverses as the match kind of drifts along without a purpose. Shawn comes back on HHH with his flying forearm, and he kips up. Jericho immediately bulldogs him and gets another lionsault, but this one only gets two. You can see the subtle manipulation by HHH and Michaels there, I hope—it insinuates that Booker and Kane weren't good enough to *kick out of a midcard finisher, but Michaels was. Anyway, Shawn gets a moonsault press on Jericho for two, and then a Boston crab, but HHH breaks it up with a DDT. Jericho gets two, but HHH wants the pin, and they fight over it. HHH clotheslines him and gets a facecrusher for two. A KICK WHAM PEDIGREE is reversed by Jericho to the walls of Jericho, but Shawn superkicks him like a sitting duck and eliminates him at 30:42.*

That leaves HHH and Shawn Michaels, and they start slugging it out. HHH gets a MAIN EVENT SPINEBUSTER for two. HHH backdrops him onto the grating, but once there Shawn tries his own version of the pedigree, which allows HHH to reverse into a catapult that puts Shawn through the Plexiglas in much less impressive fashion than Jericho went through it. Back in, that gets two. HHH hammers him down again and keeps slugging on the cut, but Shawn makes the comeback. One thing Shawn always had was great timing for that stuff. HHH gets another facecrusher to end that rally, and clotheslines him back onto the grating again. That's something like four times Shawn has taken that bump in this match, and it looks weak each time. HHH tries a Pedigree, but Shawn reverses to a catapult into the cage. Shawn clotheslines him back in, and heads up to the top of the little cage for a flying elbow. There's just not enough headroom to do that stuff in this cage. He eschews the cover and sets up for the superkick instead, but HHH blocks it and hits the Pedigree. Much like any challenger, he also makes Shawn lay there for a minute before covering, but Shawn gets to kick out at two. Shawn makes another comeback, but HHH tries another Pedigree, which Shawn reverses out of and finishes with the superkick at 39:20. That gets a big nostalgia pop from

the MSG crowd, but it meant nothing in the long run. The match was obviously carried by Jericho, and multiple viewings and hindsight have left me underwhelmed by the drama of the last ten minutes between Shawn and HHH. ★★★

HHH took the next night off to rest his vocal cords, but was back the next week on RAW to announce himself as the supreme deity of several other prominent religions and prevent RVD from winning the title from Michaels, a move that would have actually elevated both the belt and Van Dam instead of setting up yet another title match between HHH and Michaels. Even sillier was that the HBK Nostalgia Tour was not moving ratings like Hogan and/or Flair could if used properly—RAW's ratings continued to sag with an average of 3.4 for the month of November, and stayed there all through December as well. The fanbase was simply not interested in what Shawn was selling any longer. They tried everything from "shoot" interviews between the men to a silly angle involving Shawn jumping at HHH into a garbage truck that was obviously filled with padding, but couldn't do anything to stimulate interest in their rematch. It did, however, serve as a humorous metaphor for the state of the show. However, that didn't stop them from booking a rematch anyway, as HHH regained the title in a forty-minute long borefest that featured him wrestling on one bad leg in a two out of three falls match and beating Shawn at his own game: the ladder match. I won't bother recapping it here, because really haven't we all heard enough about HHH for one chapter?

Okay, one last rant about him, and then we'll move on, I promise.

This is the deal with HHH: he used to be pretty good, in 2000. I've never argued against that point. But times changed and HHH didn't, and now he's regressed as a wrestler to the point where he's clearly Not Very Good. Furthermore, he's married to the daughter of the owner and acts as the right-hand man for said owner, actively booking his own programs and taking part in the booking of others. He has nearly absolute power on the RAW side of things and chooses to take advantage of that. If he was still having great matches night after night, I wouldn't begrudge him his fun in the least, but he's not. And now what you're left with is a clear conflict of interest, which Stephanie and the family can't even deny, only dodge. For a publicly traded, multimillion dollar company like the WWE, it's ludicrous to even suggest that what is going on is proper behavior for the people involved. All that I, and many, are asking HHH to do is step down to the midcard, since it's not like his job is in jeopardy or anything, and make some new stars. *Any* new stars. Anything is preferable to holding onto the World title like a security blanket, when clearly he can book himself back to the main event whenever he wants. In fact, early in 2003, in discussions of a feud with Booker T, he was heard to comment openly that the only person he would be willing to drop the title to was Kevin Nash. If he's truly the biggest star of the show, then it shouldn't matter if he has the belt or not—both Rock and Austin are secure enough in their star power to go for months at a time without the belt, and they still headlined shows against each other without one and drew more money than any show HHH could headline, with or without the belt.

> **HHH did deign to drop his vanity belt to Goldberg for a few weeks in 2003, but made sure to book himself to regain it in short order. The show in question, where he regained the title, proved to be the least-bought of the modern era.**

Various injuries to HHH seem to indicate that mother nature may make the ultimate decision for him, but it'd be nice to see him step up and do it himself. But I'm not holding my breath. Until then, I'm gonna keep hammering on HHH until someone shuts me up.

And now, let's talk about someone else. Please. Like, say, Linda McMahon.

14.

Odds and Sods

There's a sucker born every minute.
—Attributed to P. T. Barnum, although not actually said by him

One of the interesting drawbacks in being a public company is that you have to deal with the public. Now for most corporate types this wouldn't be such a huge problem, but the WWE has long been a company built on a foundation of lies and deceit, treating its paying customers like mongrel idiots who don't deserve to be there. So what you get is the company telling the paying customer one thing on TV and their own Web site, and then spinning it in an entirely different way when it comes time to brief the actual investors in their quarterly conference calls.

Take, for example, the third-quarter conference call hosted by Linda McMahon at the end of November. They do these things every three months and they're always a great source of material for people looking to mock the WWE, such as myself, because the answers to simple questions about the state of the company always yield such delightfully deluded answers,

which appear to apply only to a strange fantasy world completely unconnected to the WWE. My personal favorite, although not from this session in particular, was the assertion in 2003 that "the war" was causing all the ratings dips and when it ended things would go back to normal again.

Anyway, whereas most of the conference calls would feature clueless investors asking empty questions about the state of the product and when they'd be getting their money and stuff, this one was distinguished by someone who actually watches the product asking a question. Citing the necrophilia angle as an example of the disastrous nature of creative at that point, the repetitive women's matches, the lack of new stars, and the falling attendance, Linda was suddenly taken aback at having to tell the truth. The investor clearly blamed HHH and Stephanie (which most people do, although in reality Stephanie has been losing power to Vince since the brand extension in terms of

117

crafting the shows—it's more accurate to say that HHH influences Vince as a result of his relationship with Steph), but Linda countered this by noting HHH was Stephanie's "new" boyfriend.

Now, maybe it's just me, but when two people start dating in late 2000 and publicly admit it more than a year later, that's a pretty serious and long-term relationship. It's pretty irritating when they lie about something as easily verified as the relationship between HHH and Stephanie. Her other defense with regards to HHH was that he was a star long before the relationship, but then many other people are stars and don't get anywhere near the input as HHH does. Okay, I promised not to talk about HHH again, but my hand has been forced here.

She also noted HHH as one of the "big four" stars of the promotion carrying things, along with (get ready for this) Brock Lesnar, Shawn Michaels, and Scott Steiner. Clearly in hindsight, no one could say with a straight face that Scott Steiner is or ever was a major star as far as the WWE goes, but the Shawn Michaels addition really shows the self-delusion they were having at that point. Shawn hadn't moved ratings with his return, people weren't going to shows to see him wrestle because he didn't work house shows, and he wasn't putting new people over to create fresh opponents for himself and other people. But because he was a big star in 1996, which much of the WWE power structure remembered but none of their fanbase did, Shawn was still treated as the same star he was back then. The really funny thing is that Shawn was never that big of a ratings or money draw even when he was supposed to have been. Shawn was champion at the point when WCW's Monday Nitro show began absolutely crushing RAW week after week, and fair or not,

it's the champion who gets the credit for carrying the company or the blame for tanking it. The fourth person she named was of course Brock Lesnar, which was at least flirting with validity and rational thinking. Brock's first two PPV title defenses against Undertaker drew buyrates of approximately 300,000 buys each, where an "average" show would be expected to draw 600,000, so clearly he wasn't the driving force behind the company that they were trumpeting. But with Rock and Austin both gone, they had to take what they could get.

Moving on, she talked about the great new storylines for the women's division they had in mind and cited Victoria as a great new talent (sidenote: Since Jazz's entrance into the promotion in late 2001, there have been exactly two additions to the women's division in the two years following: Victoria in 2002 and Gail Kim in 2003. What a division, huh?). In fact, other than an attempt to elevate a new star in that division by putting the women's title on Victoria and Gail Kim for various periods of time, much of the women's action on RAW featured the same combinations of Trish Stratus, Jazz, Jacqueline, and Molly Holly over and over. The situation on Smackdown was even more ridiculous, with women solely existing as eye candy or "soap-opera" stars performing in skits with acting at the level of a bad porno. But without the porno.

Victoria has since become quite the big star in the women's division, thanks more to her tiny pants than any great talents as a wrestler.

And speaking of bad acting and no charisma, Linda also named Test as one of the top stars they were trying to create, noting that with some it takes longer than others. Well, they've been trying to make Test a top star since early 1999 (when he was introduced and immediately programmed with Rock and HHH) and as of four years later there's still no movement toward him becoming the next Hulk Hogan, so I'd have to say that one is becoming a lost cause.

Linda summed up her stance by noting that they were not WCW. I'll let you make your own judgment on that one.

Really, this call showed just how unprepared they were to deal with legitimate criticisms of their product (which is no shock to those following them before they went public), and in fact when the same investor called back at another conference call in 2003, he was immediately cut off and his questions never answered. Many people have since wondered (and a couple actually asked at a conference call) why the WWE is even a public company at this point. Aside from the obvious influx of cash, they generally appear uncomfortable divulging their financial situation, don't deal well with critical investors, have lost all footholds into expanding their market, and are actually getting close to being in a worse position than they were in when the whole thing started. In fact, Linda's big chestnut was constantly noting that the brand extension was a twelve to eighteen month plan that would revive business through international business and split PPVs, and they had it planned out all along as twelve to eighteen months. Well, we're eighteen months into the brand extension, and all the same stars are on top of the promotion, ratings are down, buyrates are *way* down, and attendance is a joke. If it's truly a long-term plan, it must be one of those really devious ones where they pull things out at the last minute and turn business around.

Linda also detailed the then-continuing legal battle with the World Wildlife Fund, as another lawsuit was in progress for damages due to reneging on the original agreement made in 1994. The fund claimed $360 million, WWE claimed $0. Vince's personal response was going to be wrestling a guy in a panda suit on the next UK-only PPV, but thankfully he was talked out of it at the last minute. But still, I think that demonstrates why he's truly the genius of the business.

And speaking of his genius, buildup began for the RAW tenth anniversary show at that point.

Now, I think this warrants a bit of explanation.

RAW of course debuted in 1993 (formerly known as "Monday Night RAW" before people apparently realized the inherent redundancy and dropped the day of the week from the title) and was a much different show at that point. In 1993, the wrestling world was on a definite downswing and RAW marked a sort of throwback to the old days, shot in front of a smaller, rowdier crowd in Manhattan and featuring a more intimate feel than the cold arena shows filmed for syndication. It also served as a kind of prelude to the rise of ECW, although obviously no one realized it would be going in that direction at the time.

Financial considerations and a lack of interest in maintaining the live feel (the show was actually taped four weeks at a time) meant that RAW reverted back to arena shows by 1994, and remained that way until a total revamp in 1997 transformed it into "RAW is WAR" as a declaration of same against Ted Turner's WCW. The years between RAW's debut and the 1997 revamp are largely ignored by history, and many fans thought an anniversary show would be a good time to revisit those years and give due to the people who toiled during the down years.

Ten years on the air for any show is a pretty big deal, and since wrestling is more preoccupied with roman numerals than most, January 2003 seemed to be an ideal time to build up a show called "RAW X," celebrating ten years of the surviving show of the Monday Night Wars. The idea, however, seemed flawed from the get go, once the format was announced. It would be a faux awards show, much like the campy and maligned Slammy Awards of the '80s and mid-'90s, presenting trophies for "achievements" on RAW over the years. This should have set off alarm bells and red flags in the minds of fans everywhere, because there's rarely an opportunity to put over current history as the "right" history that Vince won't take.

But the show seemed to have a saving grace: surprises and guest stars, and lots of 'em, according to the hype for the show. Steve Austin was on the verge of making nice with Vince after his assault conviction and most figured he'd take the opportunity to return in some role. The show was in New York City, so Mick Foley seemed like a shoo-in, and his name was all over the buildup as a part of the awards. And Rock was, well, Rock, so obviously he'd be there. As well, Bobby "The Brain" Heenan, recently featured on *Confidential* and in need of a vehicle to hype his book, was announced as a participant by Gene Okerlund. And even if those four big names couldn't or wouldn't appear, there was still ten years of history to draw from, and surely they'd think to call SOMEONE?

So after two months of hype, this then is what we got:

The show was hosted at the World, itself a dying prospect by that point, and featured two running themes throughout the night: awards and a top ten "Greatest RAW moments." The RAW moments were voted by fans on the WWE's Web site, and may or may not have been fixed. They ended up as follows:

10. This Is Your Life, Rock
9. Austin crushes Rock's truck
8. The Final Nitro, which was simulcast on RAW
7. Vince gets attacked in the hospital and we meet Mr. Socko
6. The Nation of Domination parody by D-Generation X
5. Steve Austin interrupts a Mike Tyson speech and a brawl erupts
4. D-X invades WCW in 1998
3. Rock and Hogan have a pre-Wrestlemania staredown
2. The Owen Hart tribute show
1. Austin gives Vince McMahon a beer bath

A lot of these do have merit, although trying to rank them from one to ten is a pretty arbitrary business. The Owen Hart inclusion was a bullshit political move on the part of the WWE so they could congratulate themselves on how well they handled his death—hardly an objective viewpoint on the matter. They would have handled it better by not forcing him into the rafters to die in the first place, I think. I mean, really, is there anything more crass than dropping someone to their death on live PPV, letting the show go on, and then giving yourself an award years later for the tribute show? It's like some kind of sick version of the Oscars winning an Emmy. You'd think that even after a man has DIED as a result of Vince McMahon's vision of sports entertainment that he might be able to stop and say "Yes, I admit I was wrong" rather than trying to spin everything as a crowning moment for the glorious WWE machine. Was I, as a fan, supposed to feel vindicated by seeing Jeff Jarrett crying his eyes out on live TV one day after being forced to wrestle in a comedy match after one of his best friends died in the same ring minutes before?

But I digress.

Other things on the list were clearly there as a way to suck up to the big stars who were on top at that point: Austin was featured prominently (which he should be), as was Rock (ditto) and HHH (not so fast). The Nation parody was funny at the time, but doesn't age well and most of the audience voting on this list probably wasn't even watching when it first aired. The D-X invasion of WCW also scored high, and it was featured on a piece on *Confidential* talking about the demise of WCW, so it was at least more likely to have been viewed prior to the voting.

That was actually a weird piece, just to get off on another tangent for a moment. In keeping with the "All things good stem from HHH" motif during the time when Austin was absent in 2002, history was again rewritten so that the turnaround in the Monday Night Wars came in mid-1998, when D-Generation X staged their invasion of WCW. Now, given it was huge for HHH's career, but calling it the most important moment in the war between WCW and the WWE is stretching things like Plastic Man with his dick caught in a zipper. The average fan didn't really even clue into what was going on with those skits, and besides which the ratings had turned around weeks earlier. It was WCW's own incompetence that ultimately sunk them, not some smart-ass "invasion" skit that was meant to expose the free tickets given away for the competition. But then the WCW burial got weirder, as everyone from Hulk Hogan to Big Show was trotted out to lay the blame squarely on the feet of two men: Goldberg and Bret Hart. Indeed, to hear Hulk Hogan of all people blaming Bret for being too greedy and having a contract that was too big was surreal in the extreme. I thought it was the funniest thing I was going to hear on that show until Big Show started talking about guys not earning their spot or working hard enough. Talk about the pot calling the kettle fat and lazy.

But back to RAW X again, as the evening churned along with people, like Stacy Keibler, who are barely in their twenties and have no perspective on what RAW even means to the business, telling us that gimmicks from 1995 sucked and we should feel silly for ever paying money to see them. Furthermore, the awards showed a marked lack of forethought and everything skewed toward the preceding two years. Out of a field of Sable, Sunny, Chyna, Lita, and Trish Stratus for "Diva of the Decade," Trish wins. Now, this wasn't such a big deal—how do you even WIN Diva of the Decade? And why wasn't Shawn Michaels in contention? But it showed a greater symptom: instead of acknowledging the past and maybe even throwing a bone to someone currently down on their luck and in need of *any* self-esteem boost (Sunny, I'm looking at *you*. More accurately, I'm trying not to look because it's not pleasant to do so), they simply gave the award to someone currently in the system, despite her only being a part of the WWE for two years at that point. The funny thing is that Sable returned a couple of months later, playing exactly the same character, and got an even bigger push than Trish. The silliness continued: Kurt Angle won an award for taking a bump in a cage match that no one remembers. It was simply an opportunity for his new backup, Team Angle, to get showcased as his henchman. Mick Foley wins an award for the most unbelievable moment or something, as a result of his three identities. However, he wasn't even invited to the show and wouldn't have showed up even if he was, so why give him the award? Even worse, he beat out Kane shooting fire out of the ringposts, which violates the laws of thermodynamics themselves! You'd think that at least warrants a trophy!

The most surreal moment of the show (in a show of surreal moments) came when Rock won an award for best interview and instead of showing up, was featured in a "live via satellite" (carny for "on tape") interview that the crowd dumped all over, seeing that the biggest star in the promotion couldn't even be bothered to show up for what was obviously a joke show by that point. This marked the biggest case of backlash against Rock's Hollywood career, once again by cynical New York fans, and was a large contributor to Rock's return as a heel early in 2003, since Vince pretty much listens to anything that New York fans tell him. HHH and Stephanie won a lame "best kiss" award and proceeded to engage in a spanking exhibition on stage, Mae Young giving birth to a hand was suddenly "controversial television" (in reality, it garnered no controversy and was just stupid, although the original idea of Mae giving birth to a douchebag was thankfully dropped), and a ladder match that had taken place a couple of months before and was quickly forgotten was suddenly the best match in RAW's history.

The Background: This was a four-way TLC match for the World tag titles held by Kane and Hurricane at the time, set up by a spin of a giant wheel as a part of an "all-gimmick" show from Las Vegas. The teams were mostly thrown together.

The Stipulations: TLC (tables, ladders, and chairs) matches are a variant of the standard ladder match rules, where additional objects (i.e., tables and chairs) are left for the competitors and their use encouraged. The first one to climb the ladder and grab both title belts wins.

The Overall Importance: Well, apparently it was the greatest match of the decade, although it barely made a dent in the other award ballots at the end of the year. Bubba Dudley suffered a concussion as a result of the match, and after the match concluded, HHH came down to ringside to make his infamous speech about Kane and Katie Vick, thus killing a hot crowd. So really we'd all prefer to forget it in the long run.

RAW, October 7, 2002, Las Vegas, NV

TLC match, WWE tag titles: Kane and Hurricane versus Spike & Bubba Dudley versus Rob Van Dam and Jeff Hardy versus Christian and Chris Jericho. Hurricane is absent due to an injury suffered earlier in the show, so we start without him. Some might say that three injury angles in the same show is a bit much, but obviously you don't realize the genius of the RAW writers. Jericho and Christian take advantage of a schmoz to make the first climb, but get stopped. Jeff's hankies tonight: Red and white, thus indicating that he's into Canadians, or semaphore. Hardy and RVD double-team Kane, and that backfires on them. Kane pounds Hardy on the outside, but gets hit with a railrunner. In the ring, Bubba does the old Terry Funk ladder routine, knocking everyone down before getting booted by Kane. Rob dropkicks him and dumps him, and Christian and Jericho double-team Spike and send him into the ladder. Heel miscommunication allows Bubba to get the Flip Flop and Fly, but Kane hits Christian with the flying lariat. Bubba gives him some ladder and climbs, but Kane pulls him off and chokeslams him. Spike goes after Kane, and also gets slammed. Now Jericho makes a go of it, hitting Kane with a ladder and sending him out, where he ends up on a table. Jericho and Christian take too long setting up and get a ladder in the face from RVD as a result. Now Jeff tries to put Kane through the table, as he heads to the top of the ladder and gets the LEAPFROG OF DOOM to put Kane through. Bubba drops a ladder on Kane for good measure and Bubba climbs, but we've gotta take a break, Tony! The tape machines are rolling, fans.

We return as Rob and Bubba climb dueling ladders, and Jericho and Christian follow them up. Jericho bulldogs Bubba off the ladder, and Christian takes RVD down with the inverted DDT. Now Spike climbs but gets dumped by Christian. JR declares this "wrestling purgatory." I thought that was TNA? Christian climbs and gets crotched by Kane, and Hardy gets slammed by Kane and dumped. Kane makes a go of it, but Spike hangs onto the leg. Kane gets rid of him, too. Jericho finally ends the no-selling with a chairshot, but gets hit with a spin-kick from RVD. Rob follows with the Van Terminator to put Kane out of the ring. Now it's over to Jeff suplexing Jericho onto the ladder. This is a really disorganized match—the spots aren't flowing into each other and don't really make much sense.

Christian gets slammed ugly style into the ladder and Jeff climbs, but Bubba follows him up and superplexes him off the ladder. Everyone appears to be dead. Now Rob makes the miracle revival and climbs, but Bubba knocks him off. Now Jericho climbs (and can't reach the belts—we're gonna need a bigger boat), but Spike pushes the ladder over and Jericho hits

the floor. Now Spike climbs, but gets pulled down by Christian and dumped through a table. Now Christian climbs and gets bombed down by Bubba. This is getting repetitive. RVD hits Christian with a frog splash as Bubba rolls into position to get hit with the swanton, but moves. Jeff goes through a table, Bubba gets Van Daminated, and Rob climbs, but gets chaired by Jericho and sent down. Now Kane returns and follows Jericho up, and chokeslams him off. So with everyone out of commission, Kane climbs and (being the only one tall enough to reach) retains the tag titles at 25:08.

So he no-sells everything, takes no bumps, sits out the last five minutes, and wins the titles single-handedly? Way to reward all the other bumping in the match. Anyway, the match itself was just a mess of spots one after another that were all forgotten about (by the audience and the guys supposedly selling the injuries) seconds later. I mean, yeah, you can level that criticism at all the TLC matches, but this one just seemed so sloppy and chaotic that I felt like I was watching an indy match at times. ★★★

As a fan, the whole thing left you feeling insulted that you had ever invested time in anything on the show before 1998, because no one in charge seemed willing to acknowledge that those years even happened, other than as a chance to mock them. And there's nothing worse than telling fans that they're stupid for watching your TV show.

The capper for the evening was Steve Austin winning an overall "Best in RAW History" award, which was to be presented by Vince McMahon, and then having no Austin there. Even worse, Vince essentially rubbed it in the fans' faces, casting himself as a heel owner against the face Austin again in a storyline that was dead years before and which fans no longer had any vested interest in seeing. In fact, the only guy they had interest in seeing was Austin, which you might expect because almost the entirety of the show was built around how great Austin was and all the swell things he did for the show over the years.

I know I'm spending a lot of time on a show that was stupid and ultimately meaningless in the grand scheme of things, but it was, I think, a wasted opportunity in what could have been a great chance to celebrate the past and start some new storylines for the future. But that was the theme of 2002: wasted chances.

And as 2003 began, that theme would only get more pronounced.

15.

Blown Spots

We cannot all see alike, but we can all do good.
—P. T. Barnum

The WWE, ever since Vince took over the reigns in the early '80s, has always had a unique problem in its infrastructure that has hampered it from true greatness—kind of a self-defeating mechanism, if you will. The problem is this: they tailor the workers to match the product, rather than vice versa.

I think this warrants a bit of an explanation.

For literally years on end, it seemed like all we heard from the company shills was "We're doing our best to get the cruiserweight division going," but it never seemed to. From 1997 (when the first tentative baby steps toward a viable division for 225-pound-and-under wrestlers were first taken) until 2001, they had a pretty good excuse: WCW had all the good cruiserweights under contract already. But as of March 2001, the WWE owned EVERYTHING, so you can scratch that one.

Really, it should come as no huge shock that Vince will always push big guys over small

guys. Most armchair psychologists have pinned it down to a scrawny grade school-aged Vince McMahon getting bullied by jocks and thus living out his revenge fantasies on national TV by having big muscular supermen at his beck and call. He can't accept that someone physically smaller than him could take him in a real fight, and therefore he doesn't believe that the fans would believe that, either. In fact, Vince has been heard to comment many times that he won't push Chris Benoit as a legitimate top star because of his height. Thankfully that changed in 2004.

And okay, fine, we all have our own tastes and likes when it comes to wrestling, even if you are the most powerful man in the sport. But take a trip to your local independent wrestling promotion some day. What are you gonna see? Big bruising behemoths up and down the card who weigh 300 pounds and stand 6'5"? No, of course not, because people who look like that fall into three categories:

1. Professional bodybuilder
2. Legitimate athlete, professional or otherwise
3. Someone already signed to the WWE system

In other words, the WWE machine has already swallowed up everyone decent who's available. The depth chart in the kind of talent they're looking for is woefully depleted because they've already scraped down to the bottom of the barrel. For proof of that, watch a Test match sometime. No, what you're going to see in the indy promotions (and what the market in those promotions generally demands) is smaller, quicker guys doing a more high-flying or submission-based style of match. Reality check: Before anyone freaks out and thinks that I'm declaring cruiserweights the saviors of the indy circuit and Ring of Honor the next WWE, let me clarify that no one is drawing any significant money outside of the WWE. The business is stagnant all over, and that's the truth whether you run shows with 300-pound steroid monsters on top or 200-pound high flyers. However, your chances of developing a loyal audience who will support your promotion on a regular basis are much greater if you present that simultaneously more realistic (i.e., "real wrestling") and less realistic (i.e., insane spotfest) style than just having big guys chopping each other.

So bringing this back to the WWE, what you have now is the vaunted "WWE Main Event Style," which is scripted heavily by road agents and was developed to disguise the weaknesses of top wrestlers like Undertaker and Steve Austin, but becomes almost another layer in the glass ceiling for people below it. Check out this catch-22: You can't break into the main event until you learn to work "main event style," but

> As of 2004, Ring of Honor has done quite well for themselves within their own niche, and they are one of the few indy promotions to consistently run a profit.

you can't learn "main event style" until you work a main event. Kurt Angle picked it up pretty quick because he's a freak of nature, and Chris Benoit picked it up because he can do damn near anything associated with professional wrestling (he's one of the few people who is a great technician, great brawler, and great power wrestler, sometimes all within the same match). Chris Jericho caught on within a year or so of entering the WWE in 1999, but it pretty much ruined his natural style and left him a weaker wrestler in the long run. Booker T pretty much had it down pat after joining from WCW in 2001, but was never allowed to cross the magic barrier and become a full-fledged main eventer. Brock Lesnar got it down faster than anyone thought was possible, but he, too, is something of a freak of nature. Edge kinda has it, but still doesn't seem to have the confidence in himself to carry someone to a great match.

But let's look at these names: Chris Benoit, Kurt Angle, Brock Lesnar, Chris Jericho, Booker T, and Edge. Not exactly the jacked-up freaks or larger-than-life characters that people like Rock, Steve Austin, and Undertaker represent, are they? Sure, Brock Lesnar is pretty big, but you don't see Undertaker doing shooting-star presses, do you? Whereas the previous run of top workers needed an entire style of working invented for them, this collection of wannabe main eventers is (and in some cases, has been doing so for years) fully capable of wrestling an entirely mat-based, "classic" wrestling match that the fans are all too willing to accept as something they'd pay to see. Such was the case at Royal Rumble 2003, as Kurt Angle defended his newly won WWE title against Chris Benoit.

The Background: Benoit and Angle had been forced together as tag team partners for much of 2002, despite feuding at the same time. Angle introduced Paul Heyman as his new advisor the night after winning the title in December, and immediately became the #1 heel on Smackdown again. Benoit defeated Big Show in a #1 contender match to earn the shot, and Benoit won the majority of the one-on-one meetings between himself and Angle in 2002, usually thwarting Angle's attempts at locking in his dreaded anklelock submission move. This was to be the final showdown between them, with the WWE title on the line.

The Stipulations: The winner gets the WWE title.

The Overall Importance: This was the first clear-cut contender for Match of the Year, even at that early point of 2003, and seemed to tease a new main event style focusing on "real" wrestling, which was then paid off by a match between Kurt Angle and Brock Lesnar at Wrestlemania. It also looked to be the final elevation of Chris Benoit to something meaningful, judging by the crowd's reaction to him, but that proved to be wishful thinking.

Royal Rumble 2003, January 19, 2003, Boston, MA

Smackdown World Title: Kurt Angle v. Chris Benoit. Team Angle gets the boot before we start, to ensure fairness. Benoit quickly goes for a Sharpshooter, but Angle bails to escape. Back in, Benoit grabs a headlock and kicks off an attempt at a single-leg takedown by Angle. Angle tries a sleeper, but Benoit armdrags out of it, and then legdrags Angle into another Sharpshooter attempt, which Angle again blocks and makes the ropes. Angle's knee might as well have a big "kick me" sign on it tonight, as it's braced and previously injured. Angle posts him and pounds away in the corner, into a vertical suplex that gets two. He starts throwing chops, but that's a dumb thing to try with Benoit, and he fires back and pounds on him in the corner. Angle misses a charge and Benoit hits him with a clothesline to the back and a knee to the gut that gets two. More chops as he keeps wearing Angle down, but he gets suplexed onto the top rope to break up the momentum. Benoit necksnaps him, however, and they slug it out on the apron, leading to a Benoit DDT out there. Back in, he gets two. Flying headbutt comes way too early, however, and misses.

Angle goes for the Angle Slam, and now Benoit really does get the Sharpshooter, having built up to it three times. Angle makes the ropes, however. Benoit hits him with a backdrop suplex and gets two. Angle responds with an overhead suplex and tosses Benoit, and they brawl outside. Angle wins that pretty handily and stomps away. Back in, Angle hits him with a short-arm clothesline for two. Angle goes to a chinlock and gets the hooks in, but Benoit powers out and armdrags him. He walks into another suplex, however, and can't get the momentum going again. Angle drops him with a backdrop suplex for two. Back to the chinlock, but Benoit powers out again. This move actually serves two purposes within the match: it works on the surgically repaired neck of Benoit and it causes him to expend energy escaping the hold. They collide with clotheslines and both are out.

Benoit is up first and slugs away, and overpowers Angle into a backdrop. Rolling germans, but Angle reverses and starts throwing his own. Benoit then reverses after the first one thrown by Angle and throws his own, winning the battle four suplexes to one. Benoit goes up after blowing snot on him (not just a great athlete, but a true gentleman), but Angle pops up with the superplex for two. Now that's guts—taking a snot rocket for the sake of selling the injury. Benoit reverses the Angle Slam into the crossface, dead center of the ring, and Angle looks to be in trouble. He makes the ropes, however. Benoit then switches to an anklelock, but as generally happens, Angle counters that into his own version of the move. Benoit counters back into the crossface, but Angle rolls him over for two to escape. Benoit keeps coming, however, taking him down with another crossface. Angle rolls him over again, but Benoit adjusts this time and hangs on, so Angle adjusts to that and uses the Angle Slam, but Benoit kicks out at two.

Angle gets pissed and grabs another anklelock, but Benoit rolls through and counters Angle into the corner, and then rolls him up off a reversed german suplex for two. He starts throwing more suplexes, but Angle switches and hits his own. Benoit then tops him by throwing him 180 degrees in the air and onto his head. Angle is three-quarters of the way across the ring, so naturally Benoit hits him with the flying headbutt from all the way over there. He gets two as the crowd starts to get seriously into the match. Back to the crossface, but Angle rolls out of it and tries a powerbomb, then drops Benoit neckfirst onto the top rope, into

another Angle Slam for two. That was a guaranteed finish in any other match, which only made Benoit a bigger babyface with the crowd. Benoit takes him down again with the crossface and Angle is about to tap, but he spins into another anklelock instead. Benoit kicks him off, but Angle hangs on tenaciously, thinking one move ahead.

Benoit finally powers out, but is too weak to fight him off again, and kicking off won't work a second time because Angle can anticipate now. Benoit goes for the ropes, but Angle pulls him off and turns it into a heel hook (a more painful variation where Angle wraps his legs around the knee) and that's enough to tap Benoit at 19:47. Just a great hybrid of pure mat-wrestling and mixed martial arts psychology that not only got Angle's shooter image over, but made Benoit into a huge babyface . . . for about two weeks, at which point they pissed it all away again. ★★★★¾ Benoit gets a standing ovation after the loss, and even limps back to the dressing room, selling the ankle injury the whole time.

Still a great match, still the same rating, because I couldn't quite put it over the top as a perfect match. It still cleaned up in most of the year-end awards polls for 2003, winning Match of the Year in pretty much all but the *Wrestling Observer Newsletter*'s awards. That's quite amazing for a match that took place in January, when voting is in November!

You'll note that the match drew rave reviews and was effective in getting the crowd worked into a frenzy (even after an HHH match that nearly put the entire crowd to sleep), and without the need for ref bumps or chairshots or brawling into the crowd or run-ins. In fact, the point was specifically made here that there would be *no* run-ins, and the match would be won on the strength of the victor's wrestling skill. And on that night, Angle was the better wrestler, so he won. That sort of attitude was the philosophy of Paul Heyman with regards to the Smackdown brand. Unfortunately, that attitude couldn't last.

Paul Heyman can be considered in some ways a genius. Hell, he's probably smart enough to qualify for MENSA on intellectual merit alone, but I'm talking the elusive "wrestling genius" tag that Vince McMahon has several times chosen to award himself and himself alone. But like all geniuses, if you don't agree with his view of The Way Things Should Be, be prepared for an argument. And while arguing with Vince will sometimes earn you respect, most of the time it just earns you a ticket to the unemployment line. Unfortunately for Paul, his frequent clashes with the other members of the creative team and frequent disagreements with Vince on the direction and content of Smackdown led to him being giving a "consulting job" in February (which is carny for "sit at home and think about how grateful you should be to have a job at all when we own the entire market") and taken off TV after being "injured" by Brock Lesnar.

Now, just to chime in with my two cents Canadian (1.5 cents U.S.), I have a love-hate relationship with Heyman and his previous works in our so-called sport. As a manager, I always thought he was one of the best, playing the fast-talking psycho yuppie in WCW, but even there he rubbed people the wrong way and ended up

starting a fight with WCW VP Bill Watts that he couldn't finish, in 1992. That resulted in him living out his dream and moving to Philadelphia to start ECW with pawn shop owner Tod Gordon (originally Eastern Championship Wrestling in 1993, when Heyman took over controlling interest in 1995 it was renamed Extreme Championship Wrestling), with the idea being to evolve the sport with a fast-paced product both in the ring and in the interviews. Matches were high impact and bloody, and interviews were more of an exercise in thumbing their nose at the other two promotions than any kind of serious money-drawing angles.

Their whole goal was to build a loyal and fanatic audience who, to paraphrase Jim Ross, would be willing to drink Heyman's Kool-Aid. And while that worked, it worked at the expense of potential national coverage because most of the major markets were terrified of picking up the show for fear of having someone die on the show or say something so offensive that the Bible Belt would spontaneously combust. The short version of the long story is that while ECW got a national TV deal in 1999 with TNN, by then the company was the walking dead and only surviving because of millions of dollars in money from Heyman's rich parents and secret payments from Vince McMahon. It folded for good in 2001, millions in debt and with months' worth of unpaid money owed to the roster.

So while on one level Heyman is a booking genius, on another the entire purpose of wrestling is to make money, and he did just the opposite. I still hold a soft spot in my heart for him because of his ability to disguise the weaknesses of his wrestlers and recognize fan reactions to great wrestling, but having him running a company full time is tantamount to suicide. With that being said, given the high level of talent on top of the Smackdown brand, I think the WWE made entirely the wrong decision in jettisoning him to save Vince's hurt feelings, and it was a case of Vince thinking with his ego instead of stopping to look at the bigger picture.

> **Paul would, however, return later in 2003 in a very effective role as the new general manager of Smackdown, so maybe he's smarter than I thought.**

And then there's another guy who would have benefited from stopping to look at the bigger picture: Jeff Hardy. Hardy was truly one of the saddest cases in wrestling, because everyone seemed to know how badly he needed help, except for the people who could help him. As strange a case of transforming personality as there ever was in the WWE, Jeff debuted in 1999 with brother Matt as a standard pretty-boy tag team, doing high-flying moves and making the girls squeal. By 2001, two things had started to happen that would dramatically affect both of their careers: Jeff was becoming more and more regressed as a worker, relying on high-spots and squealing crowds to maintain his standing in the promotion. And Matt was wanting to turn heel and move away from the team, seeing what was happening to his brother.

Drugs in wrestling are an accepted thing by this point, I should point out. People don't really flinch much when the details of painkillers, steroids, and recreational drugs are revealed, and we have become conditioned not to care when someone else dies from an overdose.

While Brian Pillman's death in 1997 sent shockwaves through the industry and fanbase, Rick Rude's death under similar circumstances in 1999 barely caused an eyelash to bat. Davey Boy Smith's death in 2002 was almost expected given the way his life was falling apart. Curt Hennig's misadventure with cocaine in 2003 was just a sad coda on the funeral dirge of his career in the previous year. I think it's almost easier to ignore the immediate effects of the drugs because you rarely see them firsthand due to the larger-than-life nature of the people involved. They hide their pain and addictions with big muscles and macho interviews, and fans go on treating them the same because otherwise it might cost someone money if they don't.

But then you have someone like Jeff Hardy, who weighs maybe 200 pounds soaking wet, and is built like a regular guy. And yet he throws himself through furniture, gets tossed around the ring like a ragdoll, and generally takes risks that no sane human being would even consider. How can someone like that function without the crutch of drugs? Jeff Hardy is one of the rare cases where you can actually watch him week to week from his peak in 2000 until early 2003 and see him degenerating, physically and mentally, every step of the way. You can watch him week to week like that because Vince McMahon kept pushing him on TV week to week in order to keep the squealing girls buying their tickets.

And it's not like Jeff was out there busting his ass night after night, either: by 2001, he had become one of the lazier workers in the business, so burned out by painkillers and his lifestyle that he would work the same match every night, repeating the same spots to the point where anyone else should have them memorized and be able to hit them in his sleep. But then it got worse, because not only was he repeating stuff, he was missing it or doing it so badly that putting him on TV was becoming an embarrassment. When asked to do promos for live TV shows, he would deliver them in a bored, rambling monologue and move on to the next match. This was obviously someone in no condition to work, to use the euphemism that the WWE loves so much, but the merchandise was all-important and thus he had to be there. Matt Hardy even recounted a story late in 2002 about Jeff's Christmas present to him: A dead fish with "Mattitude Follower #1" written on it.

By the time the evidence had piled up to the point where even pushing Hardy as the new Shawn Michaels and having him feud with Chris Jericho couldn't hide his problems any longer, then the WWE offered him a chance to check into rehab to help himself. And that's carny for "check in for a couple of weeks and then hit the road again," so you can imagine how messed up the guy had to be to turn down that offer and instead take his release from the WWE. Here's a guy who had everything in the world handed to him on a silver platter by the promotion, who could show up late whenever he wanted and still get pushed on TV the next week, who was put in high-level programs with top stars of both the past and present, but was so burned out on the business that he decided to walk away from it because the drugs had consumed the passion he used to have for wrestling. Jeff Hardy is more the symptom than the cause, but it's a troubling trend nonetheless.

Another disturbing trend, in the same vein, was the welcoming back of Steve Austin after a well-publicized run-in with the law and well-publicized drinking problems. Not to mention walking out on the company. Twice. Now for anyone else that would be career death, but Austin has more money than he can ever spend in two lifetimes anyway, and Vince enjoys having more money, so when the WWE started getting desperate again at the beginning of the new year, Austin was the guy they called. They also tied it into the TV product, as Vince McMahon gave RAW GM Eric Bischoff a "thirty-day ultimatum" to shake RAW up. This ultimatum mysteriously became twenty-eight days when someone realized that it wouldn't line up with a Monday otherwise. This also marked an annoying trend of burying the show you're trying to sell on TV, as Vince called the RAW brand boring during his speech to Bischoff. He also did that while getting rid of Ric Flair back in June (ironically the time when Austin left the promotion) and it made RAW seem like a stupid show to be watching—Vince was basically telling you that you were stupid for devoting time and energy to watching it all those months, since he thought it was boring. Well, HHH was, but I don't think that's what Vince had in mind exactly. At any rate, "shaking things up" soon became interpreted as "sign Steve Austin back to RAW," even though Vince never said at any point that he wanted that. The end result was that Bischoff couldn't meet the deadline and took out his frustrations by firing Jim Ross before getting fired by Vince later in the same show. However, this being wrestling, Vince reversed both decisions (maybe the referee was out at the time, who knows) and made JR an announcer again and Bischoff the GM again, with the caveat that he had to fight Steve Austin in his return match at the No Way Out PPV in February. It was a short squash for Austin, of course, but even from that small sample and the way he had trouble moving around the ring, it was apparent that things weren't right with Austin any longer. By Wrestlemania, we'd find out how bad his medical situation really was.

As for Bischoff, perhaps inspired by Vince's failures with the XFL, Smackdown Records, and the wrestling-themed nightclub, he decided to contact the people behind the Girls Gone Wild franchise about partnering on their upcoming PPV. While at first it looked as though Bischoff was only going to be lending his business acumen to the project, soon it caught fire within Vince and he was pushing the show as a full GGW-WWE coproject and hyping the involvement of several WWE women as well as readying the WWE production guys to lend a hand with the live presentation. Now, most of the people without their lips surgically attached to Vince's ass realized what a cockamamie idea this was from the start, but apparently Vince enjoys proving people wrong by taking the stupidest concepts humanly possible and making something out of them. He was fighting an uphill battle with this one, though. The show was originally supposed to emanate from Florida, but authorities there threatened to bring the police in if the show went ahead, so it moved to Texas.

Now, I'm going to assume that you, gentle reader, are of a more refined stock than someone like myself and thus are not aware of the basic concept behind Girls Gone Wild, and if so, the idea is that A1 sleaze peddler Joe Francis would carry around a video camera and talk chicks on Spring Break to flash for him. That's about it, actually. Now, this would seem to be a very hard concept to either find fault with or screw up, but the WWE did both. First of all, they decided that what was needed was a beauty pageant. And instead of hundreds of random girls flashing, there should only be ten. And they shouldn't really flash. Oh, and Snoop Dogg would be a judge and drinks would be on the house. A true recipe for disaster, the show was horribly received, a critical and financial bomb,

and featured Torrie Wilson (who bared all in *Playboy* early in 2003) balking at flashing her breasts and instead working an angle with former stripper Nidia that ended with no one getting naked. As a funny coda to this sad story, Joe Francis was arrested a couple of months later when it was revealed that one of the girls on the show was actually sixteen and thus he was not only a sleazeball, but a pederast. Well, shoot for the moon, I always say.

I think in all this, the saddest story of them all on another level entirely was that of Brian Kendrick. Kendrick was a student of Shawn Michaels, hired under a developmental contract back when the WWE still gave a crap about keeping Shawn happy, and then cut when Shawn screwed up one of his many inspirational returns (this was back in the days when he was more likely to find Jim Bean than Jesus). Not content to be rejected by the WWE, Kendrick (who wrestled under the name Spanky) worked any indy promotion that would hire him, building up a reputation as a crazy guy who would work his ass off every night, do whatever it took to get over, and bust out innovative offense and selling all the time. After a stint with the Ring of Honor promotion in Philadelphia, Kendrick was signed back to the WWE again and immediately turned into a case study in humiliation. He was originally given a lame gimmick where he'd wrestle nontelevised matches under a mask and have an identity related to whatever city they were in that night for the cheap pop (i.e., in Nashville he would wrestle as "The Titan," in Pittsburgh he'd be "The Penguin," etc.) but when that apparently proved to be too intellectual to catch on, he was finally put on TV as plain Brian Kendrick. Oh, except his first appearance saw him dressed in a bellhop uniform and delivering a singing telegram to Undertaker before getting destroyed. He moved up the ladder a bit with a bit where he took advice from Sean O'Haire (then doing an evil motivational speaker gimmick) and streaked into the arena wearing only a scarf in an homage to the Nike commercial. It was not only stupid, but unoriginal—when the announcers are coming right now and saying that he's spoofing the commercial, it kind of takes away from the impact of it.

See, Brian is small and a great worker. You can see how this would cause a problem in not knowing how to use him, being that it's not like there's a title just for cruiserweights or anything. Well, there was such a title, but it was being held by Matt Hardy, a heavyweight pretending to be a cruiserweight, who was feuding with Rey Mysterio, a cruiserweight pretending to be a heavyweight. So missing the vital two-week window of having a gimmick the writers can't screw up, Kendrick ended up as an opening match jobber back in nontelevised matches, after only one PPV appearance, right back where he started. Maybe he should have stuck with the mask. This is the one that really bugs me for some reason, maybe because in a sport filled with idiots like Kevin Nash who collect their paycheck and complain to management about every job they have to do, it was refreshing to see someone willing to truly bust ass and do anything to get over, and then get punished for it when he did get over. In fact, shortly after Kendrick debuted, another wrestler the same size, but missing a leg, was signed.

Funny story behind that: Zach Gowen, who wrestled on the independent circuit as Tenacious Z, did a show for the NWA-TNA promotion and was on the verge of getting national press for the company due to his handicapped state and the fact that he could do moonsaults and high-flying stuff with one leg. However, Vince caught wind of the twenty-year-old kid and told agent John Laurinaitis to "sign the one-legged guy." John, having no idea who Gowen was, interpreted that as ANOTHER one-legged wrestler in the WWE developmental universe, Steve Chamberlain, who was being trained by Steve Keirn in Florida and is about twice as big as Gowen and $\frac{1}{100}$ as talented. So Chamberlain gets a developmental contract (apparently a shock to him), and that's a few thousand dollars down the toilet for the WWE, because he signed the contract before they could discover who he was. And people wonder why Vince wants to handle everything personally. Gowen eventually signed with the WWE, thus completing the sideshow atmosphere of the promotion. Not surprisingly, Zach was programmed into a feud with Vince himself, because if there's one thing Vince's image was lacking it was that of "Guy who beats up crippled kids fresh out of high school."

As a coda to the whole saga, both Kendrick and Gowen were released in a financial bloodletting in early 2004, along with Chris Kanyon.

By Wrestlemania, it would be "Guy who puts himself into the main event of the biggest show of the year with another senior citizen and then wonders why it didn't draw."

16.

Racism and Retirement

Advertising is like learning—a little is a dangerous thing.
—P. T. Barnum

I think it's only fitting that we wrap up our tale of woe with the biggest show of the year for the WWE, Wrestlemania XIX, which also ended up being one of the most disappointing.

And as much as I don't want to keep bringing things back to HHH again and giving him even more airtime than he already gives himself, I said at the very beginning that this was the story of HHH and Austin, and it's somehow equally fitting that we return to that theme as we end.

So back to HHH we go.

Now, not to disrespect all the hard work of Scott Steiner (okay, who am I kidding here, that's exactly why) but I'm gonna skim over a couple of months' worth of torture by noting that HHH tried to draw money by defending the belt TWICE against Steiner, and the result was a really painfully bad match both times out. The first one took place at Royal Rumble 2003, and the buildup was, shall we say, less than 100 percent heterosexually fulfilling, as they engaged in just about every fakeout possible to prevent from having them meet in the ring before the PPV. And while this is generally good business sense, HHH's idea of exciting buildup included an arm-wrestling match, a weightlifting exhibition, and most notably a bodybuilding contest.

Now, you might not see the big deal about the bodybuilding contest, but look at it this way: HHH is a huge mark for that stuff. He'll admit it, too. He did color commentary on the Mr. Olympia contest telecast that year and has been featured in a few bodybuilding magazines throughout his career. Scott Steiner, while having freakishly large-proportioned muscles, is not what you'd call your classic bodybuilder type. So the bizarre result was HHH arranging the contest so that, for the ten people in the audience who understood bodybuilding, he clearly out-classed Steiner in all the professional categories in terms of physique, poses, and execution. The problem was that no one gave a crap about the finer points of a bodybuilding contest, and it just came across as a couple of guys out there bumping into each other while posing. Not exactly the most macho way to pass the time, indeed. But in HHH's mind, this was the grand heel plan to show up the babyface or something. The result was a match at Royal Rumble so bad that the crowd turned on Steiner after only a few minutes, as HHH went out of his way to expose every weakness that Steiner had (i.e., making him work a long match and forcing him to do the brunt of the work on power moves) and thus completely cut the legs out from underneath him as a future challenger. The match ended in a DQ to set up a rematch the next month, but by that point it was clearly second-banana to a Rock-Hogan rematch in the main event. As a rule, HHH's title defenses generally rank second to the "real" main event. Point being, they spent whatever ungodly sum of money to bring in WCW reject Scott Steiner, and his only worth (drawing money for a big match against HHH right out of the gates) was now shot. Steiner was, for all intents and purposes, a dead issue leading into Wrestlemania, so HHH needed a new challenger.

Enter Booker T.

Now, in case you haven't noticed, Booker T is black. I know, seems like an obvious assumption, but in the words of Samuel L. Jackson, when you make an assumption, you make an ass out of "u" and "umption." Okay, so obvious notes aside, the point is that everyone who isn't blind and deaf can tell that Booker T is black. It shouldn't be an issue, because in theory wrestling moved forward into the twenty-first century along with the rest of the world. So when Booker won a battle royale on RAW to earn a title shot at HHH on the big show (Wrestlemania, not to be confused with the Big Show), people were somewhat puzzled as to the reasons behind the WWE's strategy of building that match up the next week. Booker was not only sent out to die, verbally speaking, with no bullet points to hit in his interview aside from his former dealings as a criminal in real life, but then HHH interrupted his promo, pointed out that his five former WCW World title reigns were a joke since David Arquette was a former holder of that title, and accused "his kind of people" of not being ready to hold the oh-so-prestigious RAW World title. Now, the first one is kind of a valid point, but why do you take the time to go on TV and point out that your next big challenger is a nobody? People are already trained to think that HHH never loses as is, outright *telling* them that no one else is in the same class strikes me as a wee bit counterproductive. But the second point?

Well, to put this in perspective, think back on all the great black WWE World champions of years past. There's the Rock, kind of, although he's mostly Samoan. There's Ron Simmons (Faarooq), back when the WCW World title still existed and meant something. And that, my friends, is it. In fact, not only are blacks almost completely neglected when it comes to having someone in the main event to cheer for, there have rarely been any black stars in wrestling at all. Junkyard Dog is a notable exception, but his own problems destroyed his career. Ahmed Johnson came close in the mid-'90s, but again self-destructed. I suppose Bad News Brown in the '80s, but most of his schtick was the stereotypical "scary Harlem badass" routine in order to frighten us white people. This isn't an affirmative action speech—the most talented people should get the push, not the blackest, in my opinion—but wrestling has a long history of whiteness, and those in the audience who are black and are looking for someone to relate to know this.

Which brings me back to HHH's speech. Reading between the lines, he was attempting to recreate an angle originally done by Ole Anderson in the '80s, and again by Harley Race and Ron Simmons in WCW in the '90s, whereby you'll have a racist manager cutting promos on a black star to insinuate that he's not good enough to carry the same belt as the white champion, which in theory draws instant heel heat for the champion until the black star overcomes him and wins the title to prove everyone wrong.

Yeah, and pigs fly.

The Background: Standard WWE back-and-forth buildup booking with a twist, as Booker wins a battle royal and gets accused of not being white enough to be the champion. The racist stuff is tapered off in the week before the show, and Booker is even given a pinfall victory over HHH in a tag match (just in case the NAACP watches wrestling, I guess), but this was clearly pretty far down the card and neither guy collected main event money from the show as a result.

The Stipulations: The winner gets the RAW World title.

The Overall Importance: Just like I seem to type before every match involving HHH, this proved to be Booker's only shot at the big belt, as HHH deemed him not worthy of being a prime-time guy and thus showed that he was indeed correct about Booker not being in the same class. Booker shot back down into mid-card purgatory afterward, getting stuck in a feud with Christian for months following this.

Wrestlemania XIX, March 30, 2003, Seattle, WA

RAW World title: HHH versus Booker T. Jerry Lawler's commentary is immediately perplexing, as he completely buries not only Booker T, but WCW in general. The time for cheapshots at the former competition is probably not when its biggest former star is challenging for the World title. They fight over a lockup to start and Booker slugs him out of the corner and starts chopping. They exchange shots and Booker backdrops him and keeps chopping. He runs into an elbow, however, and HHH goes up. Booker armdrags him off the top and they hit the floor, where Booker sends him into the post. Back in, HHH grabs a headlock and overpowers him, but gets clotheslined down for two. Booker uses high kicks to stun him, but he charges and gets dumped. HHH sends him into the post for good measure and they brawl outside. Booker meets the stairs, and HHH stomps him on the way back in. Lawler continues to bury Booker far beyond the call of a heel commentator.

HHH knees him down and gets a neckbreaker for two. They exchange shots in the corner, but Booker falls victim to a MAIN EVENT SPINEBUSTER, for two. Corner clothesline gets two. HHH chokes away and they slug it out, but Booker gets kneed down before coming back with a DDT. They slug it out, which Booker gets the best of, and a leg lariat sets up a sideslam. Flying forearm gets two. More chops and HHH tries a sleeper, but Booker sends him into the turnbuckle to break. HHH uses the POWER OF THE KNEE, however, and gets two. For years the joke was that HHH only had four moves, and they all involved his knee. Facecrusher, but Booker comes back with his own spinebuster and gets two. HHH tries going up, but Booker kicks him on the way down for two. He tries for the axe kick, but whiffs and crotches himself on the top rope, and Ric Flair adds to the punishment by dropping him on the stairs, knee first. This puts HHH firmly in control and begins the heel heat segment, as HHH goes for the knee with an Indian deathlock. This was during the period when HHH was trying to get a resthold from the fifties over as a serious submission move, and not doing very well at it. Poor Jim Ross has to sell it like it's Ric Flair himself doing a figure-four on a guy with a broken leg. The move, for those who don't know, is basically crossing the opponent's legs together and bending them slightly at the knee. It's not exactly UFC-level submission wrestling, in other words.

HHH keeps working on the knee in the corner, and Booker's knee collapses on a simple Irish whip. That's a nice bit of selling that you don't see often, since Irish whips violate a dozen laws of physics to begin with. Booker has a hope spot with a sunset flip for two, but HHH pounds him down again into a Pedigree position. Booker breaks it, but the ref is bumped mildly, as Booker gets a rollup for two. HHH nails the knee again, but Booker catches him with a reverse elbow. An axe kick follows (which is a bit silly since the knee is supposed to be seriously injured and it involves hitting the opponent with the damaged leg) for two. Booker goes up, fighting off Flair in the process, but HHH knocks him down to set up a superplex attempt. Booker blocks that and fights him off, as well as Flair, and the Harlem Hangover (somersault legdrop, his finisher) hits, but further injures the knee. It gets two, but Flair gets HHH's foot on the ropes. Booker is slow to recover and go for the kill due to the knee, and his knee collapses again, allowing HHH to finish with the Pedigree (hitting the move and then making Booker lay there for a while selling the devastation of the move) at 18:47. A supremely anticlimactic finish, but the story of the match made sense, with HHH injuring the knee and Booker costing himself the match by doing a high-flying move that only served to further injure the knee. Unfortunately, HHH forced Booker to wrestle his match, and the results were pretty dull. ★★¾

The original rating was ★★½, so it's a bit better on the second go, but not much. HHH's slow pace is still a killer.

The thinking in keeping the title on HHH (when clearly there were no babyface challengers even left—as three months of Kevin Nash would prove) was that he needed to be kept strong to build to a match with newcomer Goldberg, for a feud that would have to carry the summer. Of course, months later, HHH got out of the original match scheduled for the June PPV and had it moved to the September PPV, thus reclaiming his REAL World title—that of The Smartest Man in Wrestling—from Hulk Hogan, who had come back for a feud with Vince McMahon but was clearly running out of steam as a top-level babyface. Hogan and McMahon spent weeks building up to their match at Wrestlemania, which was a "dream match" that no one had actually dreamed about, by giving dueling promos about who was more responsible for the WWE's success in the '80s and who helped and hurt who at the steroid trials in the '90s and so on. In other words, twenty-year-old dirty laundry being aired on a show watched by fourteen year olds.

Vince, being Vince, was arrogant enough to presume that by pushing his match with Hogan as the *real* main event of the show—complete with their staredown on the video cover later on—he could actually boost the buyrate of the show. While a decent overbooked brawl between two senior citizens (complete with a surprise appearance from a *third* senior citizen: Rowdy Roddy Piper), it failed to capture the imagination of the wrestling world like they thought it would, and the result was one of the lowest buyrates for Wrestlemania in years. Both Hogan and Piper were gone again from the promotion by June.

And speaking of gone again, Rock was getting ready to leave for another movie, so he made his yearly foray back into the WWE to save the show again. The deal this time was that he would get his win back on Hogan at the February PPV, No Way Out, leading up to a true dream match against Goldberg at Wrestlemania. Goldberg didn't sign in time for that to happen, but they were prepping Rock for him anyway in hopes of creating a new monster babyface star in Goldberg. To do so, they played into the natural charisma of the Rock and the fans' increasing backlash toward him and his Hollywood leanings. The result was an awesome heel character, with an over-the-top entrance video featuring a helicopter doing a flyby of Hollywood, and Rock began refining his heel mannerisms as well, mocking the fans who chose to still cheer him and egging on the ones who joined in with the boos. Much of what he did wasn't in the ring, however, as he concentrated his efforts on promos and backstage interviews, trying to "give the rub" to young stars

like dorky wannabe superhero Hurricane by treating them as a threat to him and backing down from their bluster. Unfortunately, that proved to be a short-term boost to Hurricane, as Rock himself knows how to play the game and only lost to him in the ring because of interference and distraction, treating him as an afterthought rather than a person on the same level. The distraction was caused by Steve Austin.

Austin was always notoriously quiet about his injuries in the past (so quiet in WCW that he got fired over it, in fact) and as he made his big return in 2003, it proved to be no exception to the rule. When he had his big tantrum and left in 2002, he was suffering from the cumulative effects of neck surgeries and endless bumps on a bad back, and the thinking was that with seven months to rest up and heal to 100 percent again, he would be able to undertake a full schedule again and contribute to the rapidly declining house show business. And with Goldberg not ready for Wrestlemania yet, the only use for Rock seemed to be in a rematch with Steve Austin, who held a 2-0 record at Wrestlemania over Rock (winning the WWE World title from him both times, in fact) and who Rock wanted to beat to prove that he could hang with Austin on the big stage.

The Background: As noted, Austin held a 2-0 advantage over Rock at Wrestlemania. This match featured a bizarre build as well, with Rock doing a "Rock Concert" and singing songs to rile up Austin, who in turn smashed Rock's guitar as his big act of revenge. This was a notably anemic build to what proved to be a very historic match indeed.

The Stipulations: None.

The Overall Importance: We'll get to that in a bit.

Wrestlemania XIX, March 30, 2003, Seattle, WA

The Rock versus Steve Austin. JR's over-the-top commentary about Austin's greatness and destiny and stuff makes a lot more sense given the events following this. They slug it out to start, and Austin kicks his ass and goes for a quick stunner, but neglects the KICK WHAM, which allows Rock to bail. They brawl outside and Austin gets the better of that, and Rock meets the stairs and gets chopped. Austin drops him on the railing and Rock makes a break for the ring to escape, but Austin drops him on the railing again and back into the stairs. Back in, Austin stomps away and gets in his face, and gets a backdrop suplex for two. He whips Rock around and clotheslines him coming out of the corner, and chokes him on the ropes. Rock goes low, however, while Austin is chatting with the ref, and then clips him on the outside as they head out there. Rock uses the remains of a previously destroyed table for some punishment, and they head back in, where Rock goes for the leg again.

He wraps the leg around the post, but Austin fights back with punches. Rock catches him coming off the ropes, however, and kicks the knee again to drop him. Rock goes into the Scorpion King Deathlock (which, unlike HHH's Indian deathlock, is at least over as a finish), but Austin makes the ropes. Rock keeps on it, wrapping it around the post again, and then going for the ultimate insult by stealing Austin's vest. Austin fights back and kills Rock with a clothesline for the sleight, and slugs back on him to set up the Thesz Press and F-U elbow. That gets two. Austin stomps a mudhole and walks it dry, but Rock nails him with a lariat and kips up to end the rally. He turns around after

jawing with the fans, however, and Austin gives him Rock Bottom for two. Rock, proving why he's awesome, adjusts the vest while fighting to his feet, and then blocks the stunner with his own version of the move, for two.

Rock slugs away on him, but Austin plays rope-a-dope and gets a KICK WHAM STUNNER out of nowhere. It only gets two, however. Austin is reenergized, but Rock goes low to counter his burst of energy, and tries the People's Elbow, but it misses. Austin goes for another stunner, but Rock catches him with a spine-buster and gets the People's Elbow on take two. It only gets two. Rock stops to insult the crowd and then proceeds to hit another Rock Bottom for two. But the damage was done, and another Rock Bottom gets two after a fight from Austin. And after all that, Austin has no comebacks left, and a third one finishes at 17:52. A very hard-hitting, intense "main event style" match that loses points for Austin, who ignored the knee injury after a certain point, but was very well executed otherwise. ★★★ ½

> **Same rating as the original—which kind of surprised me because I thought I'd like it more afterward, but I didn't. The psychology still wasn't there, and Austin is just too limited as a performer in his last days.**

However, soon enough the truth about Austin's involvement in the match and career in general came out: He was wrestling without medical clearance, because he couldn't get it.

His neck injury had in fact not healed up during his hiatus, and in fact was now worsened to the point where no more tricky referrals and second opinions were going to save his career. Doctors told Austin point-blank to retire, and he was left with little choice but to call it a career. This was the worst news possible for the WWE, who had now lost the biggest star in their history and were forced to use him in a non-wrestling role as Eric Bischoff's babyface foil. It also gave the match with Rock added significance, as it proved to be Austin's final match, and a match where he put Rock over clean as a sheet and got destroyed in the process, truly passing the torch and ending an era.

And that's where we'll end our little tale.

Conclusion

How were the receipts today at Madison Square Garden?
—P. T. Barnum's dying words

In case you hadn't picked up on it by now, I've been not-very-subtly comparing Vince McMahon to P. T. Barnum throughout this book. Vince has always fancied himself the great ringmaster, heir apparent to the throne of Barnum, and general god among flim-flam men. But 100 years from now will people still be quoting Vince McMahon or attributing things to him? I somehow don't think so.

In his book *There's a Customer Born Every Minute: P. T. Barnum's Secrets to Business Success*, Joe Vitale outlines ten basic principles of business that Barnum used:

1. He believed there was a customer born every minute
2. He believed in using skyrockets
3. He believed in giving people more than their money's worth
4. He believed in persistently advertising
5. He fearlessly believed in the power of "printer's ink"
6. He believed in people helping people to get results
7. He believed in negotiating creatively and treating employees and performers with respect
8. He believed all was well
9. He believed in the power of the written word
10. He believed in the power of speaking

Let's see how our ringmasters compare, shall we?

He believed there was a customer born every minute. Both Vince McMahon and P. T. Barnum understood the main thing that propelled their business: constantly creating new fans, who would in turn spread the word to their friends, and so on. And both men understood that touring America wasn't enough: global touring would constantly refresh the audiences, because they wouldn't have seen what you're offering yet.

He believed in using skyrockets. Neither man was ever averse to using cheap publicity stunts to draw in new fans. Barnum was fond of grand exhibitions with large animals, Vince was more drawn to celebrities hyping his shows. Either way, the theory is the same: make the hoi polloi stop and gawk at the freakshow, and then hook them with the main product.

He believed in giving people more than their money's worth. Again, another tenet that both men followed to a tee. Whereas Barnum would search out the greatest acts on earth to populate his circus, Vince would constantly be trying to push the envelope of what was expected in a wrestling show, with gaudier entrances, bigger pyro, and more dangerous matches.

He believed in persistently advertising. Barnum set the very model of advertising that continues to this day in wrestling. Barnum's saturation of brightly colored posters and hype set the tone for the carnivals and early wrestling promoters, which in turn evolved over the years into TV shows that hype PPV specials. Same principle, just a different media.

He fearlessly believed in the power of "printer's ink." Here's where things start to differ. Whereas Barnum always knew how to befriend the media and use them as an ally, Vince took a more adversarial approach to things and viewed the media as an enemy who he could trick into promoting his events for him. In the '80s, it often worked, but as the company fell into a down-cycle again in the new century, the press became more

indifferent than anything after failures like the XFL, and Vince started taking open shots at them and refusing to grant access to his WWE superstars.

He believed in people helping people to get results. And now we go all the way into different directions, as Barnum was a man of the people who used his friendships in high places to gain greater respect for his circus and a lasting name for himself. Vince, on the other hand, is endlessly paranoid, generally refuses help from anyone outside his immediate family, and is openly hostile to those he perceives as against him.

He believed in negotiating creatively and treating employees and performers with respect. Do I even need to elaborate on this one? Or is Vince very publicly screwing Bret Hart in Montreal over a contract he intentionally breached and then lied about enough?

He believed all was well. Barnum was an optimist who looked at the bright side of any situation and rolled with the misfortunes life dealt him, building a stronger business as a result. Vince blames the media, critics, fans, employees, "the cyclical nature of the business," Wall Street, his lawyers, his childhood, and anyone who's standing within ten feet of him any time the ratings drop a half-point. He's also so arrogant and supremely self-confident that he believes his genius will save the company no matter what the situation, but I don't know if that's always a positive.

He believed in the power of the written word. Barnum was not only an accomplished showman, but a prolific writer as well. Vince, as noted, hates the media, edits the autobiographies of his wrestlers with a chainsaw to make himself sound better, and eschews the Internet because it's so negative.

He believed in the power of speaking. Barnum could not only captivate his own audience, but could also hold his own with any public speaker of the day and discuss a variety of issues. Vince is a great wrestling promo, but has an endless list of stupid things he's said while giving interviews outside of his own circle of power.

I think it's pretty easy to see why Vince can never be perceived as anything but a joke by the mainstream media he hates so much—the guidelines for the proper way to capture the imagination of the general public were pretty much set 100 years ago, and although Vince thinks of himself as a modern-day version of Barnum, he's more like the evil twin of Barnum.

Vince's sideshow has all the pizzaz of the circus with none of the childlike glee and innocence that the circus represents. Drug use is rampant. People suffer serious neck injuries at a staggering rate. Deaths occur so often that any legitimate sport would collapse under the weight of scrutiny given the same fatality rate. People sign downsized contracts without the benefit of a union because times are tight, while Vince goes public and pays himself millions in bonuses while retaining his daughter as the head writer and her husband as the #1 star of the show.

For those wondering why the company that was on top of the wrestling world in 2001 could tumble so dramatically by 2003 and beyond, look no further than the lessons taught by a fellow huckster a century before.

What does the future hold? Buy a ticket and step right up and see.

To be continued. . . .

Appendix A:

Title Histories, 2001-2004

This appendix covers all the title changes from November 2001 (the period where the book begins) until November 2003.

1. Undisputed WWF World Title

Won by	Won from	Location	Date
Chris Jericho	Steve Austin[1]	San Diego, CA	December 9, 2001
HHH	Chris Jericho	Toronto, ON	March 17, 2002
Hulk Hogan	HHH	Kansas City, KS	April 21, 2002
Undertaker	Hulk Hogan	Nashville, TN	May 19, 2002
The Rock	Undertaker[2]	Detroit, MI	July 21, 2002
Brock Lesnar[3]	The Rock	Uniondale, NY	August 25, 2002

1. Jericho defeated the Rock to win the former WCW World title earlier in the evening, and defeated Steve Austin in the main event to unify that belt with the WWF World title.

2. This was a three-way match that saw Rock pin Kurt Angle to win the belt. Undertaker was not involved in the finish.

3. From here, the belt splits off into two titles: The World Heavyweight title, a.k.a. RAW World title, and the WWE Heavyweight title, a.k.a. Smackdown World title.

2. World Heavyweight Title/RAW World Title

Won by	Won from	Location	Date
HHH	Awarded[1]	Milwaukee, WI	September 2, 2002
Shawn Michaels	HHH[2]	New York, NY	November 17, 2002
HHH	Shawn Michaels	Ft. Lauderdale, FL	December 15, 2002
Goldberg	HHH	Hershey, PA	September 3, 2003
HHH	Goldberg	Orlando, FL	December 14, 2003

1. HHH was given the title by RAW general manager Eric Bischoff partly because he had defeated Undertaker in a #1 contender match the week before, and partly because he was just such a swell guy, I guess.

2. This was a six-way Elmination Chamber match also featuring Booker T, Kane, Chris Jericho, and Rob Van Dam.

3. WWE World Title/Smackdown World Title

Won by	Won from	Location	Date
Brock Lesnar	The Rock	Uniondale, NY	August 25, 2002
Big Show	Brock Lesnar	New York, NY	November 17, 2002
Kurt Angle	Big Show	Ft. Lauderdale, FL	December 15, 2002
Brock Lesnar	Kurt Angle	Seattle, WA	March 30, 2003
Kurt Angle	Brock Lesnar	Denver, CO	July 27, 2003
Brock Lesnar	Kurt Angle	Raleigh, NC	September 16, 2003
Eddie Guerrero	Brock Lesnar	San Francisco, CA	February 15, 2004

4. WWF World Tag Team Titles

Won by	Won from	Location	Date
The Dudley Boyz	The Hardy Boyz[1]	Greensboro, NC	November 18, 2001
Tazz and Spike Dudley	The Dudley Boyz	New York, NY	January 7, 2002
Billy Gunn and Chuck Palumbo	Tazz and Spike Dudley	Rockford, IL	February 19, 2002
Rikishi & Rico	Billy Gunn and Chuck Palumbo	Nashville, TN	May 19, 2002
Billy Gunn and Chuck Palumbo	Rikishi and Rico	Oklahoma City, OK	June 4, 2002
Hulk Hogan and Edge	Billy Gunn and Chuck Palumbo	Boston, MA	July 2, 2002
Lance Storm and Christian	Hulk Hogan and Edge	Detroit, MI	July 21, 2002
Kane and Hurricane[2]	Lance Storm and Christian	Anaheim, CA	September 23, 2002

1. The Dudley Boyz (D-Von and Bubba Ray) defeated the Hardy Boyz (Matt and Jeff) to unify the WCW and WWF World tag titles.

2. At this point, the titles become recognized as the World tag team titles (a.k.a. RAW World titles), while Smackdown has a tournament to crown its own champions.

5. World Tag Team Titles/RAW World Tag Team Titles

Won by	Won from	Location	Date
Chris Jericho and Christian	Kane and Hurricane	Montreal, QC	October 14, 2002
Booker T and Goldust	Chris Jericho and Christian[1]	Ft. Lauderdale, FL	December 15, 2002
Lance Storm and William Regal	Booker T and Goldust	Phoenix, AZ	January 6, 2003
The Dudley Boyz	Lance Storm and William Regal	Boston, MA	January 19, 2003
Lance Storm and William Regal	The Dudley Boyz	Providence, RI	January 20, 2003
Sean Morley and Lance Storm	Awarded[2]	Sacramento, CA	March 24, 2003
Kane and Rob Van Dam	Sean Morley and Lance Storm[3]	San Jose, CA	March 31, 2003
La Resistance (Sylvain Grenier and Renee Dupree)	Kane and Rob Van Dam	Houston, TX	June 15, 2003
The Dudley Boyz	La Resistance[4]	Hershey, PA	September 21, 2003

1. This was a four-way elimination match also featuring the Dudley Boyz and the team of Lance Storm and William Regal.

2. William Regal suffered a severe stomach infection on a trip to India and retired, allowing "Chief" Morley to award himself and Storm the tag titles in the interim.

3. This was a three-way match also involving the Dudley Boyz.

4. This was a six-man tag match with Rob Conway and Spike Dudley also involved.

6. WWE Tag Team Titles/Smackdown Tag Team Titles

Won by	Won from	Location	Date
Chris Benoit and Kurt Angle	Rey Mysterio and Edge[1]	Little Rock, AR	October 20, 2002
Rey Mysterio and Edge	Chris Benoit and Edge	Manchester, NH	November 5, 2002
Eddie and Chavo Guerrero	Rey Mysterio and Edge[2]	New York, NY	November 17, 2002
Shelton Benjamin and Charlie Haas	Eddie and Chavo Guerrero	Philadelphia, PA	February 24, 2003
Eddie Guerrero and Tajiri	Shelton Benjamin and Charlie Haas	Charlotte, NC	May 18, 2003
Shelton Benjamin and Charlie Haas	Eddie Guerrero and Tajiri	Rochester, NY	July 1, 2003
Eddie and Chavo Guerrero	Shelton Benjamin and Charlie Haas	Raleigh, NC	September 16, 2003
Doug and Danny Basham	Eddie and Chavo Guerrero	Albany, NY	October 21, 2003

1. This was a tournament final.

2. This was a three-way match also involving Chris Benoit and Kurt Angle.

7. WWE Intercontinental Title

Won by	Won from	Location	Date
Edge	Test[1]	Greensboro, NC	November 18, 2001
William Regal	Edge	Atlanta, GA	January 20, 2002
Rob Van Dam	William Regal	Toronto, ON	March 17, 2002
Eddie Guerrero	Rob Van Dam	Kansas City, MO	April 21, 2002
Rob Van Dam	Eddie Guerrero	Edmonton, AB	May 26, 2002
Chris Benoit	Rob Van Dam	Greensboro, NC	July 29, 2002
Rob Van Dam	Chris Benoit	Uniondale, NY	August 25, 2002
Chris Jericho	Rob Van Dam	Denver, CO	September 16, 2002
Kane[2]	Chris Jericho	Houston, TX	September 30, 2002
Title "abandoned"			
Christian[3]		Charlotte, NC	May 18, 2003
Booker T	Christian	Montreal, QC	July 7, 2003
Christian	Booker T	Des Moines, IA	August 10, 2003
Rob Van Dam	Christian	Rosemont, IL	September 29, 2003
Chris Jericho	Rob Van Dam	Fayetteville, NC	October 27, 2003
Rob Van Dam	Chris Jericho	Fayetteville, NC	October 27, 2003[4]

1. U.S. champion Edge defeated Intercontinental champion Test to unify the titles into the Intercontinental title.

2. Kane lost to World champion HHH in a unification match and it was immediately abandoned.

3. The title was resurrected in May 2003 and awarded to Christian for winning a battle royal of former champions. He eliminated Booker T, who was never champion to that point.

4. Yes, both of these changes took place on the same show.

8. WWE United States title

Won by	Won from	Location	Date
Eddie Guerrero	Chris Benoit[1]	Denver, CO	July 27, 2003
Big Show	Eddie Guerrero	Baltimore, MD	October 19, 2003

1. This was a tournament final when the title was revived for Smackdown in 2003.

9. WWE Cruiserweight Title

Won by	Won from	Location	Date
Tajiri	Billy Kidman	Kansas City, MO	October 22, 2001
Billy Kidman	Tajiri	Rochester, NY	April 4, 2002
Tajiri	Billy Kidman	Kansas City, MO	April 21, 2002
Hurricane	Tajiri	Montreal, QC	May 14, 2002
Jamie Noble	Hurricane	Columbus, OH	June 23, 2002
Billy Kidman	Jamie Noble	New York, NY	November 17, 2002
Matt Hardy	Billy Kidman	Montreal, QC	February 23, 2003
Rey Mysterio	Matt Hardy	Anaheim, CA	June 3, 2003
Tajiri	Rey Mysterio	Philadelphia, PA	September 23, 2003

10. WWE Women's Title

Won by	Won from	Location	Date
Trish Stratus	Awarded[1]	Greensboro, NC	November 18, 2001
Jazz	Trish Stratus	Las Vegas, NV	February 4, 2002
Trish Stratus	Jazz	Toronto, ON	May 13, 2002
Molly Holly	Trish Stratus	Columbus, OH	June 23, 2002
Trish Stratus	Molly Holly	Los Angeles, CA	September 22, 2002
Victoria	Trish Stratus	New York, NY	November 17, 2002
Trish Stratus	Victoria[2]	Seattle, WA	March 30, 2003
Jazz	Trish Stratus	Worcester, MA	April 27, 2003
Gail Kim	Jazz[3]	Buffalo, NY	June 30, 2003
Molly Holly	Gail Kim	Colorado Springs, CO	July 28, 2003

1. Trish defeated Jazz, Ivory, Jacqueline, Lita, and Molly Holly in a six-way match to claim the vacant title.

2. This was a three-way match also involving Jazz.

3. This was a battle royale for the title.

Appendix B:

Pay-per-View History, November 2001–November 2003:

Results, Buyrates, and Attendance

The following are the number of homes who bought WWE PPV shows (i.e., "buys") during the period covered by the book, along with live attendance for each show, the advertised main event, and full results.

Please note, all buyrate numbers are approximations provided by the WWE corporate Web site. Any number around or above 400,000 would be considered average, although as of April 2002, PPV prices jumped from $29.95 to $34.95, giving them a higher revenue stream of less buys. The actual buyrate (percentage of people buying the show) follows the number of buys in parentheses, which is obtained by dividing the number of buys by 400,000 (the baseline number).

In the case of the results, "d." is an abbreviation for "defeated," thus "William Regal d. Tajiri" should be read "William Regal defeated Tajiri." The time of the match follows, with "DQ" occasionally noting a disqualification finish, as well as a star rating for each match, where applicable. "DUD" is equal to zero stars, five stars is the highest, and matches even more insulting than zero stars can go into negative numbers. I don't rate battle royales or midget matches. Any discrepancies between these ratings and those listed earlier in the book are because of wizards.

2001

Survivor Series

From: Greensboro, NC
Date: November 18, 2001
Attendance: 10,142
Buyrate: 475,000 buys (1.1)
Advertised Main Event: Team WWF v. Team Alliance
Results: Christian d. Al Snow (6:31, ★★¼), William Regal d. Tajiri (2:59, ★½), Edge d. Test to unify U.S. and Intercontinental titles (11:17, ★★★), The Dudley Boyz d. The Hardy Boyz to unify the WCW and WWF tag titles (15:41, ★★¾), Test wins the immunity battle royale (7:41, no rating), Trish wins six-way women's match (4:22, ¾★), Big Show, Undertaker, Kane, Chris Jericho, and The Rock d. Shane McMahon, Steve Austin, Kurt Angle, Rob Van Dam, and Booker T (44:55, ★★★★).

Vengeance

From: San Diego, CA
Date: December 9, 2001
Attendance: 10,699
Buyrate: 310,000 buys (0.78)
Advertised Main Event: Winner of Rock-Jericho v. winner of Austin-Angle
Results: Scott 2 Hotty and Albert d. Test and Christian (6:19, ★), Edge d. William Regal (9:07, ★★), Jeff Hardy d. Matt Hardy (12:29, ★½), The Dudley Boyz d. Big Show and Kane (6:50, –☆), The Undertaker d. Hard-core champion Rob Van Dam (11:05, ★★★), Women's champion Trish Stratus d. Jacqueline (3:35, DUD), WWF champion Steve Austin d. Kurt Angle (15:01, ★★★¼), Chris Jericho d. WCW champion The Rock (19:05, ★★★★½), WCW champion Chris Jericho d. WWF champion Steve Austin to unify the titles (12:37, ★★★).

2002

Royal Rumble

From: Atlanta, GA
Date: January 20, 2002
Attendance: 12,915
Buyrate: 640,000 buys (1.6)
Advertised Main Event: The Royal Rumble match
Results: WWF tag team champions Tazz and Spike Dudley d. The Dudley Boyz (5:06, ★★), William Regal d. Intercontinental champion Edge (9:44, ★★¼), Women's champion Trish Stratus d. Jazz (3:42, ½★), Ric Flair d. Vince McMahon (14:54, ★★★), WWF Undisputed champion Chris Jericho d. The Rock (18:41, ★★★★¼), HHH wins the Royal Rumble, eliminating Kurt Angle (69:16, ★★★¾).

No Way Out

From: Milwaukee, WI
Date: February 17, 2002
Attendance: 15,235
Buyrate: 550,000 buys (1.4)
Advertised Main Event: Chris Jericho v. Steve Austin
Results: Scotty 2 Hotty and Albert d. Christian and Lance Storm (2:56, ½★), The Hardy Boyz d. Christian and Lance Storm (2:50, ½★), The Hardy Boyz d. The Dudley Boyz (4:06, ★¼), Billy and Chuck d. The Hardy Boyz (0:33, DUD), The APA d. Billy and Chuck (3:49, ½★), Rob Van Dam d. Goldust (11:04, ★★½), WWF tag team champions Tazz and Spike Dudley d. Booker T and Test (7:17, ★½), Intercontinental champion William Regal d. Edge (10:27, ★★), Rock d. Undertaker (17:25, ★½), Kurt Angle d. HHH (14:40, ★★½), WWF Undisputed champion Chris Jericho d. Steve Austin (21:33, ★★★).

Wrestlemania X-8

From: Toronto, Ontario, Canada
Date: March 17, 2002
Attendance: 68,237

Buyrate: 850,000 buys (2.1)
Advertised Main Event: The Rock v. Hulk Hogan
Results: Rob Van Dam d. Intercontinental champion William Regal (6:19, ★★½), European champion Diamond Dallas Page d. Christian (6:10, ★★¼), Spike Dudley d. Hardcore champion Maven (3:18, no rating), Kurt Angle d. Kane (10:51, ★★½), Undertaker d. Ric Flair (18:45, ★★★), Edge d. Booker T (6:31, ★★), Steve Austin d. Scott Hall (9:51, ★), WWF tag team champions Billy and Chuck d. APA, Hardy Boyz and Dudley Boyz (13:50, ½★), The Rock d. Hulk Hogan (16:22, ★★), WWF Women's champion Jazz d. Lita and Trish Stratus (6:15, ½★), HHH d. WWF Undisputed champion Chris Jericho (18:41, ★★★¼).

Backlash

From: Kansas City, KS
Date: April 21, 2002
Attendance: 12,489
Buyrate: 400,000 buys (1.0)
Advertised Main Event: Hulk Hogan v. HHH
Results: Tajiri d. Cruiserweight champion Billy Kidman (9:07, ★★★½), Scott Hall d. Bradshaw (5:07, DUD), WWF Women's champion Jazz d. Trish Stratus (4:25, ★½), Brock Lesnar d. Jeff Hardy (5:32, ½★), Kurt Angle d. Edge (13:23, ★★★★¼), Eddie Guerrero d. Intercontinental champion Rob Van Dam (11:42, ★★★½), Undertaker d. Steve Austin (26:58, ★), WWF tag team champions Billy & Chuck d. Al Snow & Maven (6:00, ½★), Hulk Hogan d. WWF Undisputed champion HHH (22:08, ½★)
(*Note:* At this point, the WWF becomes the WWE, along with all the titles)

Judgment Day

From: Nashville, TN
Date: May 20, 2002
Attendance: Unknown
Buyrate: 375,000 buys (0.94)

Advertised Main Event: Hulk Hogan v. Undertaker
Results: Intercontinental champion Eddie Guerrero d. Rob Van Dam (10:57, ★★★★¼), WWE Women's champion Trish Stratus d. Stacy Keibler (2:52, DUD), Brock Lesnar and Paul Heyman d. The Hardy Boyz (4:58, ¼★), Steve Austin d. Big Show and Ric Flair (15:38, ★★★), Edge d. Kurt Angle (15:29, ★★★½), HHH d. Chris Jericho in a Hell in the Cell match (24:31, ★★★), Rico and Rikishi d. WWE tag team champions Billy and Chuck (3:54, DUD), Undertaker d. WWE Undisputed champion Hulk Hogan (12:30, DUD).

King of the Ring

From: Columbus, OH
Date: June 23, 2002
Attendance: 14,000
Buyrate: 325,000 buys (0.81)
Advertised Main Event: HHH v. Undertaker
Results: King of the Ring Semifinal match: Rob Van Dam d. Chris Jericho (14:31, ★★★), King of the Ring Semifinal match: Brock Lesnar d. Test (8:17, ★), Jamie Noble d. Cruiserweight champion The Hurricane (11:56, ★★½), Ric Flair d. Eddie Guerrero (16:59, ★★), Molly Holly d. WWE Women's champion Trish Stratus (5:33, ★★¾), Kurt Angle d. Hulk Hogan (12:09, ¾★), King of the Ring Final: Brock Lesnar d. Rob Van Dam (5:42, ½★), WWE Undisputed champion Undertaker d. HHH (23:43, –☆☆).

Vengeance

From: Detroit, MI
Date: July 21, 2002
Attendance: 12,000
Buyrate: 375,000 buys (0.94)
Advertised Main Event: The Rock v. Undertaker v. Kurt Angle
Results: Bubba Ray and Spike Dudley d. Chris Benoit and Eddie Guerrero in a tables match

(14:59, ★★¼), Cruiserweight champion Jamie Noble d. Billy Kidman (7:35, ★★½), European champion Jeff Hardy d. William Regal (4:15, ★), John Cena d. Chris Jericho (6:16, ★★), Intercontinental champion Rob Van Dam d. Brock Lesnar (DQ, 9:30, ★½), Booker T d. Big Show (6:12, ★), Lance Storm and Christian d. WWE tag team champions Hulk Hogan and Edge (9:58, ★½), The Rock d. WWE Undisputed champion Undertaker and Kurt Angle (19:34, ★★★¾).

Summerslam

From: Uniondale, NY
Date: August 25, 2002
Attendance: 14,797
Buyrate: 525,000 buys (1.31)
Advertised Main Event: The Rock v. Brock Lesnar
Results: Kurt Angle d. Rey Mysterio (9:20, ★★★), Ric Flair d. Chris Jericho (10:23, ★★), Edge d. Eddie Guerrero (11:45, (★★★¼), WWE tag team champions Lance Storm and Christian d. Booker T and Goldust (9:36, ★★), Rob Van Dam d. Intercontinental champion Chris Benoit (16:29, ★★★¾), Undertaker d. Test (8:18, ½★), Shawn Michaels d. HHH (27:23, ★★★★), Brock Lesnar d. WWE Undisputed champion The Rock (16:03, ★★★★).

Unforgiven

From: Los Angeles, CA
Date: September 22, 2002
Attendance: 16,000
Buyrate: 275,000 buys (0.68)
Advertised Main Event: Brock Lesnar v. Undertaker
Results: Kane, Goldust, Bubba Dudley, and Booker T d. Lance Storm, Christian, William Regal, and Test (9:59, ★★¾), Intercontinental champion Chris Jericho d. Ric Flair (6:17, ★★½), Eddie Guerrero d. Edge (11:54, ★★★★), Rosey and Jamal d. Billy and Chuck (6:38, ★),

RAW World champion HHH d. Rob Van Dam (18:19, ★★¼), Trish Stratus d. WWE Women's champion Molly Holly (5:46, ★½), Chris Benoit d. Kurt Angle (13:55, ★★★★½), Smackdown World champion Brock Lesnar draw Undertaker (Double DQ, 20:23, ★½)

No Mercy

From: Little Rock, AR
Date: October 20, 2002
Attendance: 10,000
Buyrate: 300,000 buys (0.75)
Advertised Main Event: Brock Lesnar v. Undertaker
Results: RAW tag team champions Chris Jericho and Christian d. Booker T and Goldust (8:47, ★★¼), Torrie Wilson d. Dawn Marie (4:40, –☆☆), Rob Van Dam d. Ric Flair (7:58, ★¼), Cruiserweight champion Jamie Noble d. Tajiri (8:14, ★★½), RAW World champion HHH d. Intercontinental champion Kane to unify the titles (16:09, ★½), Smackdown tag title tournament final: Chris Benoit and Kurt Angle d. Rey Mysterio and Edge (22:03, ★★★★★), WWE Women's champion Trish Stratus d. Victoria (5:33, ½★), Smackdown World champion Brock Lesnar d. Undertaker in a Hell in the Cell match (27:14, ★★★).

Survivor Series

From: New York, NY
Date: November 17, 2002
Attendance: 17,930
Buyrate: 330,000 buys (0.83)
Advertised Main Event: The Elimination Chamber
Results: Jeff Hardy, Bubba Dudley, and Spike Dudley d. Jamal, Rosey, and Rico in a tables match (14:19, ★★¾), Billy Kidman d. Cruiserweight champion Jamie Noble (7:28, ★★½), Victoria d. WWE Women's champion Trish Stratus (7:00, ★★¼), Big Show d. Smackdown World

champion Brock Lesnar (4:18, ★), Eddie and Chavo Guerrero d. Smackdown tag team champions Edge and Rey Mysterio and Chris Benoit and Kurt Angle in a three-way match (19:25, ★★★½), Shawn Michaels d. RAW World champion HHH, Booker T, Kane, Chris Jericho, and Rob Van Dam in the Elimination Chamber match (39:21, ★★★¼).

Armageddon

From: Ft. Lauderdale, FL
Date: December 16, 2002
Attendance: 7,000
Buyrate: 330,000 (0.83)
Advertised Main Event: Shawn Michaels v. HHH and Big Show v. Kurt Angle
Results: Booker T and Goldust d. RAW tag team champions Chris Jericho and Christian, William Regal and Lance Storm, and The Dudley Boyz in a four-way elimination match (16:44, ★★★¼), Edge d. A-Train (DQ, 7:11, ★), Chris Benoit d. Eddie Guerrero (16:48, ★★★★¼), Batista d. Kane (6:37, DUD), WWE Women's champion Victoria d. Trish Stratus and Jacqueline in a three-way match (4:29, ½★), Kurt Angle d. Smackdown World champion Big Show (12:36, ★★), HHH d. RAW World champion Shawn Michaels two falls to one (38:33, ★★½)

2003

Royal Rumble

From: Boston, MA
Date: January 19, 2003
Attendance: 14,712
Buyrate: 500,000 buys (1.25)
Advertised Main Event: The Royal Rumble match
Results: Brock Lesnar d. Big Show (6:28, ★★), The Dudley Boyz d. RAW tag team champions Lance Storm and William Regal (7:26, ★★), Torrie Wilson d. Dawn Marie (3:38, –☆), Scott

Steiner d. RAW World champion HHH (DQ, 18:13, –☆☆½), Smackdown World champion Kurt Angle d. Chris Benoit (19:47, ★★★★¾), Brock Lesnar wins the Royal Rumble, eliminating Undertaker (53:47, ★★★¾).

No Way Out

From: Montreal, QC
Date: February 23, 2003
Attendance: 16,125
Buyrate: 450,000 buys (1.13)
Advertised Main Event: The Rock v. Hulk Hogan and Steve Austin v. Eric Bischoff
Results: Chris Jericho d. Jeff Hardy (13:00, ★★★¼), RAW tag team champions William Regal and Lance Storm d. Rob Van Dam and Kane (9:21, ★★), Matt Hardy d. Cruiserweight champion Billy Kidman (9:31, ★★½), Undertaker d. Big Show (14:09, ★), Chris Benoit and Brock Lesnar d. Kurt Angle, Shelton Benjamin, and Charlie Haas (13:13, ★★★½), RAW World champion HHH d. Scott Steiner (13:00, –☆☆), Steve Austin d. Eric Bischoff (4:25, DUD), The Rock d. Hulk Hogan (12:35, -★).

Wrestlemania XIX

From: Seattle, WA
Date: March 30, 2003
Attendance: 54,097
Buyrate: 560,000 buys (1.4)
Advertised Main Event: Vince McMahon v. Hulk Hogan and The Rock v. Steve Austin
Results: Cruiserweight champion Matt Hardy d. Rey Mysterio (5:36, ★), Undertaker and Nathan Jones d. Big Show and A-Train (9:44, ¾★), Trish Stratus d. Women's champion Victoria and Jazz in a three-way match (7:17, ★★), Smackdown tag champions Shelton Benjamin and Charlie Haas d. Chris Benoit and Rhyno, Eddie and Chavo Guerrero in a three-way match (8:47, ★★¼), Shawn Michaels d. Chris Jericho (22:34, ★★★★), RAW World champion HHH d. Booker T

(18:47, ★★½), Hulk Hogan d. Vince McMahon (20:45, ★★½), The Rock d. Steve Austin (17:53, ★★★½), Brock Lesnar d. Smackdown World champion Kurt Angle (21:07, ★★★★¼).

Backlash
From: Worcester, MA
Date: April 27, 2003
Attendance: 10,000
Buyrate: 325,000 buys (0.81)
Advertised Main Event: The Rock v. Goldberg
Results: Smackdown tag champions Shelton Benjamin and Charlie Haas d. Eddie and Chavo Guerrero (15:03, ★★★), Sean O'Haire d. Rikishi (4:52, –☆½), RAW tag team champions Kane and Rob Van Dam d. The Dudley Boyz (13:01, ★½), Jazz d. WWE Women's champion Trish Stratus (5:50, ★★½), Big Show d. Rey Mysterio (3:45, DUD), Smackdown World champion Brock Lesnar d. John Cena (15:11, ★½), HHH, Chris Jericho and Ric Flair d. Booker T, Kevin Nash and Shawn Michaels (17:52, ★★½), Goldberg d. The Rock (13:04, ½★).

Judgment Day
From: Charlotte, NC
Date: May 18, 2003
Attendance: 13,000
Buyrate: 310,000 buys (0.78)
Advertised Main Event: HHH v. Kevin Nash
Results: John Cena, Chuck Palumbo, and Johnny Stamboli d. Chris Benoit, Rhyno, and Brian Kendrick (3:55, ¾★), Sylvain Grenier and Renee Dupree d. Test and Scott Steiner (6:21, ½★), Eddie Guerrero and Tajiri d. Smackdown tag team champions Shelton Benjamin and Charlie Haas in a ladder match (14:21, ★★★), Christian won the Intercontinental battle royale, eliminating Booker T (11:48, no rating), Mr. America (Hulk Hogan) d. Roddy Piper (4:43, –☆☆), Kevin Nash d. RAW World champion HHH (DQ, 7:44, DUD), Women's champion Jazz d. Trish Stratus,

Jacqueline, and Victoria in a four-way match (4:47, ¾★), Smackdown World champion Brock Lesnar d. Big Show in a stretcher match (15:27, ★★¼).

(*Note:* At this point, the shows become RAW and Smackdown exclusive, with the only crossover coming on the "Big Four" shows: Wrestlemania, Summerslam, Survivor Series, and Royal Rumble)

Bad Blood (RAW only)
From: Houston, TX
Date: June 15, 2003
Attendance: 10,000
Buyrate: 390,000 buys (0.98)
Advertised Main Event: HHH v. Kevin Nash, Hell in the Cell
Results: Chris Nowinski and Rodney Mack d. The Dudley Boyz (7:07, ★★), Scott Steiner d. Test (6:24, ★½), Booker T d. Intercontinental champion Christian (DQ, 7:52, ★★), Sylvain Grenier and Renee Dupree d. RAW tag team champions Kane and Rob Van Dam (5:46, ½★), Goldberg d. Chris Jericho (10:58, ★★★), Ric Flair d. Shawn Michaels (14:18, ★★★), RAW World champion HHH d. Kevin Nash in a Hell in the Cell match (21:01, ★★½).

Vengeance (Smackdown only)
From: Denver, CO
Date: July 27, 2003
Attendance: 9,500
Buyrate: 325,000 buys (0.81)
Advertised Main Event: Brock Lesnar v. Kurt Angle v. Big Show
Results: U.S. title tournament final: Eddie Guerrero d. Chris Benoit (22:14, ★★★★), Jamie Noble d. Billy Gunn (4:59, ★½), APA win a "bar room brawl," Smackdown tag team champions Shelton Benjamin and Charlie Haas d. Rey Mysterio and Billy Kidman (14:52, ★★★★¼), Sable d. Stephanie McMahon (6:23, ★), Undertaker d. John Cena (16:01, ★★★½), Vince McMahon d.

Zach Gowen (14:01, ★★½), Kurt Angle d. Smackdown World champion Brock Lesnar and Big Show in a three-way match (17:29, ★★★★).

Summerslam (Both brands)
From: Phoenix, AZ
Date: August 24, 2003
Attendance: 17,113
Buyrate: 410,000 buys (1.03)
Advertised Main Event: Brock Lesnar v. Kurt Angle and The Elimination Chamber II
Results: RAW tag team champions Sylvain Grenier and Renee Dupree d. The Dudley Boyz (7:49, ★½), Undertaker d. A-Train (9:19, ★), Shane McMahon d. Eric Bischoff (10:33, ½★), U.S. champion Eddie Guerrero d. Rhyno, Tajiri, and Chris Benoit in a four-way match (10:50, ★★★), Smackdown World champion Kurt Angle d. Brock Lesnar (21:19, ★★★½), Kane d. Rob Van Dam (12:51, ★★¼), RAW World champion HHH d. Goldberg, Chris Jericho, Randy Orton, Kevin Nash, and Shawn Michaels in an Elimination Chamber match (19:15, ★★★).

Unforgiven (RAW only)
From: Hershey, PA
Date: September 21, 2003
Attendance: 10,347
Buyrate: 300,000 buys (0.75)
Advertised Main Event: HHH v. Goldberg
Results: The Dudley Boyz d. RAW tag team champions Sylvain Grenier, Renee Dupree, and Rob Conway in a tables match (10:16, ★½), Test d. Scott Steiner (6:56, ½★), Randy Orton d. Shawn Michaels (19:22, ★★¾), Trish Stratus and Lita d. Gail Kim and Molly Holly (6:41, ★★½), Kane d. Shane McMahon in a Last Man Standing match (19:54, ★½), Intercontinental champion Christian d. Rob Van Dam and Chris Jericho in a three-way match (19:03, ★¾), Jonathan Coachman and Al Snow d. Jim Ross and Jerry Lawler (8:17, –☆☆), Goldberg d. RAW World champion HHH (14:56, ★½).

No Mercy (Smackdown only)
From: Baltimore, MD
Date: October 19, 2003
Attendance: 9,000
Buyrate: 240,000 buys (0.60)
Advertised Main Event: Vince McMahon v. Stephanie McMahon
Results: Cruiserweight champion Tajiri d. Rey Mysterio (12:05, ★★★), Chris Benoit d. A-Train (12:21, ★★), Zach Gowen d. Matt Hardy (6:50, ★½), Doug and Danny Basham d. The APA (8:55, ½★), Vince McMahon d. Stephanie McMahon in an "I Quit" match (9:28, DUD), Kurt Angle d. John Cena (18:24, ★★★★), Big Show d. U.S. champion Eddie Guerrero (11:22, ★), Smackdown World champion Brock Lesnar d. Undertaker (24:20, ★★).

Survivor Series (Both brands)
From: Dallas, TX
Date: November 16, 2003
Attendance: 13,487
Buyrate: 292,000 buys (0.73)
Advertised Main Event: Vince McMahon v. Undertaker
Results: John Cena, Chris Benoit, Kurt Angle, Bradshaw, and Hardcore Holly d. Big Show, Nathan Jones, Matt Morgan, Brock Lesnar, and A-Train in an elimination tag match (13:30, ★★½), Women's champion Molly Holly d. Lita (6:49, ★½), Kane d. Shane McMahon (13:29, ½★), Smackdown tag team champions Doug and Danny Basham d. Eddie and Chavo Guerrero (7:32, ★★), Mark Henry, Chris Jericho, Christian, Scott Steiner, and Randy Orton d. Shawn Michaels, Booker T, Bubba Dudley, D-Von Dudley, and Rob Van Dam in an elimination tag match (27:27, ★★★★), Vince McMahon d. Undertaker in a Buried Alive match (11:59, DUD), RAW World champion Goldberg d. HHH (11:41, ★½).

Index